a common devotional *from* a common man

by Rick Bowman

Dick,
May God Bless each and every day!
Rick B

TATE PUBLISHING, LLC

"A Common Devotional from a Common Man" by Rick Bowman

Published in the United States of America
by Tate Publishing, LLC
127 East Trade Center Terrace
Mustang, OK 73064
(888) 361–9473

ISBN: 1–9332905–3-6

"ONE GENERATION WILL COMMEND YOUR WORKS TO ANOTHER, THEY WILL TELL OF YOUR MIGHTY WORKS"
PSALM 145:4

Write a legacy of faith to future generations with "Pass it On Pages."

Dedication

I am dedicating this devotional to my Lord and Savior Jesus Christ. He has been there for me through thick and thin, and has made all things possible.

I am, also, dedicating this to my wife Rhonda and my children—Joshua, Jordan, Nathan, and Sara. They have each been of great support and encouragement. They are each special to me and to God. God has blessed me with them and God wanted me to share a special message to each of them.

To Rhonda: Do not fret because life sometimes disappoints you. Focus on God's love for you and your heart's desires will come to pass.

To Joshua: Your intelligence is very impressive, but never lose sight of who is really in control—God.

To Jordan: Laugh and continue to enjoy life. Never forget though, that God is the cornerstone of all joy and happiness.

To Nathan: Work, play, and enjoy your animals. God created living creatures and He has given you a gift of care for each of them.

To Sara: Be happy always and don't complain. God has great things in store for you, if you can learn to be content with what you have today.

May this devotional be a blessing to my family and friends. My prayer is that it becomes a source of inspiration and encouragement to all who choose to read it.

Preface

God granted me the privilege and opportunity to write on His behalf. He was very specific on the intent of this devotional. God wants to make sure that the future generations of every family know and understand how walking with God impacts life. God knows that younger children, because of a lessened life experience, do not grasp the faith of their parents, therefore it is important to leave them a legacy of faith they can read in the future. This written legacy will touch their lives at the right time and at the right moment God chooses. Enjoy this devotional and be sure to use the "Pass it on Pages" to leave the legacy of faith for generations to come.

January

January 1

"When God tells you to act—act"

Scripture: Commit your way to the Lord, trust in him, and he will do this: (Psalm 37:5)

Today I am embarking on a great adventure. While reading my devotional and studying God's Word, God spoke to me and told me to start writing. As normal, I wondered why. I thought to myself, *I don't have time for this*, but nonetheless God kept up his urging. God wanted me to act. He didn't want me to second-guess His leading, but to follow Him faithfully without reservation. I again thought to myself, *Here I am Lord, writing as you instructed, but to what end?* And as quickly as the thought popped into my head, God placed this in my spirit; "Someday," He said, "your wife and children will read this and know that I am your God and caretaker. They will know I will always be with you and your family. I will hold your hand and though you may stumble you will not fall. And, you will succeed in whatever you do, as long as you act when I say act."

Writing is not necessarily my greatest strength, but I know God will see this to the end and bring it to pass; as long as I am willing to act.

January 2

"Birthday Joy"

Scripture: let us draw near to God with a sincere heart in full assurance of faith, having our hearts sprinkled to cleanse us from a guilty conscience and having our bodies washed with pure water. (Hebrews 10:22)

When I think back to my birthday on January 1, 2000, I remember it as being a wonderful day. It was a great day to be alive and know that all was well with the world and with my soul. If you remember, it was during 1999 that all of the hype about Y2K occurred and everyone was apprehensive about what was going to happen. Was it going to be the end of the world? Were there going to be catastrophic collapses in the world economy, in the computers that run it, and in the lives we lived? Well, none of that happened. The year 1999 ended uneventful, other than a few hangovers, and 2000 started the same way.

I rejoiced that day that the Y2K bug did not bite, but I did so knowing that my life was eternally secure. I know today (as I knew then) that no millennium bug, catastrophe, or earthly situation can change my relationship with God. I am committed to Him and He to me, and so no matter what kind of hype the world wants to dish out, I know that my life is eternally safe in Jesus. Therefore, I can have birthday joy for eternity.

January 3

"Lasting Treasure"

Scripture: "Do not store up for yourselves treasures on earth, where moth and rust destroy, and where thieves break in and steal. But store up for yourselves treasures in heaven, where moth and rust do not destroy, and where thieves do not break in and steal. For where your treasure is, there your heart will be also. (Matthew 6:19–21)

There is a program on TV called *Antiques Roadshow*. On the show people bring their collectibles and so-called treasures to have them appraised by experts. Each person who comes to the show has hope that his or her item is a valuable treasure.

There are lots of treasures in life that have lasted years, decades, centuries, and even millenniums. Each treasure has its own value, which was created over time, but all eventually fade away. In the Kingdom of God, however, God has promised us treasures beyond compare that will last for all of eternity. These treasures are heavenly treasures that surpass any knowledge of value we can comprehend.

If you are looking to collect something of true lasting value, then accept Jesus. You will have collected the most valuable treasure of all.

January 4

"Persistent Prayer"

Scripture: Then Jesus told his disciples a parable to show them that they should always pray and not give up. He said: "In a certain town there was a judge who neither feared God nor cared about men. And there was a widow in that town who kept coming to him with the plea, 'Grant me justice against my adversary.' "For some time he refused. But finally he said to himself, 'Even though I don't fear God or care about men, yet because this widow keeps bothering me, I will see that she gets justice, so that she won't eventually wear me out with her coming!'" (Luke 18:1–5)

My son has an interesting way of getting what he wants. For example when he wants to invite a friend over and I tell him I need some time to think about it, he remains persistent. He will give me a few minutes and then ask again. If the question falls on deaf ears, he asks again and again until he gets his answer.

Our prayer lives need to be the same way. When we ask God to answer our prayers, do we only ask once and stop? Or do we make them a part of our daily prayer time until we receive answers? Persistent prayers get answers, just like my son gets answers from me when he is persistent.

The next time you want your prayers answered, just ask and ask and ask until God answers.

____

____

____

January 5

"God's Specifications"

Scripture: Jesus looked at him and loved him. "One thing you lack," he said. "Go, sell everything you have and give to the poor, and you will have treasure in heaven. Then come, follow me." At this the man's face fell. He went away sad, because he had great wealth. Jesus looked around and said to his disciples, "How hard it is for the rich to enter the kingdom of God!" (Mark 10–21–23)

A machinist working in a factory and operating a sophisticated machine has to constantly make adjustments in order to keep the machine working properly. He has to calibrate every setting for the machine to operate efficiently. He has to check each part produced to make sure that it meets all tolerances and specifications. If the machine is calibrated incorrectly or if a setting is not functioning properly, parts may need to be replaced. If the machine is not recalibrated or if parts are not replaced, the parts produced will not meet the specifications and will have to be scrapped.

Our walk with God requires that we make adjustments. He asks that we check what we are producing for His Kingdom to see if it meets His specification. If not, we must make adjustments through prayer, study, and worship. We must calibrate our lives to meet God's specification so that we might add more believers to His Kingdom.

Are you out of spec with God? There is no better day than today to adjust your mind and attitude for His glory.

January 6

"Blessed Days"

Scripture: I know what it is to be in need, and I know what it is to have plenty. I have learned the secret of being content in any and every situation, whether well fed or hungry, whether living in plenty or in want. I can do everything through him who gives me strength. (Philippians 4:12–13)

Yesterday was a very good day. It seemed that everything went smoothly and I accomplished what I wanted and needed to do. When I returned home that evening, I was very content and felt good about the day.

As I reflected on the day, I came to realize that contentment is exactly what God wants. He wants us to be satisfied. He wants our lives to be free from stress, anxiety, worry, and fear. God wants everyday to be full of peace and harmony. Additionally, I realized how my day started. It started with reading God's Word, praising His majesty, and praying for a blessed day. I am sure that is why the day went so smoothly. Blessed days start with God.

January 7

"Daily Routine"

Scripture: Jesus answered, "It is written: 'Man does not live on bread alone, but on every word that comes from the mouth of God.'" (Matthew 4:4)

We are all creatures of routine. For example, I get up at the same time, get ready for work the same way, and leave for work at the same time every morning to avoid traffic. I carry that routine through to work, on lunch breaks, and even on to how I accomplish tasks.

Our church life is structured much the same way. We sit in the same pew, next to the same people, say the same prayer of confession, and our whole worship is scripted the same way week after week.

Routines are a necessary reality to get us through life. Without routine, we have chaos and confusion; and the devil can manipulate chaos and confusion into fear. Recognizing that a routine is an important structure to our day, let's use it to our advantage. Let's put God at the center of our lives through the daily reading of his word, through prayer, and through devotion. By placing God at the center of our daily routines, our days will be more complete and more satisfying, so, let's add God to our daily routine starting today.

January 8

"White as Snow"

Scripture: "Come now, let us reason together," the LORD. "Though your sins are like scarlet, they shall be as white as snow; though they are red as crimson, they shall be like wool." (Isaiah 1:18)

We had a snowstorm yesterday and as I awoke and looked outside the dingy winter landscape had been transformed. A fresh new blanket of snow had covered all of the brown, dirty scenery around the house.

Thinking about the new fallen snow reminded me of God's mercy towards us. We were dirty and dingy with sin yet God, through His Son Jesus, removed our sin and made us as pure as the new fallen snow. Our sin was removed never to be brought up again.

Before long the snow will melt and the dingy landscape of winter will once again be revealed, but God will never reveal our confessed sin. Thank you, God for transforming us from sinners to children of a living God through the blood of your Son, Jesus.

____

____

____

January 9

"Thou Shall Not"

Scripture: "A new command I give you: Love one another. As I have loved you, so you must love one another. By this all men will know that you are my disciples, if you love one another." (John 13:34–35)

Recently there have been a number of signs "from God" around the city. One sign said, "Thou shall not kill! I meant that—God," and another said, "Thou shall not use my name in vain. If you do, I'll make your rush hour longer—God." These billboards popped up along the city roads sharing God's Word. It seems God is trying to get our attention and make sure we know His commandments. These reminders are not just to make sure we *know* His commandments, but are meant to encourage us to *practice* them as part of our daily lives.

The Ten Commandments, even if you ask Christians, are hard to remember. And if you can't remember them, how can you live them? God knew that, so He sent His Son to give us the greatest commandment that encapsulates them all, "Love one another as I have loved you . . ." (John 3:34). Jesus gave us this commandment, because He knew if we truly loved someone, we could not break the commandments of God.

I thank you God for your recent signs reminding us to obey your commandments.

January 10

"Written Truth"

Scripture: There came a man who was sent from God; his name was John. He came as a witness to testify concerning that light, so that through him all men might believe. He himself was not the light; he came only as a witness to the light. The true light that gives light to every man was coming into the world. (John 1:6–9)

Newspapers are one way we receive local, national, and international news. Many of us read the newspaper to gain knowledge of what has recently transpired. We read these reports from journalists of events that have taken place. We seem to accept these reports at face value and we believe them to be completely true. We accept the reporting and quotes of eyewitnesses without question and believe them as truth as well.

God has provided each and every one of us an article. It is an article of truth written by several reporters and has been verified by eyewitnesses. So why do we have so much trouble accepting His report as fact? The Bible is a written account of events that occurred and it was inspired by God. God collaborated all of the events with witnesses. He used quotes from all of the parties involved and His reports are filled with truthful facts, so why not believe them? If you can accept a report from a journalist in the newspaper, then you can surely accept the report of a living God. It is the truth!

January 11

"THAT DOES NOT COMPUTE"

Scripture: And the LORD said to Joshua, "Today I will begin to exalt you in the eyes of all Israel, so they may know that I am with you as I was with Moses. (Joshua 3:7)

Computers have become a standard in today's society. It seems that the whole world would shut down if some type of failure occurred in the government or banking computers. Many people live their lives based on the computer. They track their stocks, get weather reports, follow financial indicators, and check what is playing at the movies. The internet has entered the majority of homes and has made a major impact on how wc make purchases, pay bills, and gain information. We have gained so much from computers that we trust them for practically everything.

Ultimately, however, there is only one in whom we can place our full trust to make our lives better. His wisdom far exceeds that of the greatest data base and His ability to assess situations and make corrections is far vaster than the most powerful computer. His information is so great that He knows even the future. He knows so much that He granted the knowledge to have computers invented.

Computers have added great value to the way we live, but they are far from being the greatest trusting factor in our lives. God made everything and in Him we can be assured that He is in control of our whole world. Trust in Him and He will lead your life even when the computer does not compute.

January 12

"Faithful 100%"

Scripture: Know therefore that the LORD your God is God; he is the faithful God, keeping his covenant of love to a thousand generations of those who love him and keep his commands. (Deuteronomy 7:9)

"An elephant faithful 100%," touted by Horton the elephant in a Dr. Suess classic children's story.[1] It is the story of an elephant that agrees to sit on an egg for a dodo bird. The elephant made a promise to do the job and to sit on the nest. It didn't matter if it rained, snowed, or stormed the elephant was faithful to its promise - 100%.

God is that way. He has made promises and He is faithful to keep those promises. It does not matter what kinds of storms we face in life He is there. No matter how much garbage we have accumulated He cleans the house. No matter what our past reveals and what sins we've committed He forgives us. God is a 100% faithful God.

Promises are broken daily in this world, but God never ever breaks His promises. He is there and will always be there for all of eternity—100% faithful.

[1]Dr. Seuss, "Horton Hatches the Egg", Random House, 1968

January 13

"Blanket of Love"

Scripture: This is love: not that we loved God, but that he loved us and sent his Son as an atoning sacrifice for our sins. Dear friends, since God so loved us, we also ought to love one another. No one has ever seen God; but if we love one another, God lives in us and his love is made complete in us. (1 John 4:10–12)

It has been very cold the last few days. The temperatures have been near zero with wind chills making it below. Walking the dog early in the morning is a frigid experience, even with a coat, hat, and gloves. The cold seems to cut you right to the bone. Once our walk is over and we come into the house, the warmth seems to surround me. Like a blanket it starts from the outside and then engulfs me. What a great feeling to be warm and cozy again.

God's love is like that. When we are separated from God everything around us and within us is cold. Our relationships, our attitudes, and our feelings are cold. People don't want to be near us because of the cold. God's love, however, warms us. It radiates from us like a heater. Everything around us warms to our touch. God's love is truly a warm blanket around our lives.

January 14

"Smooth Paths"

Scripture: He guides me in paths of righteousness for his name's sake. Even though I walk through the valley of the shadow of death, I will fear no evil, for you are with me; your rod and your staff, they comfort me. (Psalm 23:3–4)

Now that we have a dog, walks are very common. We walk all around our neighborhood and our best walks occur in the woods. Our walks in the woods take us through, over, and around many obstacles. We walk through briars, over logs, and traverse small streams. Sometimes the paths are less taken and the footing is more treacherous. On occasion, we lose our paths altogether, stumble through trees, and stumble over rocks. It can be challenging to get back to a path more easily traveled.

Walking in the world is like walking through the woods. We often face obstacles. Briars and thorns tear at our flesh slowing us down and are a constant annoyance, like the wearing of life itself. The logs of our lives are a little more difficult. They sometimes block our entire path, force us to go around, and to take a new, uncharted path where fear of the unknown creeps in. Our footing is always a problem. We try not to slip, stumble or fall, which is like sin that causes us to stumble out of God's righteousness.

We can make our paths smoother and more easily traveled. All we need to do is seek God. He will make our paths straight, and if we stumble, we will not fall. He will also lighten our load. Since we have to travel these paths of life, then let's do it as smoothly as we can. Let's have God direct our paths.

January 15

"Holy Spirit Fire"

Scripture: When the day of Pentecost came, they were all together in one place. Suddenly a sound like the blowing of a violent wind came from heaven and filled the whole house where they were sitting. They saw what seemed to be tongues of fire that separated and came to rest on each of them. All of them were filled with the Holy Spirit and began to speak in other tongues as the Spirit enabled them. (Acts 2:1–4)

Last night I built a fire in the fireplace. I didn't have much kindling, so the logs took longer to catch. I had to work harder than normal feeding the fire with newspaper and the kindling I had, but finally I created enough heat that the logs ignited.

God's work in us, through His Holy Spirit, can be the same. When we accept Jesus as Savior, God sends His Holy Spirit to dwell within us. Our Christian life catches fire, but often the flames dwindle. We smolder without flames and only have a few glowing embers. God's holy breath blows the coals to keep it burning. As we mature in our Christian walk, the glowing embers finally combust showing our Holy Spirit fire, light, and warmth to everyone around us. Then and only then are we truly baptized with fire; the fire of the Holy Spirit.

January 16

"Small Blessings, Giant Results"

Scripture: You will be blessed in the city and blessed in the country. The fruit of your womb will be blessed, and the crops of your land and the young of your livestock—the calves of your herds and the lambs of your flocks. Your basket and your kneading trough will be blessed. You will be blessed when you come in and blessed when you go out. (Deuteronomy 28:3–6)

God is always doing great and wonderful things in our midst. Sometimes they are grand and easily recognized, and these are things for which we are eager to thank Him. However, sometimes they are small and we miss them and take them for granted.

My youngest son got sick yesterday. Nothing major, but as a parent, when one of your children gets sick you are very concerned. In light of this minor illness, I realized just how healthy our family truly is. God has blessed us for years with good health. Sure we have a few sniffles and sneezes every now and then, but overall we are healthy.

There are many blessings God has for us each and everyday. They may not be mountain-top experiences, but they still reflect the love and care of an awesome God. I thank you God for your small blessings that have giant results.

January 17

"Second Chances"

Scripture: The law was added so that the trespass might increase. But where sin increased, grace increased all the more, so that, just as sin reigned in death, so also grace might reign through righteousness to bring eternal life through Jesus Christ our Lord. (Romans 5:20–21)

This week *The Early Show* aired a program about "Second Chances." The program was based on individuals who, even though successful in their present vocation, heard a small voice inside calling them to do something different. Oddly enough, the two stories I watched were about women who were called to change their lives and go a different direction. One was a successful engineer for a firm and was destined to become president of the company. One day an instant urging came from within and she gave up the security of her career to go into the priesthood. She said she knew that it was a second chance in life to do what God had intended for her to do. The second women gave up a career in TV commercial production to pursue a new career as a stand-up comic. She knew beyond doubt that she was called and had been given a second chance to make people laugh. Both women were given a second chance to do what was intended for them to do.

Our God is a God of second chances. I know in my life of poor judgments and decisions, mistakes and blunders God has been there to forgive me and give me a second chance to do better. And because He is willing to do that, I find that I give Him control over my judgments and decisions. Now, instead of my decisions being wrong, they are wonderfully right.

If you have chosen the wrong path, made bad choices, and sinned against God and man, know that God is waiting patiently for you to come and receive a second chance. He will accept you just the way you are and will help you transform into what He wants you to be.

January 18

"ALWAYS WELCOME"

Scripture: "The son said to him, 'Father, I have sinned against heaven and against you. I am no longer worthy to be called your son.' "But the father said to his servants, 'Quick! Bring the best robe and put it on him. Put a ring on his finger and sandals on his feet. Bring the fattened calf and kill it. Let's have a feast and celebrate. For this son of mine was dead and is alive again; he was lost and is found.' So they began to celebrate. (Luke 15:21–24)

The elders meeting the other day felt cold to me and I do not mean temperature-wise. I had not been to a meeting for about six months due to the fact that I had been involved in the building of my house and traveling for my company. Coming back put me in a position of not knowing what was happening, nor what was going on. I wasn't sure of what the elders were involved in let alone able to offer them any assistance. Out of touch, out of place, and out of the loop was the way I felt.

God never makes us feel that way. He always welcomes us with open arms. He knows that we get distracted by the things of this world and that sometimes He is put on the back burner, but He always accepts us back. God will love us and enjoy our company no matter when we return. God loves us in spite of ourselves and we are always welcome with Him.

January 19

"The Big Game"

Scripture: For if, by the trespass of the one man, death reigned through that one man, how much more will those who receive God's abundant provision of grace and of the gift of righteousness reign in life through the one man, Jesus Christ. (Romans 5:17)

The Super Bowl is a big event in our house and the United States in general. It occupies our time and conversation for weeks prior to the game. We plan parties and plan where we are going to watch the big game on TV. After all, it is the game of all games in football.

What amazes me is that we seem to put more emphasis on a football game than we put on going to church or becoming involved in God's work. God's game is more than a day it is for eternity, yet we don't place the same value on God's day as we do game day.

God is not asking us to put everything else aside and not enjoy the events of this world. He is just asking that we put Him at the center. When we make God a priority, we will be able to enjoy life and the events of life more abundantly, even when our team doesn't win the Super Bowl.

January 20

"Mold Us"

Scripture: It does not, therefore, depend on man's desire or effort, but on God's mercy. 17For the Scripture says to Pharaoh: "I raised you up for this very purpose, that I might display my power in you and that my name might be proclaimed in all the earth." Therefore God has mercy on whom he wants to have mercy, and he hardens whom he wants to harden. One of you will say to me: "Then why does God still blame us? For who resists his will?" But who are you, O man, to talk back to God? "Shall what is formed say to him who formed it, 'Why did you make me like this?'" Does not the potter have the right to make out of the same lump of clay some pottery for noble purposes and some for common use? (Romans 9:16–21)

We humans are basically creatures of habit. We have routines for everything. We have routines for getting ready for work, routines at work, routines at church, and even routines that revolve around watching TV. It seems routines give us some level of security and comfort.

Overall routines are good things, however, if we become so attached to our routines that we become inflexible and unwilling to change, routines can be bad things. Routines are great in our prayer life and our devotions, but as we grow in God we must let the master mold us into the vessel of His choosing even if it means breaking a routine we're used to following. God has a great and wonderful work in progress in us and if we become too rigid He cannot mold us into what He wants. God has to shape us into mature Christians in order for us to be capable of doing His will. So God, mold us and make us into what you want us to be.

____

____

____

January 21

"Speak to Me God"

Scripture: "Do not be afraid, O man highly esteemed," he said. "Peace! Be strong now; be strong." When he spoke to me, I was strengthened and said, "Speak, my lord, since you have given me strength." (Daniel 10:19)

"Speak to me God." We have all made this statement at some time in our lives. It may not have been as a direct request, but we offer up prayers asking the same thing. We want God to speak to us through signs, through others, or if God chooses, directly to us through His Holy Spirit.

God speaks to me, but many times I am too busy to hear. He has a lot He wants to tell us. Can we and will we slow down enough to get the message? This question reminds me of my voice mail. Many times I have to play my voice message over and over again to get all of the details. It is because my mind is too distracted and on too many things. We cannot replay God's message, therefore, we had better do a better job of listening, because what He has to say is very important. Find a time everyday when you and God can communicate. Be quiet in the presence of God and He will speak to you.

January 22

"Praise Edition"

Scripture: Then the high priest and all his associates, who were members of the party of the Sadducees, were filled with jealousy. They arrested the apostles and put them in the public jail. 19But during the night an angel of the Lord opened the doors of the jail and brought them out. "Go, stand in the temple courts," he said, "and tell the people the full message of this new life." (Acts 5:17–20)

Every Wednesday I try to listen to a program called, "Praise Edition" on Christian radio. Whenever I do, I get a true blessing from hearing the testimonies of others. Hearing their stories of praise to God lifts me up and encourages me to be a better witness for Him.

God knows that witnessing and testifying to each other about His blessings builds up the church. It strengthens the church to do more for His glory. In turn, when God is glorified; those being blessed by God want to tell it. Like a rock rolling down a hill, once praise starts, it continues to roll, thus we get to the point where we are praising God constantly.

I once heard a story about the angels in Heaven singing glories and praises to God. When they sang, the radiance of God engulfed Heaven in a spectacle too wonderful for expression. When the angels saw this awesome display, they sang over again and again and again glorifying and praising God.

When we learn to praise our wonderful God, we will see His radiance in every day of our lives.

January 23

"Blessing of Children"

Scripture: Children's children are a crown to the aged; parents are the pride of their children. (Proverbs 17:6)

Last night, as I was getting ready for bed, the pictures of our four children, when they were babies, caught my eye. They immediately took me back to the time when they were that age and the joy that each one of them brought as they were born. The pictures gave me a sense of pride, brought a lump to my throat, and caused me to realize what a blessing they are.

God enriches our lives as He blesses us with children. Each one adds a new dimension to the family and each one provides the family with new character. Each child brings a new love that each one of us receives.

I thank God for my children and for the blessing each one has given me. I know that the blessings will continue in my golden years as they add to our family with their children. I look forward to that day and the blessing each will bring.

January 24

"Earthly Arrogance"

Scripture: "I know that you can do all things; no plan of yours can be thwarted. You asked, 'Who is this that obscures my counsel without knowledge?' Surely I spoke of things I did not understand, things too wonderful for me to know. (Job 42:2–3)

Our generation was born in an era where we sometimes believe we know everything. Our education, our access to books, the internet, and other resources give us the ability to learn much. The more we learn, the more knowledge we gain, the more we think we are in control.

Reading in the book of Job, Job thought he had figured everything out with his friends. He thought he had all of the answers to the cause of his problems and thought he knew why his life was turned upside down. Job thought he knew God and why God allowed all of these life-changing things to happen to him. Shortly after Job arrogantly thought he had figured out his circumstance and God, God came to Job and asked him to answer a few questions. God proceeded to ask Job about the creation of the universe, the formation of the earth, the beasts, and all that was in the world. As God riddled him with question after question, Job was humbled because he could not answer even one. Job then realized that all knowledge, truth, and understanding come from God the creator and author of all.

Earthly arrogance only proves that we think we know more than God. Don't be caught in this trap, but humble yourself before God and He will provide you with the knowledge for life.

January 25

"God Speaks"

Scripture: On that day Gad went to David and said to him, "Go up and build an altar to the LORD on the threshing floor of Araunah the Jebusite." So David went up, as the LORD had commanded through Gad. (2 Samuel 24:18–19)

How does God speak to you? Can you hear His voice? Does He call your name?

God speaks to us in many ways. He speaks to us through His Holy word, through situations good and bad, and through people He chooses. God wants us to know and understand what He is saying; therefore, He uses people most of all. He uses people to relay His message to make it clear and understandable. Sometimes God uses people who don't realize they are being the deliverer of an important message and other times He sends someone direct. However, when God chooses to speak, one thing is clear: our spirit will verify the truth.

God loves us and wants to speak to us. So the next time we are approached and someone imparts some pearls of wisdom, we must listen to what is said and then check to see if what we are told lines up with our spirit.

January 26

"Are You Listening?"

Scripture: "Be still, and know that I am God; I will be exalted among the nations, I will be exalted in the earth." (Psalm 46:10)

The world is constantly bombarding our ears with information. Our family, job, sports, TV, and radio are always competing for our attention. We get so busy trying to pay attention to what is being said that it all just gets jumbled and confused. We seem to be so distracted that we fail to listen and gain the details of the message. God is speaking to us, but are we listening? He has invaluable knowledge and wisdom, but if we are distracted by information overload, how can we gain from what God is trying to say?

Make time in your schedule to listen to the Spirit of God within you. Turn off the TV and radio, get out of earshot of the family, and sequester yourself from the noisy world. Then be still and listen. In the stillness you will recognize God's presence and receive clear direction for your life—that is, if you are listening.

January 27

"The Simple Truth"

Scripture: I am astonished that you are so quickly deserting the one who called you by the grace of Christ and are turning to a different gospel—which is really no gospel at all. Evidently some people are throwing you into confusion and are trying to pervert the gospel of Christ. But even if we or an angel from heaven should preach a gospel other than the one we preached to you, let him be eternally condemned! As we have already said, so now I say again: If anybody is preaching to you a gospel other than what you accepted, let him be eternally condemned! (Galatians 1:6–9)

Do you know what really steams me? It is when I hear about a church that wants to change the Gospel. They want to change the Good News of Jesus into something today's society will accept. Now, I am all for reaching the lost and using Paul's philosophy of finding common ground, but not for the sake of political correctness.

The plain and simple truth is that you can't distort it, change it, sugar coat it, or make it more acceptable. God sent His one and only Son to take our sins upon him. He gave His life that we might have eternal life. So no matter what you hear from others, God is the same yesterday, today, and forever. He offers each of us a free gift of salvation by believing in the life, death, and resurrection of Jesus Christ. This is the Good News, the Gospel, and the simple truth.

January 28

"Godly Compassion"

Scripture: Shout for joy, O heavens; rejoice, O earth; burst into song, O mountains! For the LORD comforts his people and will have compassion on his afflicted ones. (Isaiah 49:13)

Compassion is very difficult for some of us. We see the warmth and caring nature of others, but struggle to be that way ourselves. Are we so self-centered, that we don't really care? I think and hope not. In my case, I have been focused on providing for my family, working hard, and surviving this world. I had no time or place for anyone or anything to distract me until . . .

God through Jesus showed me true compassion. He showed me by His own love, mercy, grace, and sacrifice that compassion didn't distract me, but enhanced me. It graced me with new horizons and a better understanding of how to be compassionate to others. It would not be phony or insincere, but true, genuine compassion for my fellow man.

Praise be to God that He can take our worldly personality and add to it with Godly compassion.

____

____

____

January 29

"Health, Happiness, and Prosperity"

Scripture: So be careful to do what the LORD your God has commanded you; do not turn aside to the right or to the left. Walk in all the way that the LORD your God has commanded you, so that you may live and prosper and prolong your days in the land that you will possess. (Deuteronomy 5:32–33)

In today's society we are constantly tempted. We are bombarded with advertisements coaxing us to buy all sorts of things, to become more beautiful, to become more prosperous, and to be sexy. These advertisements beckon us and try to make us believe that if we buy that stock, wear those clothes, and drive a specific car our lives will be better than ever before. We are constantly tempted to chase after these items because society portrays them as our only hope for health, happiness, and prosperity.

The truth is there is only one hope that truly accomplishes what we seek—Jesus Christ. He can and does deliver on His promises. Jesus is the same yesterday, today, and forever. His promises will never run out nor wear out, but will be there to replenish themselves year in and year out. So instead of chasing after meaningless trivial trinkets, get the real thing that supplies all—Jesus—and when you do you will have your heart's desires. You will have your health, happiness, and prosperity.

January 30

"What's Your Decision?"

Scripture: But if serving the LORD seems undesirable to you, then choose for yourselves this day whom you will serve, whether the gods your forefathers served beyond the River, or the gods of the Amorites, in whose land you are living. But as for me and my household, we will serve the LORD. (Joshua 24:15)

Each and everyday we live we are faced with decisions. They start the moment we wake until we go to bed. Decision after decision, whether it is pertaining to something serious or it is an insignificant matter, has to be made.

Our decision to choose God and to serve him everyday of our lives is *not* insignificant. It is by far the most important decision we will have to make. The choice to serve God has consequences not just here and now, but eternal ones as well. It affects the quantity and quality of our day-to-day existence and provides us with eternal hope for the future.

So what decision will you make? Will you choose God or not? Will you serve God or something else? What's your decision?

January 31

"God's Strength"

Scripture: Then Samson prayed to the LORD, "O Sovereign LORD, remember me. O God, please strengthen me just once more, and let me with one blow get revenge on the Philistines for my two eyes." Then Samson reached toward the two central pillars on which the temple stood. Bracing himself against them, his right hand on the one and his left hand on the other, Samson said, "Let me die with the Philistines!" Then he pushed with all his might, and down came the temple on the rulers and all the people in it. Thus he killed many more when he died than while he lived. (Judges 16: 28–30)

Everyday we rely on our own physical strength. We move about freely, lift items, and participate in athletic endeavors. Many of us take our physical strength for granted. There are many, however, who cannot. They are afflicted by an illness or a disability that prevents them from using their own strength. Even though they can't use their physical strength, many remain strong in other ways. They face their disabilities and afflictions with more courage and mental strength than most of us who have all of our faculties.

I have learned over the years that true strength comes from God. He has granted each and every one of us the strength we need to face any situation. He often uses our weaknesses to give us unique strength to overcome and glorify Him. God is my strength.

February

February 1

"Fully Committed"

Scripture: But Ruth replied, "Don't urge me to leave you or to turn back from you. Where you go I will go, and where you stay I will stay. Your people will be my people and your God my God. Where you die I will die, and there I will be buried. May the LORD deal with me, be it ever so severely, if anything but death separates you and me." When Naomi realized that Ruth was determined to go with her, she stopped urging her. (Ruth 1:16–18)

Fully committed—what does that really mean today? We live in a society where the divorce rate is 50% and single parents are trying to raise their children alone without the support of the other parent. We find that loyalty takes a back seat to greed and profit. People do not want to make a full commitment, instead they want a loophole and/or a back door to every relationship they have.

God honors commitment and loyalty. He blesses and binds marriages of those who work at it and stay together. God blesses and recognizes loyalty, because He is loyal. Through the sacrifice of His Son, God committed Himself to insuring that every one of us do not face eternal damnation, but instead experience eternal hope. God wants commitment from us and in turn, He gives it to us forever. God is fully committed and expects us to be as well.

February 2

"Living or Lifeless?"

Scripture: As the body without the spirit is dead, so faith without deeds is dead. (James 2:26)

Growing up in a farm community allowed me to experience life on the farm. Many farms had ponds to water livestock. These ponds usually fit into two basic categories: one was a beautiful, living pond; and the other, a lifeless mess of moss and pond scum. Evaluating the ponds more closely, I noticed the ponds that were beautiful and full of life were ponds that had one stream feeding into them and one leading away from them. The streams seemed to be rejuvenating the ponds by the exchange of water flowing through them.

What a great analogy for our lives as Christians. Our faith without works is lifeless and cold, but if we share ourselves in Christian love through works, our lives are beautiful and full of life. The exchange of God's Spirit flowing through our lives keeps them healthy and vibrant. It allows us to support other life by being encouraging and helpful. It is our choice to be a stagnant pond of faith alone or a beautiful spring of life through God's work. What do you want to be—wonderfully alive or lifeless?

____

____

____

February 3

"Is Your Radio On?"

Scripture: So Eli told Samuel, "Go and lie down, and if he calls you, say, 'Speak, LORD, for your servant is listening.'" So Samuel went and lay down in his place. The LORD came and stood there, calling as at the other times, "Samuel! Samuel!" Samuel said, "Speak, for your servant is listening." (1 Samuel 3:9–10)

How does God speak to you? With life's hectic pace of parenting, working, and chasing after the American Dream, how can God speak to us? It is incredibly hard to find a few minutes to be quiet and allow God an audience. He wants to speak to us and we want to hear what God has to say, but then again would we listen?

God, at least to me, is like a giant radio beacon. He is always transmitting messages and programs He wants me to hear and all I need to do is tune in. At times, I have to adjust my antenna to receive the truth that God has for me. He is broadcasting 24 hours a day, 7 days a week, and 365 days per year and no matter where I am or what I am doing he has a message for me—so, in the words of an old gospel song, "Turn Your Radio On."

February 4

“Saving Light”

Scripture: When Jesus spoke again to the people, he said, “I am the light of the world. Whoever follows me will never walk in darkness, but will have the light of life.” (John 8:12)

Augustine Fresnel was the inventor of a lens used to focus and concentrate light into a beam that can be seen for over 20 miles. This invention, because of its unique focus, was used in lighthouses all over the world and consequently has saved many ships from crashing onto rocky shores.

Jesus is the focused “Light for this world.” Like the Fresnel lens, His teachings and Word shine like a beacon into the darkness. They point the way so that we may avoid danger and the rocky shores of the world, and so that we do not end up broken, crumbled, and lost. Just as the Fresnel lens saved many ships from crashing into rocks and undergoing a disastrous, total loss, Jesus can save our battered, wrecked, and damaged souls if we heed His warnings and follow His light to safety.

I am glad God chose to show His light throughout the world through Jesus and that Jesus’ light saved me from the rocky shores of catastrophe and death.

February 5

"Two Lane Road"

Scripture: In his heart a man plans his course, but the LORD determines his steps. (Proverbs 16:9)

I was driving down the road one day on a narrow, two-lane road and came to a new realization about following God's plan and guidance. The road I was on was narrow with hills, curves, and the usual person in front of me who wanted to mosey along at a much slower pace than I cared to go. I watched for a chance to pass, but with the hills, curves, and oncoming traffic I found little opportunity to do so. Finally, I came to a stretch of road seemingly vacant of cars, hills, and curves, so I started to pass when suddenly, from behind a rise, a car appeared, coming straight for me. Fortunately, I had plenty of time to get back into my lane, but in that moment of surprise God taught me this lesson.

Life's roads have all types of hills, curves, and obscured cars. As we travel, we may grow impatient of traveling the road God has mapped for us. Our first inkling is to take off on our own and pass slower traffic. The truth is God knows every bump in the road. He knows that the road that seems to be open and smooth can actually lead to death, just like a two-lane road. Therefore, we would be wise to stay on God's path, even if it seems to take us a bit longer to travel.

February 6

"Slay Your Goliath"

Scripture: David said to the Philistine, "You come against me with sword and spear and javelin, but I come against you in the name of the LORD Almighty, the God of the armies of Israel, whom you have defied. This day the LORD will hand you over to me, and I'll strike you down and cut off your head. Today I will give the carcasses of the Philistine army to the birds of the air and the beasts of the earth, and the whole world will know that there is a God in Israel. All those gathered here will know that it is not by sword or spear that the LORD saves; for the battle is the LORD's, and he will give all of you into our hands." (1 Samuel 17:45–47)

This morning I was reading about David and Goliath. It amazed me how God gave David the strength and faith to know he would be protected from his enemy. Through faith, David approached a fierce enemy, an enemy with proper battle training and equipment to fight, yet David was unafraid. David defeated Goliath and glorified God in doing so. David knew without a doubt that God would protect him, which gave him the confidence he needed to succeed.

Each of us faces some type of Goliath in our lives. It may be lust, greed, disease, or perhaps fear itself. We try to face these on our own, with our own strength, when what we need to realize is that God is there to help. All we need to do is place our "Goliath" before God and trust Him to help us to slay it. God is faithful and will not let us down.

February 7

"Take the Road Less Traveled"

Scripture: Then Jesus went through the towns and villages, teaching as he made his way to Jerusalem. Someone asked him, "Lord, are only a few people going to be saved?" He said to them, "Make every effort to enter through the narrow door, because many, I tell you, will try to enter and will not be able to. Once the owner of the house gets up and closes the door, you will stand outside knocking and pleading, 'Sir, open the door for us.' (Luke 13:22–25)

Interstate, expressways, and toll roads are all wonderful ways to move people commuting from one point to another quickly and efficiently. Millions of people use these highway systems everyday to go to work and to transport goods from town to town. These kinds of roads were uniquely conceived to bypass the cluttered little communities and the less traveled smaller roads. When we travel we have a choice: we can use the high-speed highway system or the road less traveled. I find many times that the road less traveled has many blessings unseen by most people.

Our walk with God takes us down a road less traveled. It provides us with an alternative to the fast-paced worldly roads by giving us a road with less traffic and many other blessings. The road is less traveled, because of our choice to follow God rather than the world. Our choice to be guided by God, at the pace God wants and over the road He knows is best, is not what the people of the world want. Instead of taking the smooth, safe, and blessed road that God has paved for us, they want to get there, get there fast, and in so doing miss the true blessing of life. So the next time you are faced with the choice of going down either God's less-traveled road or going the way the high-speed world goes, choose God and receive his eternal blessings.

February 8

“Enduring Love”

Scripture: Give thanks to the LORD, for he is good. His love endures forever. 2Give thanks to the God of gods. His love endures forever. 3Give thanks to the Lord of lords: His love endures forever. (Psalm 136:1–3)

God’s love is truly amazing. We go through life thinking that we are in control and that we are the makers of our own destinies. We will only give our love, when we get love. God is actually the one who controls and decides our fate and unlike us, He loved us even before we were created. He loves us in our rebellion. He loves us when we turn our backs on Him. He loves us when we sin against Him and our fellow man. He never ever stops loving us. He is there, as a patient Father, hoping someday that His love will be returned, but even if we don’t return His love, He will love us regardless.

I have been through a lot in my life. I have had glad times and bad times. I have had smooth sailing and tragedy. And, through it all I have learned one very important thing—God’s love endures forever.

February 9

"Stop, Look and Listen"

Scripture: The man said to me, "Son of man, look with your eyes and hear with your ears and pay attention to everything I am going to show you, for that is why you have been brought here. Tell the house of Israel everything you see." (Ezekiel 40:4)

In recent years, after God got my attention through a very trying time, I have tried to keep my ear inclined to Him. I actively seek Him to reveal new things to me regarding what He wants for my life. I have found He has many things He wants to say to me and all I need do is stop, look, and listen. I make it a point as I commute to turn the radio off and concentrate on the issues of the day. Sure there are work and family-related issues to ponder, but given enough time all of that clears and God speaks to my Spirit what He feels is important for the day. Some of these revelations are about work, family, and spiritual growth, and some are a sense of abundant peace. Whatever the message is, He makes Himself very clear.

God has revealed Himself in many ways to the Saints and Prophets. He speaks through His undeniable Spirit, through visions, and through circumstances, but He definitely wants to communicate. If you want to hear God, stop, look, and listen and God will speak to you.

February 10

"Who Wants to Be a Millionaire?"

Scripture: I rejoice greatly in the Lord that at last you have renewed your concern for me. Indeed, you have been concerned, but you had no opportunity to show it. I am not saying this because I am in need, for I have learned to be content whatever the circumstances. I know what it is to be in need, and I know what it is to have plenty. I have learned the secret of being content in any and every situation, whether well fed or hungry, whether living in plenty or in want. I can do everything through him who gives me strength. (Philippians 4:10–13)

America is truly a land of opportunity. We, as citizens, enjoy the freedom to worship, speak, and do everything we choose without fear of persecution. We can do pretty much what we want, when we want to do it. In this land of freedom, abundance, and opportunity, however, there is an undertow and current of evil that threatens to destroy the freedom we hold so dear. That evil is greed.

Currently, there are more lottery dollars collected than ever before all because of the enticement of becoming a millionaire. There are at least six or more television shows that pit people against a game or other people for the almighty millionaire status; and let us not forget our own ambitions steering us towards becoming rich.

Money itself and what can be done with it is not evil, but the love of money at all cost is. God teaches us that He provides all things therefore we need to be content in all situations. We need to thank God for our freedoms, for our opportunities, and for His plans for our lives. When we finally put God first and give Him control, we gain a wealth that far exceeds this world. It is an eternal treasure which provides riches beyond our wildest dreams, and it will never diminish, so who wants to be a millionaire?

February 11

"The Bread and Water of Life"

Scripture: Jesus answered, "It is written: 'Man does not live on bread alone, but on every word that comes from the mouth of God.'" (Matthew 4:4)

We are living in the age of the infomercial. There are many of these paid advertisement programs that tout health food and vitamins. They talk, endorse, and interview users that portray the benefits of their products. They are all confident that their products will improve your health and quality of life. Each claim builds the expectation of a long, healthy, and happy life and all at a low cost.

It is true we need to eat right, exercise, and make sure we have the proper vitamins and minerals, but we cannot forget that what truly sustains us is God. God is the bread and water of life. God sustains us and fortifies us for each day and without Him we will miss a vital part of what we need. So let's start each day with the bread of life—God's Word—and the life-giving waters of Jesus to satisfy our thirst. In doing so, we will improve the quality of our lives.

February 12

"Rebuilding the Walls"

Scripture: So the wall was completed on the twenty-fifth of Elul, in fifty-two days. When all our enemies heard about this, all the surrounding nations were afraid and lost their self-confidence, because they realized that this work had been done with the help of our God. (Nehemiah 6:15–16)

Fear and doubt grip our lives everyday. We go to work thinking about being downsized. We participate in programs at arms length, so we won't get hurt. We wonder about terror and when it may strike. And, we even hold back from trusting God, because we do not want to lose control, that is, if we really had any in the first place. The fear and doubt keep God from doing a marvelous work in us and through us. Instead of trusting God and allowing Him to govern our actions, we hold on and hold out thinking we are at the reigns.

Nehemiah was given the awesome task of rebuilding Jerusalem's walls after years of enemy destruction. If he had relied on his own abilities and strength, the task would not be complete even today. But, Nehemiah trusted God and partnered with others who trusted God, and as a result, the walls were built in 52 days.

I do not know what walls in your life have been reduced to rubble and have to be rebuilt, but I do know that without God it is impossible to do it timely and effectively. Trust God and He will help you rebuild your walls to His glory.

February 13

"Family"

Scripture: While Jesus was still talking to the crowd, his mother and brothers stood outside, wanting to speak to him. Someone told him, "Your mother and brothers are standing outside, wanting to speak to you." He replied to him, "Who is my mother, and who are my brothers?" 49Pointing to his disciples, he said, "Here are my mother and my brothers. For whoever does the will of my Father in heaven is my brother and sister and mother." (Matthew 12:46–50)

America is a great proponent of individualism. America tells people to march to the beat of their own drummer. Do what you want, say what you want and when you want are all mottos in today's society. This concept of individualism teaches a message that is tearing apart the basic fabric of the nation—family.

I have noticed my children expressing some of these symptoms, especially my oldest. When he was around seventeen he wanted to spend most of his waking hours in his room on the computer totally disassociated from the rest of the family. It was an extremely difficult issue to deal with, so instead of guilting him into spending time with the family, we simply made sure to include him. We sat at the table and had dinner. We would take him to the movies and to church with us and we made sure that he was confident that he was a vital part of our family.

God knows what is best, because now my oldest is in college and spending summers away working. His attitude toward his family has changed. He now comes home to be part of his family, to be included, and to enjoy what the family has to offer. God wants us all to belong and to have a sense of family. He wants us to marry and have children, to enjoy and be fulfilled. If we do not have a family, he wants us to know He is our Father and that our fellow believers are our brothers and sisters. God wants us all to be in His family and to live in confidence, comfort, and healthy well-being.

February 14

"Holiday of Love"

Scripture: Love is patient, love is kind. It does not envy, it does not boast, it is not proud. It is not rude, it is not self-seeking, it is not easily angered, it keeps no record of wrongs. Love does not delight in evil but rejoices with the truth. It always protects, always trusts, always hopes, always perseveres. (1 Corinthians 13:4–7)

St. Valentines Day is a day when we express our love towards those special persons in our lives. Our wife, husband, mother, father, girlfriend, or boyfriend are all greeted this day with cards, candy, and flowers. We want to show our love in a special way to insure they realize the breadth, width, and depth of our love.

How we view love or express love is often the result of observing our parents' relationship. That is good, but what about those who haven't been blessed by seeing parents who were truly in love?

God offers and shows us true love. God's love stands the test of time. His love looks past the exterior or the personality one may present to the world and goes right to the heart. God sees *who* we are and *what* we are and loves us in spite of all of that. He really knows and shows us how to love, not only on St. Valentines Day, but every day of our lives.

____

____

____

February 15

"The Cock Crows"

Scripture: Then Jesus answered, "Will you really lay down your life for me? I tell you the truth, before the rooster crows, you will disown me three times! (John 13:38)

Have you ever been is a situation or circumstance where you denied that you were a Christian? Maybe you were at work or with a group of your peers and instead of standing on your Christian principles you let things pass. You knew the discussion was contrary to what you knew as truth, but instead of speaking up, you stood silent or even agreed with what was being said. I'm sure that when you knew that you had done wrong, you felt horrible and you were convicted, convinced you had committed a sin.

All of us have been in times, places, or circumstances where we didn't stand up for what was right or what we believed. Our faith took a back seat to the world. Silence came over us and we didn't stand up to be counted as a Christian. Instead, we denied our Father, our salvation, and Jesus.

The good news is you and I are in good company. Peter did the same thing, but he compounded the error by telling Jesus he would lay down his life for Him. Peter upped the stakes considerably. Peter feared persecution and fear for his own life, so he denied knowing Jesus three times. Jesus knew he would do it and predicted it, but Jesus loved Peter and He made provision for him to go from being the man who denied Jesus three times to the man Jesus used to build His church. Jesus can take the worst circumstance and create good, so, as we confess the times we have not stood up for the truth and for Jesus, Jesus will erase our sin.

February 16

"Test Everything"

Scripture: We have heard that some went out from us without our authorization and disturbed you, troubling your minds by what they said. So we all agreed to choose some men and send them to you with our dear friends Barnabas and Paul—men who have risked their lives for the name of our Lord Jesus Christ. Therefore we are sending Judas and Silas to confirm by word of mouth what we are writing. It seemed good to the Holy Spirit and to us not to burden you with anything beyond the following requirements: You are to abstain from food sacrificed to idols, from blood, from the meat of strangled animals and from sexual immorality. You will do well to avoid these things. (Acts 15:24–29)

Have you ever attended a church or worship service that troubled you? Ever attended a service where you did not understand the events that occurred and even had thoughts about their place in worship? Ever had suspicions about the relevance of something that happened in a service and wondered whether what happened was truly the way God wanted to be worshiped?

I experienced such an event. I attended a worship service where it was prevalent for the congregation to speak and worship in tongues. When I first experienced the act, my trip home was filled with confusion. Was this of God? What this experience did do was force me to research God's Word and the pertinence of the gifts of the Holy Spirit. After my study, I returned to the service and experienced the worship from a whole new perspective.

Everything we want and need to know about God, His worship, and what He wants for our lives is in His Word. So never be close-minded to what you see and experience, but rather test whatever you see and experience with God's Word and you will never be misled.

February 17

"Heart Attack"

Scripture: Praise awaits you, O God, in Zion; to you our vows will be fulfilled. O you who hear prayer, to you all men will come. When we were overwhelmed by sins, you forgave our transgressions. Blessed are those you choose and bring near to live in your courts! We are filled with the good things of your house, of your holy temple. (Psalm 65:1–4)

Sin is a horrible thing. We often commit sin and then try to justify it by saying that no harm has been done. One day, however, God opens our hearts and we realize that our hearts have been scarred by the sin we've committed. Each time that we sin another scar is left, then another, and another, until one day our hearts are full of scars.

Similarly, a heart attack leaves a scar on the heart. It actually damages part of the heart muscle and that part of the muscle ceases to function. If the heart is scarred enough times, the result is death. Sin does the same thing to our heart. The more we sin, the more scars it creates and eventually death occurs, not physically, but spiritually.

God does not want our hearts to be damaged and spiritual death to occur. He has provided His Son, Jesus, to take away our scars and to renew our hearts, so that we can love Him with whole, renewed, and pure hearts.

February 18

"Plans, Whose Plans?"

Scripture: For I know the plans I have for you," declares the LORD, "plans to prosper you and not to harm you, plans to give you hope and a future. Then you will call upon me and come and pray to me, and I will listen to you. (Jeremiah 29:11–12)

We all make plans. We plan our lives, our jobs, and our families. We even plan to make our dreams come true. More times than not, however, our plans end up in disappointment. The reason is because they are *our* plans, not God's. We orchestrate such plans because we believe they are all within our control.

There was a time not so long ago when I felt in complete control. I planned and worked, worked and planned only to come up short. The truth of the matter is that everything ended up in shambles. Then, one day, as I drove down the road, I noticed a sign for a church starting a new building. At the bottom of the sign announcing the church project the verse of Jeremiah 29:11 declared, "For I know the plans I have for you." In that very moment, I realized that my plans were my plans and that if God was not orchestrating them, my plans were futile.

Now God has my plans and I count on Him to bring those plans to fruition. I have found that my stress has been eliminated and my plans succeed almost effortlessly. Thank you, God, for the plans that you have for me.

February 19

"Futility"

Scripture: Now all has been heard; here is the conclusion of the matter: Fear God and keep his commandments, for this is the whole duty of man. For God will bring every deed into judgment, including every hidden thing, whether it is good or evil. (Ecclesiastes 12:13–14)

I was reading the book of Ecclesiastes the other day and found it to be somewhat disturbing. Written by Solomon who was one of the wisest men ever, the book paints a very futile picture of life. Solomon points out that the things we do in this life are in vain. It does not matter whether we are rich or poor, famous or infamous, righteous or sinful; we all end up in the same place in this world—dead.

The truth in the book, to me, was this: a life without God, even though it seems meaningless today, will be revealed in the Day of Judgment. At that time God will give a report, and then and only then will we really know how we truly lived our lives. Therefore, if we strive to uphold God's commands we will find that our lives are not lived in vain.

February 20

"Jesus' Face"

Scripture: For God, who said, "Let light shine out of darkness," made his light shine in our hearts to give us the light of the knowledge of the glory of God in the face of Christ. (2 Corinthians 4:6)

I was just sitting and thinking about the day I got married. Everything seemed to be going okay until it got closer to time for the ceremony. I remember being at the front of the church along with the groomsmen, waiting for the bride to appear when a thought popped into my head: Am I doing the right thing? And then, at that very instant, I saw my bride's face and it all became very clear. I did make the right decision to make this wonderful woman a part of my life forever.

Living a life in Christ is similar in many ways. We go through circumstances and situations where we question our decision of becoming a Christian. We see other people around us without Christ gain and grow, which fuels our doubt. But, our spirit reinforces our decision and in our hearts we know that our choice to live for God is right. So we continue day by day waiting for the time when we will see the face of Christ; for it is in that instant that we will know that we made the right decision to make Him part of our lives for eternity.

February 21

"Soul Insurance"

Scripture: That if you confess with your mouth, "Jesus is Lord," and believe in your heart that God raised him from the dead, you will be saved. For it is with your heart that you believe and are justified, and it is with your mouth that you confess and are saved. (Romans 10:9–10)

I came to a realization today after watching countless television ads for insurance. I noticed that there is insurance for our cars, insurance for our house, life insurance, health insurance, extended warranty insurance and disability insurance; all portrayed to be a necessity. "You never want to be uninsured," they tout. But, of all the insurance in the world none can prevent catastrophe from happening. Insurance just helps us with recovery after the fact. So with all of the insurance out there, where is the insurance for our souls?

Well, here is some good news: Eternal insurance is available. This insurance covers our souls. This insurance is much different than other policies, because it prevents catastrophe, it encourages, it supports, and it even comforts. Better yet, it is free. We have no premiums to pay, because the policy was purchased and paid for in full by a loving and caring God through the sacrifice of His Son, Jesus. You know by the form of payment that this policy is valuable and will cover everything—all of our sin including past, present, and future.

If you are not sure whether or not your soul is covered, get some insurance—the insurance that only comes in knowing and accepting Jesus' saving grace.

February 22

"Slow Down"

Scripture: As Jesus and his disciples were on their way, he came to a village where a woman named Martha opened her home to him. She had a sister called Mary, who sat at the Lord's feet listening to what he said. But Martha was distracted by all the preparations that had to be made. She came to him and asked, "Lord, don't you care that my sister has left me to do the work by myself? Tell her to help me!" "Martha, Martha," the Lord answered, "you are worried and upset about many things, but only one thing is needed. Mary has chosen what is better, and it will not be taken away from her." (Luke 10:38–42)

I don't know about you, but my life seems to be overwhelmed with things that need to be done. I have four kids, a cat, a dog, a wife, and a job that requires me to travel and all of them need my attention, never mind the things that I want to do for myself. And, then what about time for God? Where does He fit in the scheme of events that control my life?

I am sure everyone faces the same dilemmas. It is hard to stay in balance. It is important to make time for the things we think are important and none of them are bad, but how can we make time for them all?

Sometimes I feel like I am coming apart at the seams, so instead of trying to speed up to get more done, I slow down. Instead of concerning myself with my family or my job, I stop and commune with God. I allow God's Spirit to take charge, to prioritize and organize the chaos, and put everything in order. It is true that all things are possible for those who believe. So the next time your calendar is full, and you are feeling overwhelmed, just slow down and let God take control.

February 23

"A Message for All People"

Scripture: While Peter was still speaking these words, the Holy Spirit came on all who heard the message. The circumcised believers who had come with Peter were astonished that the gift of the Holy Spirit had been poured out even on the Gentiles. For they heard them speaking in tongues and praising God. Peter said, "Can anyone keep these people from being baptized with water? They have received the Holy Spirit just as we have." So he ordered that they be baptized in the name of Jesus Christ. Then they asked Peter to stay with them for a few days. The apostles and the brothers throughout Judea heard that the Gentiles also had received the word of God. So when Peter went up to Jerusalem, the circumcised believers criticized him and said, "You went into the house of uncircumcised men and ate with them." (Acts 10:44–48, 11:1–3)

God's message is for all people. He does not discriminate, choose by origin, or choose by denomination who should receive Him. His forgiveness is for all who listen.

If you think that this world is prejudice these days, you are right! But in Jesus' day no one of Jewish faith was even allowed in the presence of a person of another nationality let alone allowed to talk to him or her. The Jews felt that these people were impure, unclean, and unholy. They made this determination not by getting to know the person, but only by where the person lived.

God opened the door through Jesus that all may enter. It does not matter what color your skin, what country you are from, or what sins you have committed, Jesus has cleared the way. He wants us to be in the family of God. He wants us to come and eat at the banquet He has prepared for us in Heaven, so don't let anyone, anything, or any circumstance keep you from accepting God's love.

February 24

"Let God's Love Shine"

Scripture: Though I am free and belong to no man, I make myself a slave to everyone, to win as many as possible. (1 Corinthians 9:19)

Living in Christ does not come without responsibility. We are commanded to love one another. This command does not mean for us to just love our brother or sister in Christ, but also the tattooed, ear-pierced boy next door, the Hispanic man at work, the girl that walks around half-exposed, and the rude neighbor who annoys us constantly. God wants us to show His love to everyone, so that they may be saved.

I have heard many times that "we may be the only Jesus a person may see" or "we each have at least one person we can reach for Jesus". If these statements are true, then we need to be prepared to be loving and caring to all people. Let yourself be used by God and make yourself just as common as the ones you are trying to reach. Find that common ground and let God's love shine.

February 25

"Recurring Sin"

Scripture: We know that the law is spiritual; but I am unspiritual, sold as a slave to sin. 15I do not understand what I do. For what I want to do I do not do, but what I hate I do. And if I do what I do not want to do, I agree that the law is good. As it is, it is no longer I myself who do it, but it is sin living in me. I know that nothing good lives in me, that is, in my sinful nature. For I have the desire to do what is good, but I cannot carry it out. For what I do is not the good I want to do; no, the evil I do not want to do—this I keep on doing. Now if I do what I do not want to do, it is no longer I who do it, but it is sin living in me that does it. (Romans 7:14–20)

How do you deal with recurring sin? You try and work hard to be spiritual, you pray regularly, you read God's Word, but still you sin. With me it is not just sin itself, but it is the same sin over and over again. I struggled with it for decades and sometimes do very well going weeks and even months without committing this sin, but then in a weak moment . . . Bang!!! There I am back where I didn't want to be.

I am going to acknowledge this committed and recurring sin that I have within me to all of you so that you can pray for me. The sin is lust. It's not that I physically desire other women, but I sin through looking at highly suggestive and sometimes explicit movies and pictures. I see a glimpse of bare skin and there I go. It seems to get more difficult as every television show, movie, and magazine adds to my temptation.

Lord, I know Paul struggled with his sinful nature and that you helped him to overcome it. So Lord I stand ready and willing to be purged of this sin, so that I can live in your light. Please let it be so today.

I do not know what type sin you struggle with or if it is a constant recurring problem like mine, but I do know that our God can and will forgive us. We must also learn to know what tempts us and avoid it at all cost and with God's help we will overcome our sin.

February 26

"Fertile Ground"

Scripture: That same day Jesus went out of the house and sat by the lake. Such large crowds gathered around him that he got into a boat and sat in it, while all the people stood on the shore. Then he told them many things in parables, saying: "A farmer went out to sow his seed. As he was scattering the seed, some fell along the path, and the birds came and ate it up. Some fell on rocky places, where it did not have much soil. It sprang up quickly, because the soil was shallow. But when the sun came up, the plants were scorched, and they withered because they had no root. 7Other seed fell among thorns, which grew up and choked the plants. Still other seed fell on good soil, where it produced a crop—a hundred, sixty or thirty times what was sown. He who has ears, let him hear." (Matthew 13:1–9)

Many times while driving down the road, I turn on the radio and listen to all the different preachers. Some of the messages are very uplifting and touch my heart. Others are encouraging and let me know God loves me and everything will be all right. And, still others are informative and stimulate me to want to make changes in my life. The question I often face is: Do I really want to change? My intentions are always good at first and maybe for a few days, or even a week I am compelled to do what I set out to do. After that short period is over though, my enthusiasm usually diminishes and I abandon my cause.

Bearing fruit with God's Word is difficult. It takes a full commitment on our part and we must discipline ourselves to see it through. In my life I know whatever God plants in my spirit stays and produces fruit in abundance. I look at my prayer to God, prior to taking on the challenge, as soil preparation, because if I plant the seed without His blessing, it does not grow, but when God fertilizes my spirit the request produces an abundant harvest. Therefore, before I take something on, I first take an attitude of prayer to see what God wants. Only then will I know the soil is prepared, fertile, and will bear fruit.

February 27

"Birthday Blessing"

Scripture: Children's children are a crown to the aged, and parents are the pride of their children. (Proverbs 17:6)

It is February 27, and my daughter's birthday. God has blessed us with four children and one of these special blessings was the gift of a daughter. My wife and I always wanted a girl, but it wasn't until our fourth child that the gift came.

Our children all hold a special place in our hearts and we know that each is a gift from God. In God blessing us with children, we recognize how truly special we are to Him. He loves us so much that He made provision for our sin. He loves us so much that He made us heirs to the throne. He loves us so much that He lavished His blessings upon us and one of those, for my wife and I, was a daughter.

Thank you Lord for the precious gift you granted us—our daughter.

___

___

___

February 28

"Unbroken Promises"

Scripture: "Now I am about to go the way of all the earth. You know with all your heart and soul that not one of all the good promises the LORD your God gave you has failed. Every promise has been fulfilled; not one has failed. (Job 23:14)

"I promise" only to be followed by "I am sorry" is a common way of life anymore. The two seem to go hand-in-hand as promises are broken time and time again and people think everything will be okay if they just say "I am sorry". The problem is people say "I am sorry" so much that it has become nothing more than a cliché. Promises are broken so frequently that people have become cynical of the idea of being promised anything at all. It seems no one wants to be held accountable for their word and it is too easy to say "I am sorry" when they don't keep their word. No sincerity and no sense of responsibility make for a bad combination.

God has made promises too. He has promised never to leave us or forsake us. He has promised to be with us always until the end of the age, but living in a world of broken promises how can we be sure that God will be true to His?

Faith and trust coincide with a promise. Faith and trust provide the confidence we need in order to know a promise will be kept. God has never broken a promise and He never will. He has proven Himself from the beginning of time to our current day. So you ask, "How do you know God will keep His promises?" Because, God said my life would change if I accepted His Son, Jesus, as my personal Savior and it did; therefore I am a firsthand witness to God's promise.

March

March 1

"Your Choice"

Scripture: You did not choose me, but I chose you and appointed you to go and bear fruit—fruit that will last. Then the Father will give you whatever you ask in my name. (John 15:16)

Traveling for the company I work for can get pretty trying on occasion. On one trip I was faced with many hurdles to get back home. It seemed the airlines had a union slow down and there was also bad weather, which impeded a number of flights. Schedules became impossible to keep; flights were changed and even cancelled. I was forced to make choices about my travel. To get back home, circumstances dictated that I take a flight west in order to go east. What should have been a six hour trip took over twenty.

Delays and changes occur everyday in our lives. It seems to be par for the course to have our circumstances force or limit our choices. Yet when God offers the choice that will change our lives for eternity, we resist and even turn the other way. God grants us the ability to choose our course. He grants us free will and blesses us as we make those choices. With God, we are not forced to make choices by circumstance. Instead we have the opportunity to seek Him and allow Him to lead us. If we do so, He will bless us with life, health, and prosperity. It is your choice.

March 2

"Does God Ever Give Up?"

Scripture: In him we have redemption through his blood, the forgiveness of sins, in accordance with the riches of God's grace. (Ephesians 1:7)

Does God ever get tired of His children committing sin? Knowing we all sin time and time again, is there a point when God gives up?

The good news is God never gives up. He knew from the fall of Adam and Eve that we would never be free from sin. He knew if He did not provide a way for us to reconcile our sin, we would all perish. Therefore, He decided to be born of flesh and blood in the form of Jesus. He came into this world not to condemn it, but to save it. He came to present Himself as a living sacrifice by bearing all of our sins—past, present, and future—through crucifixion on the cross.

God does not want us to sin; He wants us to overcome sin in our lives. Inasmuch as He wants this, however, He knows as humans we will fail time and time again. That is why, through His grace, He made it possible for us to come to Him time and time again for forgiveness and through repentance be embraced by His love once more.

____

____

____

March 3

"God's Best"

Scripture: To keep me from becoming conceited because of these surpassingly great revelations, there was given me a thorn in my flesh, a messenger of Satan, to torment me.

Three times I pleaded with the Lord to take it away from me. But he said to me, "my grace is sufficient for you, for my power is made perfect in weakness." Therefore I will boast all the more gladly about my weaknesses, so that Christ's power may rest on me. That is why, for Christ's sake, I delight in weaknesses, in insults, in hardships, in persecutions, in difficulties. For when I am weak, then I am strong. (2 Corinthians 12:7–10)

Everyday I come to realize how difficult it must have been for the saints to be persecuted for Christ's sake. Not that I have shared in such sufferings, but I have been subject to rejection because of my own sin. The rejection I felt was my own guilt and the feeling of being inadequate to be a part of God's family. I suffered with that guilt, my helplessness, my hopelessness, and how truly weak I was. I do not have the power to reverse the sins I have committed nor do I have the power to forget them. Therefore, I have been plagued by the guilt and shame of my sin.

God knew this would happen. He knew I would eventually recognize my weakness and shortcomings, which would lead me to Him. I realize now that God's "grace is sufficient" and His power "is made perfect in my weakness". For when I am weak, God is strong; and when I am at my worst, God is at His best.

March 4

"Godly Satisfaction"

Scripture: Then the eleven disciples went to Galilee, to the mountain where Jesus had told them to go. When they saw him, they worshiped him; but some doubted. Then Jesus came to them and said, "All authority in heaven and on earth has been given to me. Therefore go and make disciples of all nations, baptizing them in the name of the Father and of the Son and of the Holy Spirit, and teaching them to obey everything I have commanded you. And surely I am with you always, to the very end of the age." (Matthew 28:16–20)

I have been preparing to do some painting around the house. Because it is not something I like to do, it takes me awhile to prepare. I have to get out drop cloths, paintbrushes, caulking, and finally force myself to start the project. Starting is always the hardest part, but when the job is finally complete, I feel a wonderful sense of accomplishment and satisfaction.

Discipleship too requires preparation. We must read and study God's Word. We must learn to seek our Father's advice and wisdom. And, we must devote ourselves to becoming more like Christ. The preparation requires gaining truth that only comes through God, boldness from His Holy Spirit, and the strength of righteousness through Jesus. This preparation molds us into true disciples and enables us to be witnesses for Christ. Once we have prepared and shared, we gain a wonderful sense of accomplishment and satisfaction that comes from God's Spirit as well as a resounding, "Well done" from the Lord.

March 5

"Just Forgiven"

Scripture: I tell you the truth, all the sins and blasphemies of men will be forgiven them. (Mark 3:28)

I saw a very interesting bumper sticker the other day. It read: "Christians aren't perfect, just forgiven." No truer words were ever spoken. I have been around people who think Christians believe themselves to be superior. Maybe they get that opinion because of the confidence Christians exude from knowing the truth, or maybe they feel guilt because they do not live in the truth themselves.

As Christians, we are thankful for God's saving grace and the fact that we can live our lives with confidence, peace, and boldness. We recognize the price paid for our forgiveness and realize that Jesus was the only sinless person who ever lived here on earth. We acknowledge that we are not perfect and that we fall short of the glory of God, but we know that in our imperfection we can still be saved.

"Christians aren't perfect, just forgiven."

March 6

"Jesus is Lord"

Scripture: So as the Holy Spirit says: "Today, if you hear his voice, do not harden your hearts as you did in the rebellion, the time of testing in the desert, where your fathers tested and tried me and for forty years saw what I did. That is why I was angry with that generation, I said, 'Their hearts are always going astray, they have not known my ways.' So I declared on oath in my anger, 'They shall never enter my rest.'" (Hebrews 3:7–11)

What do you believe? Why do you honor our Lord? These profound questions require us to search our hearts. Our intellect tells us it cannot be that God made everything and through Him all things were made. Science has worked for years to dispel everything the Bible says about God's creation and then there are our own misconceptions that threaten the teachings of God. With all of this fighting against the Word, why do we believe?

Jesus told the disciples in John 15:26, "When the Counselor comes, whom I will send to you from the Father, the Spirit of truth who goes out from the Father, he will testify about me." The Holy Spirit is with us by our profession of faith and Jesus confirms above all else that God's Word is true. So guard against unbelief, your intellect, your deceitful heart, and your sin that tears down the Spirit which testifies that Jesus is Lord!

March 7

"Be Positive"

Scripture: Be joyful always; pray continually; give thanks in all circumstances, for this is God's will for you in Christ Jesus. (1 Thessalonians 5:16–18)

When faced with situations or circumstance to difficult to bear have you ever made or received either of these statements: "It will be okay" or "Everything will be all right"? The truth is we do not really know things will turn out positively, but we say these kinds of statements as a way of encouraging others. We believe that a positive, confident attitude will prevail to see us through and that our unswerving attitude will withstand and help us move on with life, but is that enough?

God can help us overcome our circumstances and situations and can help us persevere. He may not remove the challenge, because it builds our character, but He does give us instruction and encouragement to handle it and helps us to remain positive. It is best put by Paul in a letter to the Thessalonians. He knew it would be difficult for them to hold to their faith, to ward off other religions, and to cling to God's teachings, so he gave them some instructions and encouragement. He sums it up at the end of his letter in a most powerful way—the way we need to follow as we face life's challenges. We need to grasp these three lessons:

1) Be joyful always in all circumstances and situations,
2) Pray continually for God to be with us and
3) Give thanks in all things knowing that we are not alone.

These steps will help us maintain our attitude and help us overcome whatever life wants to dish out.

____

____

____

March 8

"War is Eminent"

Scripture: Finally, be strong in the Lord and in his mighty power. Put on the full armor of God so that you can take your stand against the devil's schemes. For our struggle is not against flesh and blood, but against the rulers, against the authorities, against the powers of this dark world and against the spiritual forces of evil in the heavenly realms. Therefore put on the full armor of God, so that when the day of evil comes, you may be able to stand your ground, and after you have done everything, to stand. Stand firm then, with the belt of truth buckled around your waist, with the breast-plate of righteousness in place, and with your feet fitted with the readiness that comes from the gospel of peace. In addition to all this, take up the shield of faith, with which you can extinguish all the flaming arrows of the evil one. Take the helmet of salvation and the sword of the Spirit, which is the word of God. And pray in the Spirit on all occasions with all kinds of prayers and requests. With this in mind, be alert and always keep on praying for all the saints. (Ephesians 6:10–18)

Everyday when we pick up a newspaper or watch the news much of what we see and hear is about war. It may be country against country or race against race, but it is still war. War is defined as a raging controversy between two factions, so I guess war surrounds us more than we ever realized.

God knew that we too would be at war, even if there was world peace. God knew the devil and his army of destruction would be out there waging war for our very souls. The devil is crafty. He attacks covertly by subtly bombarding our minds with smut and filth. He also attacks with a full frontal assault hoping that he can overwhelm us and that we will surrender. One thing is for certain; since he is fighting for your soul, he will attack and attack and attack.

Soldiers always prepare for battle. They ready their equipment and drill again and again so that they can react instinctively when under attack. Their preparation is paramount to winning the battle and as a soldier prepares for warfare, so we too need to be prepared. God is our drill sergeant and will instruct us and hone our skills to be victorious in the war over eternal death. We need to heed His instruction, drill fervently, and ready our equipment for war is eminent.

March 9

"No Joke"

Scripture: The entire law is summed up in a single command: "Love your neighbor as yourself." (Galatians 5:14)

There was a Jew, a Catholic, and a Protestant traveling together discussing religion. I know it sounds like the beginning of a joke, but there is no joke as I was the Protestant. Anyway, we were traveling along, when our conversation turned to religion. Each of us made our particular points and even when our discussion got quite intense, everyone respected each other's opinion. When the trip concluded, each of us had a new appreciation for the other's beliefs and religion.

We are all God's children. He made us all even though our beliefs may be many. And, most beliefs, at least Judaism, Christianity, and Islam, are all founded on God's Word. I know that Christians, because of God's saving grace, feel that they are the only ones who have the key to God's Kingdom. The truth is God and God alone makes that decision. He grants entry to Heaven on His terms. Yes, He gives us guidelines to get us there, but He alone opens the door. That is why He gave us the greatest commandment, "Love your neighbor as yourself" and leave the judgment to God.

March 10

"Burning Bush"

Scripture: Now Moses was tending the flock of Jethro his father-in-law, the priest of Midian, and he led the flock to the far side of the desert and came to Horeb, the mountain of God. There the angel of the LORD appeared to him in flames of fire from within a bush. Moses saw that though the bush was on fire it did not burn up. So Moses thought, "I will go over and see this strange sight—why the bush does not burn up." When the LORD saw that he had gone over to look, God called to him from within the bush, "Moses! Moses!" Moses said, "Here I am." (Exodus 3:1–4)

One of my favorite shrubs is a "burning bush". I just love the brilliant red leaves that appear in the fall—they are absolutely beautiful. The shrub's name was derived from its beautiful fiery red leaves and from the bush that introduced God to Moses.

Wonders come in many fashions, like the beauty of the burning bush and the remarkable introduction of God to Moses. Why doesn't God appear in like fashion today? It would be marvelous to see such a dramatic presentation that testifies to the presence of God. It would be confirmation of our beliefs and reassurance for our faith. God does show His presence constantly. It may not be in the dramatic flame-engulfing event, but in the subtle simple visions of nature, like the "burning bush".

March 11

"What Are We Known For?"

Scripture: While Jesus was in Bethany in the home of a man known as Simon the Leper, a woman came to him with an alabaster jar of very expensive perfume, which she poured on his head as he was reclining at the table. When the disciples saw this, they were indignant. "Why this waste?" they asked. "This perfume could have been sold at a high price and the money given to the poor." Aware of this, Jesus said to them, "Why are you bothering this woman? She has done a beautiful thing to me. The poor you will always have with you, but you will not always have me. When she poured this perfume on my body, she did it to prepare me for burial. I tell you the truth, wherever this gospel is preached throughout the world, what she has done will also be told, in memory of her." (Matthew 26:6–13)

What do you want to be known for? George Washington was considered the "Father of our nation" and was known for not telling a lie. Benjamin Franklin accomplished a lot of things in his life, but is most known for discovering electricity. General Macarthur, even though a brilliant military strategist was known for a statement to the Filipinos, "I shall return." Many famous people have left their mark on the earth, but what about you?

Jesus made it clear that to love another is the greatest thing for which to be remembered. By knowing Jesus and showing others the love He has shown us solidifies His existence and demonstrates that He is present and with us today. Acts of random kindness and love would be a great heritage. I guess if I were to be known for anything that would be enough for me.

March 12

"The Covenant"

Scripture: And God said, "This is the sign of the covenant I am making between me and you and every living creature with you, a covenant for all generations to come: I have set my rainbow in the clouds, and it will be the sign of the covenant between me and the earth. Whenever I bring clouds over the earth and the rainbow appears in the clouds, I will remember my covenant between me and you and all living creatures of every kind. Never again will the waters become a flood to destroy all life. Whenever the rainbow appears in the clouds, I will see it and remember the everlasting covenant between God and all living creatures of every kind on the earth." (Genesis 9:12–16)

I recently made a trip to Chicago and as I drove through a rainstorm and got to the other side, the sun came out and a beautiful rainbow appeared. I gazed intently at the beautiful sight and remembered the story of Noah. It is wonderful to have God's assurance and seeing a rainbow provides just that. God made a covenant with Noah and with all people for all time that He would be their God and they would be His people and He would never destroy mankind or creatures again by flood.

The next time you see a rainbow remember God's covenant of love. Remember not only His covenant of the rainbow, but the eternal covenant granted through Jesus. The rainbow is a sign of God and His presence; and it is the reassurance that He is the God of all.

March 13

"Calm Seas"

Scripture: Even though I walk through the valley of the shadow of death, I will fear no evil, for you are with me; your rod and your staff, they comfort me. (Psalm 23:4)

We recently received word that a brother in Christ was diagnosed with lung cancer. It devastated us all. The news was unexpected and, at least for me, made me stop and give thanks that it wasn't me.

Tragedies occur in everyone's life and they would be totally overwhelming, if it weren't for God. He sees us through tough times. He loves us and comforts us through the valley of death and when life deals us a bad hand. Without God there would be no hope.

If you don't have God in your life, I pray that you find Him before you face tragedy. God is the anchor in all rough seas and He anchors us to the rock of Jesus. He is there and wants to help, but will not do so without being invited. Don't get caught in a storm today. Call upon God to come into your life and calm the seas of tragedy, doubt, and fear.

March 14

"Burning Coals"

Scripture: Do not repay anyone evil for evil. Be careful to do what is right in the eyes of everybody. If it is possible, as far as it depends on you, live at peace with everyone. Do not take revenge, my friends, but leave room for God's wrath, for it is written: "It is mine to avenge; I will repay," says the Lord. On the contrary: "If your enemy is hungry, feed him; if he is thirsty, give him something to drink. In doing this, you will heap burning coals on his head." (Romans 12:17–20)

Back many years ago I built custom homes. It seemed to be an admirable career. I was taking ideas, materials, and plans and building something that someone would call home. I was creating a place for that person to enjoy with his or her family and friends.

I built homes of all sizes and for all types of people. One of the common threads that appeared from client to client was they took the building process way to serious. The process took possession of them to the point they dogged me for updates on the progress daily. It consumed them totally and completely. I even had a few who were determined to make my life a living hell. These people diminished any enjoyment there was in the building process both for them and for me. It sometimes got to the point of being almost adversarial.

One day in Sunday school we studied a Scripture that showed me clearly how to deal with these difficult clients. The passage was Romans 12:17–20. It showed me to be kind, to do as God instructs, and to let Him deal with them. To this day, when I face people who want to make situations unbearable, these scriptures come to mind and the concept of "heaping burning coals on their head" found in verse 20 seems to get me through.

March 15

"Give Generously"

Scripture: Now he who supplies seed to the sower and bread for food will also supply and increase your store of seed and will enlarge the harvest of your righteousness. You will be made rich in every way so that you can be generous on every occasion, and through us your generosity will result in thanksgiving to God. (2 Corinthians 9:10–11)

I was listening to the radio on my way to work one morning and a program caught my attention. The program format was all about praise, and the host invited people to call in to give God praise for what He had done in their lives. The program referenced a Scripture to set the tone for praise and people would call to witness how God had moved in their lives.

One caller called to praise God for placing his family in ministry. He said they had dedicated themselves to furthering God's Kingdom and they would go wherever God called. He mentioned a year where they had exhausted their financial resources and were down to forty-two cents and a can of beans, but God saw them through.

In that moment, God touched my Spirit. God revealed to me how He divided us all into certain areas to further His Kingdom. He made some preachers, some teachers, some prophets, and some supporters of ministries. God needs each of us to do our part. So when God calls you to give, give generously. If you don't know what God has called you to do, give generously! If God has shown you your own ministry, give generously. Partners in ministry are needed, so do your part, because God will supply the increase.

March 16

"Becoming Children of Light"

Scripture: Do not let any unwholesome talk come out of your mouths, but only what is helpful for building others up according to their needs, that it may benefit those who listen. And do not grieve the Holy Spirit of God, with whom you were sealed for the day of redemption. Get rid of all bitterness, rage and anger, brawling and slander, along with every form of malice. Be kind and compassionate to one another, forgiving each other, just as in Christ God forgave you. Be imitators of God, therefore, as dearly loved children and live a life of love, just as Christ loved us and gave himself up for us as a fragrant offering and sacrifice to God. (Ephesians 4:29–32, 5:1–2)

So what do we do after we accept Christ and start on our path of being a Christian? There are many different ideas on what we should do after accepting God's gift, but for me knowing what to do wasn't that easy. I knew I was a sinner saved by grace, that Jesus died for me and was raised from the dead on the third day, but my question was "Where do I go from there?"

Church is a great place to start, but could I really grow with three hours of worship and study per week? Reading God's Word is a way for me to grow and mature, but reading without action—is that enough? Praying and talking to a living God is important, but can prayers mature me and mold me into the Christian God wants me to be?

The truth is it takes all three of these things and much, much more. To be a Christian and child of God is to do God's will. We must be doers of God's Word, improve our minds through study, commune with God in prayer, and live for God each day. We need to be Christ-like in action and attitude. Then and only then will we be true children of light.

March 17

"Don't Judge, Love"

Scripture: Hearing that Jesus had silenced the Sadducees, the Pharisees got together. 35 One of them, an expert in the law, tested him with this question: "Teacher, which is the greatest commandment in the Law?" Jesus replied: "'Love the Lord your God with all your heart and with all your soul and with all your mind.' This is the first and greatest commandment. 39And the second is like it: 'Love your neighbor as yourself.' All the Law and the Prophets hang on these two commandments." (Matthew 22:34–40)

We recently had a very unique worship service. At first I didn't know where our pastor was going with his sermon. He started with a lesson from Matthew about judging others. He took it from judging others to the mission trip to an Indian reservation in Nebraska, where a number of people from our church had just returned. His point was how we often judge others without even knowing them. As he neared the end of his message he asked for volunteers to come and share their experience from the trip. Seven people, both young and old, came to share how lives were changed during the trip.

Sure enough lives were changed—and not just the lives of the native Indians—the lives of those who went to serve were changed as well. Each of them came back testifying of how God had changed their lives through the experience of being caring and compassionate to others. God gave each of them a blessing only He can give, because they had fulfilled one of the greatest commandments, "Love your neighbor as yourself."

____

____

____

March 18

"Experiencing God Fully"

Scripture: Blessed is the man who listens to me, watching daily at my doors, waiting at my doorway. (Proverbs 8:34)

Each day I live I come to realize God's presence in new and different ways. God reveals himself in a loving kiss from my wife, in the laughter of my children, in the advice from my father-in-law (but don't tell him I said this), and in the dawning of a new day. I know none of these are traditional revelations of God, but each of these are Him nonetheless.

Christian maturity and experiencing God fully comes through seeing God in everyday things. Most of the time God's presence is overlooked or dismissed, because of the busyness of the day. God wants us to experience His presence in everything and wants us to see His abundant Spirit in every aspect of our lives. The challenge is to grab hold and enjoy what God has to offer instead of letting it pass us by. Today, right now can be a new beginning in experiencing God. Look around, listen, and do not let God's presence pass you by.

March 19

"Death Overcome"

Scripture: "I tell you the truth, whoever hears my word and believes him who sent me has eternal life and will not be condemned; he has crossed over from death to life. (John 5:24)

Today as I was driving to work I started thinking about my loved ones who have already passed on. Wonderful memories filled my thoughts and in that moment my spirit was touched. I felt overwhelming warmth and a smile came to my lips. God reminded me that the walk of life to death is a walk we all have to make. Yes, I thought, we all have to walk life's walk. Some walks are shorter and some are longer, but we all have to make the walk of life. The walk can be filled with fear and trepidation or with confident assurance—the assurance that can only come from knowing what lies ahead.

God has provided a look at what is ahead for those who believe. He has promised eternal life. No fear, no tears—just a life of eternal bliss which is so simply attained. All we have to do is believe Jesus was born on this earth, came to remove the death of sin through his sacrifice, and was made victorious over death through resurrection. Death is overcome by making Jesus the Lord of our lives.

____

____

____

March 20

"God is Faithful"

Scripture: A week later his disciples were in the house again, and Thomas was with them. Though the doors were locked, Jesus came and stood among them and said, "Peace be with you!" Then he said to Thomas, "Put your finger here; see my hands. Reach out your hand and put it into my side. Stop doubting and believe." (John 20:26–27)

Each day I find there are new lessons to learn. Some challenge and some amuse, but most of all they cause me to rely on God. God takes all of life's lessons and puts them into perspective. When I have doubt and fear something that is too difficult for me to handle, God is there revealing His purpose. When life's burden is overwhelming, God carries my load. When I think I have all of the answers, God provides a dose of humility.

God knows what He wants to teach. He provides the lessons that impact our learning processes, and some of those won't be easy. He knows we will have many doubts. We will doubt ourselves, our abilities and even God at some point. But, all we need to do is keep the faith and believe and God will prove His faithfulness.

March 21

"Decisions of Life and Death"

Scripture: There is a way that seems right to a man, but in the end it leads to death. (Proverbs 14:12)

My brother told me a story about his service in Vietnam. He was in a forward area right along the DMZ (Demilitarized Zone). There was always a lot of action with raids from both sides. He served as a mechanic, and his responsibility was to keep all electrical generators functioning and motorized equipment running at peak performance. He was continually asked to go into "hot LZ's" (landing zones) where equipment needed attention. Being in the Air Force, he was flown to a number of destinations, with heavy enemy concentration, to do his work. Everyday he faced uncertainty and death. His duty required him to face decisions of life or death to keep the necessary equipment running. I am certain he gave no thought to his circumstance and the risk he was under, but faced the decisions of his job with courage.

After hearing this story of his selfless acts, a Scripture came to mind. Proverbs 14:12—"There is a way that seems right to man, but in the end it leads to death."

The story and the verse taught me a valuable lesson. Only God knows what is just over the rise, in the dark or in the jungle, so I need to seek Him to avoid irreparable damage or even death. When my God is directing me, then and only then will my decisions be safe.

March 22

"Meaningful Relationships"

Scripture: There was no one to rescue them because they lived a long way from Sidon and had no relationship with anyone else. The city was in a valley near Beth Rehob. (Judges 18:28)

Relationships are a very important part of life. Our earthly success and happiness greatly depend on how we relate to others. Our marriages, friendships, and careers are all based on relationships; therefore, for those relationships to be solid we need to relate to one another in a positive way.

Today, consultants in the corporate world help companies by teaching relationship skills. Corporate America realized that many people lack the interpersonal skills to develop relationships. The consultants knew that in a fast-paced world people don't want to take time to get to know others. People especially don't want to make commitments, because they may interfere with their lives. The consultants also knew that most people are not effective communicators and effective communication is at the heart of establishing sound relationships—relationships which require people not only to share their feelings, but also to listen.

Jesus was a master at developing relationships. He was able to do so because He listened to everyone with compassion. He intently cared and gave His full attention even though He already knew the person's heart and mind. Jesus demonstrated this relationship-building skill to teach His disciples and us. A rock-solid relationship with a person comes from having a rock-solid relationship with Jesus. When Jesus is in our lives, we can learn to make the commitments necessary to develop great relationships with others.

March 23

"How Can They Tell You are a Christian?"

Scripture: But the fruit of the Spirit is love, joy, peace, patience, kindness, goodness, faithfulness, gentleness and self-control. Against such things there is no law. (Galatians 5:22–23)

How can people tell you are a Christian? Many people's professions are easily identified by the uniform they wear such as policeman, fireman, pilots, and nurses. Some Christians wear crosses or doves to designate their profession of faith. Without wearing an insignia or a sign, how can people tell if you are a Christian?

I hope people can tell you are a Christian by your countenance. I hope people notice beyond a doubt that there is something different about the way you think or act and that you truly are a caring and compassionate person.

When we decided to follow Christ, God started a new work in all of us. He is creating a new person with a new spirit that will yield fruit and this fruit will be a sign to everyone that we are in Christ and Christ is in us.

March 24

"Have You Lost Your Marbles?"

Scripture: Therefore we do not lose heart. Though outwardly we are wasting away, yet inwardly we are being renewed day by day. For our light and momentary troubles are achieving for us an eternal glory that far outweighs them all. So we fix our eyes not on what is seen, but on what is unseen. For what is seen is temporary, but what is unseen is eternal. (2 Corinthians 4:16–18)

About a decade or so Kodak had a commercial about how life seems to fly by. They had a wonderful song about turning around that was sung during a pictorial presentation of a little girl's life. When I first saw the commercial it was cute, but now that I have gotten older, the commercial rings so very true.

Life is short. Recently I heard a story about a man, Jim, who rose early every Saturday to have some time to himself. Jim really enjoyed the time and looked forward to it every week. One Saturday morning, Jim was listening to the radio, when he heard an announcer with a deep resonating voice talking to a caller who couldn't control his life. The caller was a man working sixty plus hours per week, which Jim could relate to. He admitted that he had lost all focus on the priorities of family and faith, so he asked what he was to do. After a short pause, the announcer in his deep voice gave this answer. He told the caller of a time in his own life when he felt the same way. The announcer realized that the things that were important in his life, family and faith, were slipping away at a frantic pace. The unfortunate part was that he didn't realize this until he was in his forties.

The announcer in his most forthright tone told the caller that the average life span is around seventy-five years, some more some less, and that one day he decided to take the number of estimated years he had left and multiplied them by 52, which were the number of Saturdays he had left. He figured he had about 1000 Saturdays left and wanted to make the best of them, so he went to the store and bought all the marbles they had—about 1000. The announcer, giving his best advice, went home and put them in a clear container. Each Saturday from then on, he took a marble out to visibly show how many Saturdays he had left. He told the out-of-control caller that there was no better way to prioritize one's life, because as the marbles disappeared from the jar, he saw how few he had left. It helped to focus on what things were most important, faith and family. The announcer advised the caller, "You only have so many Saturdays in your life, so make the best of them." In closing, the deep, assuring voice remarked, "Today, I took the last marble from the container, and I am taking my wife to breakfast. Each Saturday from now on is a bonus, and I will continue to make the best of them as long as God grants me life."

After absorbing the story, it came to me that I had lost my marbles. I had spent the largest part of my life chasing things that were temporary, and I needed to build on things eternal. How about you? Have you lost your marbles?

____

____

____

March 25

"Regrets"

Scripture: I rejoice greatly in the Lord that at last you have renewed your concern for me. Indeed, you have been concerned, but you had no opportunity to show it. I am not saying this because I am in need, for I have learned to be content whatever the circumstances. I know what it is to be in need, and I know what it is to have plenty. I have learned the secret of being content in any and every situation, whether well fed or hungry, whether living in plenty or in want. I can do everything through him who gives me strength. (Philippians 4:10–13)

Do you have any regrets? Many of us say we have no regrets in our lives, but as I pondered the question I came to the conclusion that I do have regrets. I regret not finishing my formal education after spending four years in college. I regret the pain I caused others in mismanaging a business that was forced to close. I regret most of all not coming to know Jesus earlier in my life. All of these regrets create serious pain in my spirit.

I think people fail to realize that it is possible to be content despite regrets. Even though I have several regrets, I am content with my life. God has taken all of the circumstances of my life, even my regrets and brought me closer to Him. Regrets, no regrets, it really doesn't matter, because with God there strengthening me I can be content with my lot in life.

March 26

"Angry Wrath"

Scripture: When the LORD heard them, he was very angry; his fire broke out against Jacob, and his wrath rose against Israel, (Psalm 78:21)

The other day I became enormously angry at our dog. We had spent hours cleaning and decorating the outside of our house for Easter. We toiled very hard and it was disheartening to see all of our Easter decorations battered, crumpled, and strewn all over the house. My anger increased to boiling, so I grabbed our dog and a handful of destroyed decorations and beat our dog severely.

When the anger subsided, God's spirit paid me a visit. I thought about how God feels when we destroy what He has so generously prepared. God brought to my mind why His wrath was unleashed on His chosen people in the Old Testament. God truly got angry with their rebellion. He took His wrath out on them and punished them in order to bring them back in line. God punished them, but His love for them never diminished.

Yes, I was angry with our dog. Yes, I punished him severely, but the bottom line is that he is still loved and is still in our house. God too gets angry with each of us for our infractions, but He still loves us. God loves us enough that He sent His Son, Jesus, to die for our transgressions. It is through His sacrifice that we can ask for forgiveness for our disobedience and will not have to experience God's devastating wrath.

March 27

"A Dose of Humility"

Scripture: Humble yourselves, therefore, under God's mighty hand, that he may lift you up in due time. Cast all your anxiety on him because he cares for you. (1 Peter 5:6–7)

Yesterday I got a full dose of humility. As an elder in our church, I was asked to take communion to one of the shut-ins. In this case, the shut-in was a younger woman who was suffering from breast cancer. She had been battling the cancer for about two years and even though at times she seemed to be getting better, her condition overall was getting worse.

Serving communion always requires prayer. I prepared the communion, bowed my head, and prayed. After the elements had been given and received, she wanted an update on church activities, my wife, and my children. I shared and reciprocated by asking about her family. The time went by and as our conversation came to a close I asked, "Is there anything I can do?"

She turned to me with a small grin on her face and said, "A cure for cancer would be nice."

Her comment cut quickly into my spirit and I realized how helpless I truly am. I searched for the right answer and as usual God's spirit answered for me. I said, "It is not possible for me, but I know someone who can."

She agreed that it was all in God's hands.

Everyone needs a dose of humility once in a while. We need to realize that what is impossible for man is possible for God and our fate is definitely in His hands.

March 28

"Daily Worship"

Scripture: For great is the LORD and most worthy of praise; he is to be feared above all gods. For all the gods of the nations are idols, but the LORD made the heavens. Splendor and majesty are before him; strength and glory are in his sanctuary. (Psalm 96:4–6)

I love to worship God. There is a joy and peace that comes over me like warm oil poured over my body. I enjoy worshiping so much I try to worship God everyday.

How you ask?

Worshiping God is an attitude. It does not require a sanctuary, a minister, a choir, or to be done only on Sunday. It does require, however, the right spirit. It means you have to put everything else aside and open your spirit to God's. With me, I start with music. I have some favorite tapes that pull me from this world and open my spirit to God's love and from there my worship begins.

God is not looking for the form or the method, but for true worshipers. John 4:23 says, "Yet a time is coming and has come when the true worshipers will worship in spirit and in truth." Don't be inhibited, worship today and everyday.

March 29

"Dire Consequences, Counseled Decisions"

Scripture: Plans fail for lack of counsel, with many advisers they succeed. (Proverbs 15:22)

The other day in youth group with 12–14 year olds, we were talking about decisions and the consequences of the decisions we make. The discussion centered on teen pregnancy, but soon migrated to include drugs, guns, and school violence. Each of these kids faces everyday situations that I never even considered when I was growing up. With these everyday issues, each of them is forced to make decisions that have dire consequences in their lives.

All of us face decisions and some of those decisions have life-changing consequences. So what are we to do? God placed in my spirit these three steps, which I shared with the kids, to help them as we face monumental decisions:

1. God wants us to seek counsel from advisers who we know and trust and who have experience on the issues we face. God has given them the talent to counsel and has called them to use their talent to benefit others.

2. God wants us to then seek Him and His wisdom to discern the counsel we received.

3. Finally, we are to take action in confidence knowing God will never leave us nor forsake us.

When we face decisions with dire consequences or we just want confirmation of what we believe, we must follow these steps. God wants us to make decisions with confidence and succeed in those decisions.

March 30

"Trust God"

Scripture: "But blessed is the man who trusts in the LORD, whose confidence is in him.

He will be like a tree planted by the water that sends out its roots by the stream. It does not fear when heat comes; its leaves are always green. It has no worries in a year of drought, and never fails to bear fruit." (Jeremiah 17:7–8)

Let me tell you a story about trust. Several years ago my wife, children, and I wanted to build a new house. Unfortunately, I had owned a business that had failed and had forced me into personal bankruptcy. The circumstance caused us to lose everything. The unusual part of the whole ordeal was that all that took place was prophesied by a Christian counselor I had sought to help me through the mess. We prayed together when we first met and before the end of our first session he prophetically announced what would transpire—that I would lose everything. I fought back at first and said that that could not happen, but my fight was in vain. As soon as I realized there was nothing I could do, my attitude changed. I decided that if that was God's will and His plan, then I would trust the outcome.

In the financial world, a bankruptcy is the kiss of death. You can't borrow any money for any reason, unless it is God's will. And in the case of us building a new house that was the case. God opened door after door, opportunity after opportunity and today we have our new house. He has restored everything we lost and much more. He has shown that trusting Him is just the beginning to the plans He has for us. As we trust God, He leads and now He graciously allows us to live in the house He built—praise be to God.

March 31

"HOPE"

Scripture: But the eyes of the LORD are on those who fear him, on those whose hope is in his unfailing love, to deliver them from death and keep them alive in famine. We wait in hope for the LORD; he is our help and our shield. In him our hearts rejoice, for we trust in his holy name. May your unfailing love rest upon us, O LORD, even as we put our hope in you. (Psalm 33:18–22)

Hope—just the sound of the word comforts and encourages. It tells each of us that there is a light at the end of tunnel. It beckons us to keep going and endure what is ahead.

God is the hope of the world. He is the light at the end of a lifetime of trials and tribulations. He beckons us to keep focusing on Him and His glory as we endure what lies ahead. In God our hope is so strong; it will last for today, tomorrow, and forever, even unto death itself.

Don't let the circumstances of this world overwhelm you. Put your hope in the Lord and He will help you, shield you, and provide you rest. Our true hope is in His unfailing love through Jesus, the sacrifice for our eternal hope.

____

____

____

April

April 1

"Clear Message of Christ"

Scripture: You know the message God sent to the people of Israel, telling the good news of peace through Jesus Christ, who is Lord of all. (Acts 10:36)

Coming back from a business trip through Ohio, I decided to turn on the radio to help the miles pass. As normal, I scanned the dial to find a clear station with music or a program that would catch my attention. As I searched the dial from one end to the other, I noticed that about every third station was a Christian station. The Christian stations were amidst the gamut of music types: rock, rap, alternative rock, oldies, classical, and country.

A few miles later the spirit of God came over me. He revealed that the Christian stations amidst all of the secular stations are like Christians in the world. Beside each Christian stands someone from another race, nationality, or someone who is spiritually lost. These people are searching for a clear message in the world of chaos and each Christian needs to be clear on the program we are transmitting. You never know who will tune in to listen, so be clear and concise and proclaim that Jesus is Lord and Savior of all.

April 2

"Life-Changing Experience"

Scripture: So Jacob was left alone, and a man wrestled with him till daybreak. When the man saw that he could not overpower him, he touched the socket of Jacob's hip so that his hip was wrenched as he wrestled with the man. (Genesis 32:24–25)

One of the biggest rages in sports is WWF (World Wrestling Federation). These bulky men with a variety of backgrounds parade around the ring insulting the announcers, enraging the crowd, and provoking their opponents. They eventually get down to using their skills for wrestling. The show goes on until someone is victorious. Either way, the crowd is entertained and each wrestler gains fans, fame, and fortune which change their lives forever.

Thinking about wrestling and how it can change lives reminds me of the story of Jacob. Jacob, unlike these wrestlers, came from a sordid past. He deceived his father with his mother's help to receive a blessing due his brother. This con led Jacob to flee his family and his community. Eventually, it led Jacob to wrestle with God. Jacob's match ended up in a judgment with God blessing him, changing his name, and making a mighty nation of him. Wrestling changed his life too.

Wrestling isn't the only way to change your life. All you really need to do is believe and trust in God. God will change your life without any broken bones or a wrenched hip. It is round one, the bell has rung, and God is waiting to change your life.

April 3

"Procrastination"

Scripture: As the Scripture says, "Anyone who trusts in him will never be put to shame." For there is no difference between Jew and Gentile—the same Lord is Lord of all and richly blesses all who call on him, for, "Everyone who calls on the name of the Lord will be saved." (Romans 10:11–13)

I recently spoke with my great nephew, a stock broker and estate planner, about investing. We discussed the pros and cons of different types of investments and decided that some type of monthly investment would best serve our investment plan. As the discussion continued, I decided that I needed some more time before I felt certain we could meet the goals financially. After I hung up, I realized that we always put things off for a better time. Sometimes the procrastination was necessary for us to make a decision, and sometimes it was just a way not to deal with it at all. As an example, people often talk about putting off college until they can save some money only to end up not going. They say they want children, but want to wait on career timing or finances. It seems we all procrastinate. The truth is that when we do act, we wonder why we didn't act sooner. If we had, we would have realized our blessings from God sooner.

God does not want us to procrastinate, because He has blessing upon blessing to give us. He has given each of us a number of days and when those days are through they are through. None of us know when our last day on earth will come, but many choose to wait and wait until it is too late. God is calling us and wants our decision. Don't procrastinate—receive God's blessing of salvation today.

April 4

"Witness of Service"

Scripture: Offer hospitality to one another without grumbling. Each one should use whatever gift he has received to serve others, faithfully administering God's grace in its various forms. (1 Peter 4:9–10)

Have you noticed a shift in the lack of service you receive when you go to the store, the bank, or a government agency? It seems the prevailing attitude is the one of inconvenience and that we should feel a sense of privilege to be served at all. It really chaps me to be treated that way.

On the other hand, look at it this way. In a society that does not want to serve, we can be of service. What better way to demonstrate God's love and be a witness of Christianity than to serve. We all have gifts and talents provided by God and we can use them to serve others. We need to be faithful and use our service as a witness to God's glory.

So when asked to serve, accept with an attitude of love. In doing so (especially in a world where service is waning), you will stand out as a beacon of Godly service and that will be a great witness.

April 5

"Intense Focus"

Scripture: Therefore, since we are surrounded by such a great cloud of witnesses, let us throw off everything that hinders and the sin that so easily entangles, and let us run with perseverance the race marked out for us. Let us fix our eyes on Jesus, the author and perfecter of our faith, who for the joy set before him endured the cross, scorning its shame, and sat down at the right hand of the throne of God. Consider him who endured such opposition from sinful men, so that you will not grow weary and lose heart. (Hebrews 12:1–3)

One of my passions, like most men, is watching sports on TV. I really enjoy a good game and the intensity of the athletes. They are extremely focused on what they have to do. I especially notice this unyielding focus in gymnastics. The athletes block out everything except the event at hand. They tune out the thousands of spectators, the media, and the other participants focusing only on their event. Each one of them has tremendous concentration and determination to do his or her best.

We need to take this approach in our Christianity and to focus on God like these athletes focus on their sport. We need to remove anything that distracts us from doing God's will. We need to train ourselves to overcome any obstacle, to tune out all the ambient distractions, and to discipline ourselves not to be hindered or hampered by the world. To do our best we need to focus intently on our faith, rely on God to encourage and help us, and keep our eyes constantly focused on Him.

April 6

"Seeing Consequences"

Scripture: Your eye is the lamp of your body. When your eyes are good, your whole body also is full of light. But when they are bad, your body also is full of darkness. (Luke 11:34)

There seems to be a lot of discussion these days about the violence in our schools and elsewhere. One opinion is that television and movies are so graphically violent that they are conditioning us to act violently without concern. Maybe, just maybe this opinion has some validity.

The Bible says in Luke 11:34 that your eye is the lamp of your body and that what you see affects who you are. If you interpret this Scripture the way I do, what you see has a direct influence on your life. Your actions are determined by those influences, therefore, what you watch does affect how you think and act.

It is our role as parents and as Christians to monitor what we watch. I am not saying that we will become violent or the programs and movies will cause us to be violent, but according to God these things do have an effect on us. If we watch violent images day in and day out without tempering them with truth and light they could have devastating consequences.

We want to be a light unto the world, so don't darken your light by watching inappropriate programs.

____

____

____

April 7

"Praise Strengthens"

Scripture: May God be gracious to us and bless us and make his face shine upon us, Selah that your ways may be known on earth, your salvation among all nations. May the peoples praise you, O God; may all the peoples praise you. May the nations be glad and sing for joy, for you rule the peoples justly and guide the nations of the earth. Selah May the peoples praise you, O God; may all the peoples praise you. Then the land will yield its harvest, and God, our God, will bless us. God will bless us, and all the ends of the earth will fear him. (Psalm 67:1–7)

I love to sing praise songs in church. They have a way of lifting my spirit and preparing my heart for worship. I guess, now that I think about it, praising God outside of song has the same effect.

I have gone through many tribulations in my life and when the times got the toughest, my praise got the strongest. It helped me combat the worry, doubt, and fear I faced. It strengthened my belief that God was there with me and would see me through. It even subdued my impatience and helped me wait on God's leading, rather than trying to get in the middle of the resolution God had already started.

The next time you are faced with problems, you are depressed, and you feel there is no where to turn, turn to God and praise Him. He will help you, guide you, strengthen you, and you will overcome. If you are not sure how or are uncomfortable with singing, then pray the Psalms, the ultimate praise of God.

____

____

____

April 8

"The Scepter"

Scripture: The seventy-two returned with joy and said, "Lord, even the demons submit to us in your name." He replied, "I saw Satan fall like lightning from heaven. I have given you authority to trample on snakes and scorpions and to overcome all the power of the enemy; nothing will harm you. However, do not rejoice that the spirits submit to you, but rejoice that your names are written in heaven." (Luke 10:17–20)

Dreams are a normal occurrence for most people. Dreams occur to some people so frequently that they seek individuals who interpret dreams and give insights into their meaning. Recently, I had a dream about a very beautiful scepter. This scepter was very valuable, because it was made of gold, silver, and was covered with precious stones. Everyone wanted it because of its spellbinding beauty and its great value. The greed overcame everyone. They wanted it and would do anything to possess it. And, once someone obtained it, they found it was Satan in disguise. Satan had fed the people's greed, and had created envy, hatred, and discord among them, so that he could control their lives. The only way Satan could be defeated was for the people to call upon Jesus and once Jesus' name was invoked he released their souls and fled.

I was not sure how to deal with this dream, so rather than seeking a worldly person to interpret it, I sought God. I was sure He was the source of the dream and could give me understanding of it. In prayer, God revealed His meaning. God showed me that we all chase idols and things we want to possess. We seek, search, and pursue them with such passion that they overcome us. When that happens, Satan moves in. He ceases the opportunity to take our souls. God said the only way to defeat Satan is through Jesus. We must accept Jesus as our personal Savior, believe in His power, and call upon Him. When we do, Satan and all his demons will flee in fear.

Jesus is the only way to defeat the ways of the world, so call upon Him today and live forever in peace.

April 9

"On My Own"

Scripture: I guide you in the way of wisdom and lead you along straight paths. (Proverbs 4:11)

Recently I was talking to a brother in Christ and he and I began comparing how our lives have been changed. Both of us, in our own way, have matured in our faith. We both recalled lessons God has taught us and we both recognized how we now strive to apply God's principles to our lives daily.

During our discussion, my spirit was stirred. We were remarking about control and how God wants us to rely on Him. We both agreed that we often want to take charge of our own circumstances and deal with issues ourselves. It struck me that, even when we do get direction from God, we forge ahead at full steam without regard for God's timing. In our impatience, we get ahead of God before He has opportunity to prepare the way.

The next time you seek God's direction and leading don't get excited about rushing ahead on your own. Instead, be patient and let God prepare the way. He will open doors and remove obstacles, so that you won't stumble and fall.

April 10

"Give Out of Love"

Scripture: As he looked up, Jesus saw the rich putting their gifts into the temple treasury. 2He also saw a poor widow put in two very small copper coins. "I tell you the truth," he said, "this poor widow has put in more than all the others. All these people gave their gifts out of their wealth; but she out of her poverty put in all she had to live on." (Luke 21:1–4)

I was asked by my brother-in-law to fill in one Sunday for his stewardship moment. He asked me about a week in advance, and as many of us do if we don't write things on our calendars, I forgot. He hadn't forgotten, however. While at a church project on the Saturday before I was to fill in for him, he reminded me of my obligation. Taken a little by surprise, I said, "Yes." However, he sensed I had forgotten, so I remarked that I work well under pressure. What I really meant was God works well under pressure, because when I am confronted with a tough situation, I run to Him.

Early that afternoon on the way home, I prayed. My prayer was, "God what do you want said?" I had no sooner got the words out of my mouth when God placed a Scripture in my mind, "The widow's offering." I had read the Scripture before, but had never really studied it.

That night and the next morning as I read and reread the Scripture, God suddenly showed me what He wanted me to say. The Scripture was not just about what was being given, but was about the heart of the giver. The widow gave out of love without concern for her well-being, because she trusted God. This was in stark contrast to the rich who gave out of their abundance and who cared only that their peers noticed.

God knows our hearts, our bank accounts, and our motives for giving. Give out of love for God, give generously, and give God the Glory.

April 11

"Use It Wisely"

Scripture: I tell you the truth, a time is coming and has now come when the dead will hear the voice of the Son of God and those who hear will live. (John 5:25)

My eyes were closed, my mind was emptied of worldly cares, my focus and attention was on God. It was my time of prayer, praise, and devotion to God. As I sat there, a song came to my mind and the words to my lips. It was a song from Sunday worship, "On Holy Ground." When I murmured the words, "standing in His presence on Holy ground," God was there with me. My mind settled again and what did I hear? It was the constant ticking of the clock next to me. All I heard was tick, tick, tick and was ready to move the clock when God touched my spirit. God said, "Listen to each tick. There, do you hear them? Remember each time the clock ticks another second is gone forever, used up, never to return. Each second I give you is precious and needed by you to further my Kingdom. Not for my sake, but for the lost souls who need a word of hope and encouragement. It is up to you what you do with each second, but remember, it is my gift, use it wisely."

The clock is ticking for each and every one of us. God has graciously given us so many seconds to use for his glory, so pray that we use them wisely.

April 12

"The Slogan"

Scripture: "So the last will be first and the first will be last." (Matthew 20:16)

As I was driving back from a business meeting, I noticed a fencing truck in front of me whose door, like most company vehicles, was labeled with the company name and a slogan. The slogan caught my attention, "The first fence to last." As I read the slogan, a Scripture came to mind. It had to do with the last will be first and the first will be last. I wasn't truly certain of the Scripture, but God touched my spirit with it. Why? What was God trying to tell me?

The next morning I grabbed my Bible to find the Scripture. Surely, I could find insight from God's Word on what He was trying to say. The Scripture was found at the end of a parable in Matthew 20:1–16 about the workers in the vineyard. As I read the parable, nothing really struck me, until I read the last verse. Yes, I finally found the Scripture that God gave me, but still I was uncertain about what God wanted me to understand. Suddenly, I realized it wasn't about the whole story, but only the last verse. I read and reread it again, when God touched me. He wanted me to know that those who are lasting in their faith through their trials and tribulations will be first in His Kingdom, but those who wane, faint, and grow away from their faith will be last. I thought that this seemed to be a little out of context, but then I understood. This is God's Word and He reveals meaning to each of us according to His will.

God wants us to be lasting and faithful in our walk with Him and He in return has prepared His Kingdom for us. That is why the slogan touched my spirit to stay steadfast, never waiver, and live life for God.

April 13

"The Writing Is On the Wall"

Scripture: Suddenly the fingers of a human hand appeared and wrote on the plaster of the wall, near the lampstand in the royal palace. The king watched the hand as it wrote. His face turned pale and he was so frightened that his knees knocked together and his legs gave way. (Daniel 5:5–6)

Have you ever wondered where we came up with an adage or saying we use? You can probably recall several, but the one that came into my thoughts was "The writing is on the wall." I had never really considered the source of such sayings until one day while reading a story in Daniel. The story was about a King. It seems that King Belshazzar was an arrogant king who worshipped gods of all types. He never realized the jeopardy he put himself and his kingdom in by doing so, until one day as he, his nobles, his wives, and his concubines drank wine from the goblets of the temple at Jerusalem when fingers of a human hand appeared and wrote on the wall. The writing was interpreted by Daniel and told of the King's demise, which did come to pass.

It seems that this adage, passed down from generation to generation, meant that when "the writing is on the wall" something is about to happen. Therefore, we use this saying in a descriptive way to predict how someone's life is about to change.

I am always amazed by how God's Word influences our lives. It seems the impact is insightful, direct, and has even woven its way into our language. I guess when it comes to God being in our lives we can say, "The writing is on the wall."

April 14

"Love Notes"

Scripture: Husbands, love your wives, just as Christ loved the church and gave himself up for her. (Ephesians 5:25)

For years I have written my wife love notes. Like most couples, who have children and who work, we both are typically going in different directions. She or I leave early for work, we get home at different times, and when we are at home, there are so many things to be accomplished that we seldom have enough time to sit and discuss the day, let alone express our love for one another. Therefore, notes of love have become an important part of our relationship.

God has provided and taught us love. He has expressed his love through His Word and has taught us how to love through Jesus. Descriptive and complete, God's Word tells of His love and how He has shown his love through the sacrifice of His Son. Jesus' compassion and sacrifice for our souls may not be notes of love, but they express His love in a way words never can. He loved us so much He gave us His life.

Learn to express love to one another. If you cannot do it physically, then do it in notes of love and God will bless and enrich your relationships.

April 15

“Sprout of Hope”

Scripture: He told them another parable: “The kingdom of heaven is like a mustard seed, which a man took and planted in his field. Though it is the smallest of all your seeds, yet when it grows, it is the largest of garden plants and becomes a tree, so that the birds of the air come and perch in its branches.” (Matthew 13:31–32)

Parenting is difficult, especially in today’s society. I try my best, but as I often tell my children, I have never done this before, so mistakes are likely. My hope is that my mistakes have little or no effect on the well-being of my kids.

One of my largest concerns is how I am doing at teaching my children about faith and God. We kept our children very active in church as they were growing up, but now, as they are getting into high school and college, church seems to have less of an impact on them. They seem to struggle with going and being involved. Some of that has to do with their schedules, some of it with my lack of forcing the issue, and some of it is just that they are not excited about what church offers. Needless to say, by not being as active in church as they once were, I fear they will make ungodly choices.

Recently I received a glimpse of hope and assurance. My oldest son, who is in college, has been faced with all types of liberal beliefs, individuals not very solid in their faith, and teaching contrary to the existence of God. Much to my joy, however, in the face of professors and faithless students, he has remarked about his faith-filled stand. His decisions, actions, and words are tempered with a moral value that can only come from God. Therefore, a small seed of faith planted in his early youth is starting to grow. I pray that this small sprout matures and bears great fruit.

Jesus knew the significance of even the smallest seed of faith and how it could grow to be of service to the world. Start planting seeds of faith in your children early. God will nurture them and allow them to grow and you will see a sprout of hope like the one I have.

April 16

"Reflections"

Scripture: Anyone who listens to the word but does not do what it says is like a man who looks at his face in a mirror and, after looking at himself, goes away and immediately forgets what he looks like. (James 1:23–24)

We all start each day by looking into a mirror. If you are like me, what I see is frightening. My hair is a mess, I need a shave, and I look like I have been sleeping in a gutter. It is clear that some things need to change before I can go to work. My appearance and my mind need to awaken to the new day, so the transformation begins.

It starts with a shave, a shower, combing my hair, and putting on my clothes. And, about thirty minutes later a transformation has occurred. I look into the mirror and see an entirely different person. The outside is presentable, but what about the inside?

The next step is prayer and devotion to make the inside presentable. It actually started in the shower as a song came to mind. It was a simple praise chorus that I repeated over and over. And, then it is on to my devotion and reading the Word of God. I digest the Scripture and gain insight from the devotion. My spirit lifts and my day has already improved. I look into the mirror again to find that the person who was there one hour ago is gone and a new person is there. It is a reflection of assurance, of confidence, and of a radiant spirit ready for the challenges of the day.

The mirror is a remarkable thing. It tends to show us where we are and it even reflects how we feel. I have learned over the years that as a mirror reflects our outside, our spirit reflects our inside; therefore, if we are not filled with God's spirit, we are not reflecting the image God wants. Allow God to envelop you and to transform the outside and inside of you, so that you will reflect the true image of God.

April 17

"Peace at 30,000 Feet"

Scripture: I will lie down and sleep in peace, for you alone, O LORD, make me dwell in safety. (Psalm 4:8)

In my profession as a sales director, I fly frequently. I travel coast to coast and from Canada to Mexico. One of the most interesting parts of my travel is the people I encounter. I tend to watch them closely and try to gain from their reactions and comments. Since 9/11 I have seen some very insightful things. There seem to be two types of people flying: those at peace and those with anxiety. I believe this is a reflection of an uncertain time and that it is the faith of the person that determines which category they fall into.

For me, I will not travel without asking for God's blessing on myself, on the hands that prepared the aircraft, and on the hands of those who pilot the aircraft. I have had times where the degree of concern of the other passengers rocked my spirit. I have felt that this day could be the day that something happens, but as soon as such a thought comes, it subsides. I know that should this be the day, I am prepared. And, as the time passes I reach a point of pure peace and know my God is with me.

God is my refuge, my safety, and my salvation; therefore I can face flying with peace even at 30,000 feet.

April 18

"Golf Lessons or God Lessons"

Scripture: "Therefore I will teach them—this time I will teach them my power and might.Then they will know my name is the LORD. (Jeremiah 16:21)

I really enjoy the game of golf. I am not very good at it and I am self taught, but I enjoy the game, because of its challenges. It is a competitive game, not necessarily against others as much as it is a game against self. It puts us in competition to improve ourselves over the last time we played.

Golf has not only supplied my need for sport, it has provided a new revelation into God. It seems as I play the game God reveals new and exciting analogies to me. For example, if I misapply the fundamentals of golf I can end up in trouble. I can slice the ball into a trap or hook it out of bounds and both have penalties. One has a penalty of play from uncertain ground which could cost me a stroke and the other costs me immediately in stroke and distance. Either way, at my level of play it is not where I want to be. The good news is once the shot is over it is over. The next shot could be forgiving, because I can place the shot in play and prevent myself from incurring additional penalties. The bad shot does not carry over to the next hole. It does impact my overall score, but the shot does not have to be discussed or thought of again.

God's mercy and grace provides the same result. When we forget to apply the fundamentals of His Word, our shots are often off target. We end up in situations and in areas that cost us a penalty or at least a setback from where God want us to be. Like golf, we must shoulder the responsibility of our errors. The good news is the last shot of sin is over and the next one can bring us back on target. God does not look back at the previous shot or bring it to our attention. It is forgotten and we are allowed to move on to better and better shots and a round of improvement for His glory.

April 19

"Crossroads"

Scripture: Jesus knew their thoughts and said to them, "Every kingdom divided against itself will be ruined, and every city or household divided against itself will not stand. (Matthew 12:25)

The United States is at a crossroad. We have seen firsthand the devastation that can occur on our own soil by terrorists who hate our ideals. We see terrorists with such hatred for the U.S. that they will sacrifice their own lives to inflict harm on our citizens. We have seen how the stronger European nations view us and work covertly to undermine our outreach to the world. We have seen our society being segmented into social liberalism and conservative Christian. We have seen our courts make law instead of interpret them as the forefathers intended. We see Hollywood and the internet removing the innocence of our children. And, we are seeing a watering down of God's principles to accommodate the ways of the world.

Yes, the United States is at a crossroad. Will we as Christians stand up and be counted for the principles God has given? We will stand on the infallible truth of God's Word or will we allow the liberal agenda to tear it apart? Will we stand and watch as the government continues to remove God from us in every way, until we have to worship in secret?

It is time for us to be counted and to put God back at the center of our lives and our government. We must speak up, stand up, and seek God, His wisdom, and His direction for a country blessed by His hand.

Oh yes, the United States is definitely at a crossroad.

April 20

"Water Color Beauty"

Scripture: One thing I ask of the LORD, this is what I seek: that I may dwell in the house of the LORD all the days of my life, to gaze upon the beauty of the LORD and to seek him in his temple. (Psalm 27:4)

Fall is a splendid time of year. I especially love to see the fall foliage in its beauty. It is as if God himself painted the landscape with brilliant water colors.

God has given us this earth to enjoy and marvel at its beauty. He has put it together in harmony. Each color blends beautifully with the other and is displayed in combination and contrast, which pleases the eye. And, if you are like me, it is definitely a feast for the optic senses.

God wants us to enjoy the earth and all that is in it. He wants us to seek Him and gaze into the landscape as if we were gazing into His eyes. So this fall enjoy God's splendor and rejoice in the watercolor beauty He provides.

April 21

"1–800-Call-God"

Scripture: And everyone who calls upon the name of the Lord will be saved. (Acts 2:21)

I was traveling by car to Chicago last week. The traffic in large cities, especially the size of Chicago, can be horrible. It is not uncommon to be stuck in traffic at some point and this day was no different. As is customary for me when I am stuck in traffic, I began checking out the cars and trucks near me. This day a semi caught my attention. I was becoming a little impatient, when I noticed the sign on the truck. It read: 1–800-Call-God. My first thought was how I would love to call God to eliminate the traffic, but I knew that the traffic was probably God's way of slowing me down and keeping me from accident or incident. But, while I continued to view the truck I saw a tag to the phone number. It read: Guaranteed On-Time Delivery. Wow, what an insightful play on words to get people's attention, I thought.

My thoughts raced as I pondered the truth of this phone number and statement. God always wants us to call upon Him. He is closer than a phone call. Just call out to Him and He will be there, but more importantly, know that it is never too late to do so. God will take a call from anyone, anytime, no matter when, where, or why they call. It doesn't matter how good or bad, righteous or sinful. God guarantees we will be delivered—all we need to do is call.

1–800-Call-God!

April 22

"Gambling"

Scripture: But among you there must not be even a hint of sexual immorality, or of any kind of impurity, or of greed, because these are improper for God's holy people. (Ephesians 5:3)

I have traveled many times to Las Vegas. Most of my travels have been work related and every time I go I am astounded at the amount of gambling that occurs. The amount of money that is thoughtlessly wagered is staggering and for what? I have often wondered what could be done for God's glory with those type funds.

Having these concerns I decided to research what God says about gambling. The Bible does not cover gambling specifically, but throughout the Bible there are many references to casting lots. Casting lots was a form of gambling, but it was utilized as a fair means of dividing everything from wealth to chores. What I did not sense in my research is that people in biblical times cast lots out of greed.

Gambling in today's society is more seductive. It appeals to the greedy side of our flesh. The lotteries entice us with jackpots of millions and the casinos that have popped up everywhere entice us with the chance of becoming wealthy. They tempt us and tell us wealth is as near as a roll of the dice or a pull of the arm on a slot machine.

God knows our hearts and when we indulge in these types of games He knows what we are after. He warns us to stay away from these types of temptations because once the door is open for them it is only a short distance to uncontrollable sin.

I thank God for some of the hard financial times I have been through, because I have learned that money is so hard to earn that I cannot stand to lose it. I pray you will not be seduced by the lure of greed and gambling and that these things do not become uncontrollable sin in your life.

April 23

"Little Prayer, Giant Results"

Scripture: Jabez cried out to the God of Israel, "Oh, that you would bless me and enlarge my territory! Let your hand be with me, and keep me from harm so that I will be free from pain." And God granted his request. (1 Chronicles 4:10)

A few years ago my mother-in-law gave me the book "The Prayer of Jabez," by Bruce Wilkerson, for Christmas. I had heard the story and others had commented about reading it, so I couldn't wait to get into it. I read it from cover to cover and it touched my spirit. I thought that the book and the concept were so insightful that I should give praying "The Prayer of Jabez" a try myself. Starting that day and everyday since, I have prayed this little prayer.

After a few months of praying it, I started to see some changes occurring. My business opportunities started to multiply. Potential customers started coming out of the woodwork and at first I couldn't imagine why. Later, I remembered that I had asked God to bless me and enlarge my territory. God was granting my request, but it didn't stop there. My spiritual life started to accelerate. God was touching my spirit with such intensity and consistency I was not sure exactly what He wanted me to accomplish. God guided me through my business and spiritual life unveiling more and more blessings. It was as if, if I thought it, God made it happen. God even orchestrated a new career opportunity granting me everything I prayed for. My income increased, I was able to work from home, and best of all God gave me the time and the timetable to complete my devotional.

I cannot speak for all who have read and prayed this prayer, but I can tell you that if you do, be prepared. It is a little prayer, but it has gigantic results and it will change your life.

April 24

"What is God Calling You to Do?"

Scripture: Then Jesus came to them and said, "All authority in heaven and on earth has been given to me. Therefore go and make disciples of all nations, baptizing them in the name of the Father and of the Son and of the Holy Spirit, (Matthew 28:18–19)

I am writing to share some serious thoughts about God's calling. God is asking and seeking his disciples to stand boldly for Him in these times. We are faced with many uncertainties and even though our community may not be directly affected, the consequences of world affairs are on our doorstep. God knows the future and has openly shared a vision of things to come in His Word, but are we paying attention? The signs of the times signal us to be aware, to be alert, and to be vigilant. It is not our safety God is concerned with, but the souls of the lost and in these times when death could be at the next corner, we must do everything within our power to reach as many people as possible and as quickly as possible.

So what is God calling you to do?

I was recently at a committee meeting when the topic of involving others into our ministry came up. The topic took several directions, but the underlying theme was that people want to be *asked* to serve. I can assure you God is asking. The invitation does not have to come from an elder, a deacon or the pastor. God himself is calling you. He wants you and needs you. Don't sit idle when there is much to be done—answer God's call.

The key is not to hold back, stay back, or wait to be asked by someone in the church, but rather to find a place, get involved, and make a difference in God's Kingdom. Time's wasting, God's calling, and the choice is yours!

April 25

"What Does it Take to Believe?"

Scripture: That which was from the beginning, which we have heard, which we have seen with our eyes, which we have looked at and our hands have touched—this we proclaim concerning the Word of life. The life appeared; we have seen it and testify to it, and we proclaim to you the eternal life, which was with the Father and has appeared to us. We proclaim to you what we have seen and heard, so that you also may have fellowship with us. And our fellowship is with the Father and with his Son, Jesus Christ. We write this to make our joy complete. (1 John 1:1–4)

I find it amazing the number of people who do not believe that Jesus existed. They believe that Jesus was a myth, a story, and a fabrication. Why do people have such a hard time believing Jesus was the Messiah?

Each and everyday we are taught something new by somebody. We take their teachings for truth, because they have laced them with logic and we accept them with no questions asked. We are so convinced that what they say is true that we believe it and pass it on. In fact sometimes we are so convinced that what we are passing on is true that we tell others that it is "the gospel truth." How ironic. Why would we refer to something as "the gospel truth" if we do not believe the gospel itself to be true?

1st John 1 bears witness to the events of Jesus. John and his partners in Christ were eyewitnesses to Jesus life, death, and resurrection and they took it upon themselves to teach others. They were so dedicated to the truth that they wrote it in the Bible for all to read. They gave an account of all of the facts using dates, times, and places. Their testimony is infallible. Yet we do not believe it as truth.

Pray today that God will open your mind and heart to the truth and know beyond doubt that Jesus does exist.

April 26

"In Jesus' Name"

Scripture: You did not choose me, but I chose you and appointed you to go and bear fruit—fruit that will last. Then the Father will give you whatever you ask in my name. (John 15:16)

In my dealings with the corporate world I have learned that it is extremely important to have an action plan. Goals cannot be accomplished unless a plan is developed and then orchestrated to completion. Therefore, to be successful for God, a plan has to be put into action, but how?

God knew that without prayer His power could not be released and we could not go in confidence. He also knew that to unleash that power we would need to ask in Jesus' name. Therefore, follow these basic steps and allow God's power to be released into the plan for your life.

Joy- Pray continuously, never ceasing, so God will make your Joy complete.

Expectations- Pray and believe that your expectations will be met.

Supply- In prayer, your answers will come and your heavenly supply will be endless.

Unveiled- The truth will be unveiled to you through your prayers.

Sustain- And, God's love will sustain you in your endeavor.

Pray every prayer in Jesus' name and it will be done.

April 27

"What Course, Oh Lord?"

Scripture: for he guards the course of the just and protects the way of his faithful ones. (Proverbs 2:8)

Imagine yourself on a lake or an ocean in a boat. You are out in the middle of this body of water with no land in sight. You have no propulsion and no rudder. You are drifting helplessly along being controlled only by the water's currents.

Your first thought is, What should I do? You assess the situation and determine that there must be land out there, but which way? Even if you make a decision on the direction to take, how can you propel the boat and keep it on course?

Many of our lives are exactly the same way. We are just floating in the middle of this world. We are trying to assess our purpose in life and are trying to choose a direction, but how can we get there? How do we get ourselves moving in the right direction and what shall we use as a compass to keep us on track? We seem to just be adrift in life going wherever the current of the world takes us.

Through God, however, everything changes. Yes, we are still in the middle of this world, but God will help us gain direction and find purpose. God will energize us to take action using our body and spirit. And, He has given us His Holy Word as a guide book to direct our course. He will provide us with the course, the propulsion, and the will to get where He purposes.

Don't spend anymore time drifting in this world. Call upon God and receive a new course that takes you to eternity.

April 28

"Seemingly Insignificant"

Scripture: The body is a unit, though it is made up of many parts; and though all its parts are many, they form one body. So it is with Christ. For we were all baptized by one Spirit into one body—whether Jews or Greeks, slave or free—and we were all given the one Spirit to drink. Now the body is not made up of one part but of many. (1 Corinthians 12:12–14)

I heard a report the other day from the National Transportation Safety Board. The announcement was regarding the cause of an airline crash. The report determined that a small pin connecting the rear stabilizer broke causing the airliner to crash. It seemed shocking to me that such a small, inexpensive piece could cause such disaster, especially with the hundreds of thousands of parts in an airplane. Yet one little, seemingly insignificant part was the key to life or death.

As Christians, we sometimes wonder what role we are to play in God's Kingdom. We seem insignificant in the context of the entire body of Christ, but the truth is we each have a part to play. We need to realize that if one part of the body is not there, the whole body is weakened. We are all individual members that make up the body but working together properly we can offer lost souls life—life everlasting. So just like the small part in the plane that determined life or death, we too determine the same outcome. Yes, we are all small parts of Christ's church, but our roles are important in giving life to God's Kingdom.

April 29

"Fuel the Lamp and Trim the Wick"

Scripture: "You are the light of the world. A city on a hill cannot be hidden. Neither do people light a lamp and put it under a bowl. Instead they put it on its stand, and it gives light to everyone in the house. In the same way, let your light shine before men, that they may see your good deeds and praise your Father in heaven. (Matthew 5:14–16)

While working in the kitchen preparing dinner, I noticed the area seemed a little dim. Upon inspection, I realized that a light bulb had burned out. It was remarkable, I thought, how one small bulb in the midst of several could diminish the light so greatly.

We are all a light for God in a world of darkness. We shine with God's love to many around us. Unlike the light bulb that has to be replaced when it burns out, we never have to be replaced. We are more like an oil lamp. Our light may grow dim for lack of fuel or our wick may need trimmed, but our light will never go out. We can replenish our fuel by reading and studying God's Word, and our wicks can be trimmed with humility to give off the light God intends. We know that God, through Jesus' spirit in our lives, can shine bright for everyone to see. So don't let your light dwindle and go out, because if your light goes out, it will be noticed. It will be just like the bulb in the midst of many, which once burned out causes the light produced around it to be less intense. Keep your light bright and brilliant with God's love and brighten a dark world.

April 30

"Free Indeed, Free at Last"

Scripture: It is for freedom that Christ has set us free. Stand firm, then, and do not let yourselves be burdened again by a yoke of slavery. (Galatians 5:1)

Our dog, Hercules, gets out occasionally without being on a leash or without his electronic collar. When he breaks free he runs and runs and runs. He knows that being free is great and that there is nothing to hold him back from exploring new horizons. Unencumbered he enjoys his freedom until he tires or we get tired of chasing him. Nonetheless there is nothing he likes more than being free.

Sin in our lives has a way of stealing our freedom. We become enslaved to our fleshly desires and it burdens us from living life as God intended, unencumbered. We are all leashed to sin as part of our earthly nature. It holds us back, keeps us from experiencing the freedom of a victorious life, and keeps us from exploring the new horizons that God has for us. We want to be free, but unless we seek forgiveness, we are slaves.

Don't be held back, leashed, and burdened by sin. Go to the Father and be set free—free from guilt, shame, and destruction. And, once you taste the freedom God can provide, you will be like Hercules, free, without care or concern. You will be free, free indeed, and free at last!

May

May 1

"What Does the Bible Have for Us?"

Scripture: For everything that was written in the past was written to teach us, so that through endurance and the encouragement of the Scriptures we might have hope. (Romans 15:4)

Many have asked what the Bible has to do with us. It was written so long ago and at a time that we cannot even comprehend that many of us have wondered what it could possibly have for us.

Paul said it best in Romans 15:4. We have the Bible to teach us hope. How profoundly simple and straightforward—to teach us hope! And then? "The God of hope will fill us with joy and peace as we trust Him" Romans 15:13a. And then? "So that we may overflow with hope by the power of the Holy Spirit" Romans 15:13b.

God wants us to have hope, so our joy and peace can be fulfilled. Our hope is generated through His Holy Word. So what does the Bible have to do with us? Joy, peace, and hope—sounds pretty good to me!

May 2

"Ants"

Scripture: They devoted themselves to the apostles' teaching and to the fellowship, to the breaking of bread and to prayer. Everyone was filled with awe, and many wonders and miraculous signs were done by the apostles. All the believers were together and had everything in common. (Acts 2:42–44)

I was sitting on the front porch, enjoying a summer afternoon, looking down into the flowerbed, and noticed a colony of ants. There was a whole line of them going from a food source to the anthill. They were taking different paths, but like a magnet they were all drawn towards the hill. Some of the ants carried a small piece and others an extremely large one in comparison to their body, but they all were working together to get the food to the colony.

Workers in God's Kingdom need to work the same way. It doesn't matter what denomination we come from or whether we want to work independently. It only matters that we each contribute to the spreading of the Good News in our own way. Some of us can take on a large task, while others a smaller one, but we are all working for God's glory. Everyone has a task to do, and we need to realize that we are all working towards the same end—everyone being fed the Good News. Take a lesson from the ants. We may not take the same path or carry the same load, but we are all working for the same colony. Don't be concerned about the paths others take, but complete the job assigned to you and you will find out that the others have gotten to the same point as you, because God leads the way.

May 3

"Pentecost Fruit"

Scripture: But the fruit of the Spirit is love, joy, peace, patience, kindness, goodness, faithfulness, gentleness and self-control. Against such things there is no law. (Galatians 5:22–23)

This past Sunday the church celebrated Pentecost. This is in honor of God's Holy Spirit descending upon His disciples. The Bible says in Acts 2:2–3 that the house where they were was filled with a rushing wind and that they saw what seemed to be tongues of fire come to rest on each of them. The disciples received God's spirit to continue the ministry Jesus had started. They all spoke in tongues of other lands and many were saved.

When most people think about Pentecost they think of speaking in tongues. Some believe that God's Holy Spirit only comes to those who speak in tongues. On the contrary, God's Spirit comes in many forms and manifests itself in a number of ways. Surely, you can recognize God's Spirit, especially when you know what to look for. Read Galatians 5:22–23, about the fruit the Spirit provides and look around to see if God isn't present around you.

The Holy Spirit is for each of us and can and should be part of our lives as Christians. He may manifest himself in a number of ways, but unless He produces fruit for God's Kingdom through you, you cannot serve God's purpose.

May 4

"Matryoshka, Story Revealed"

Scripture: Now Samuel did not yet know the LORD: The word of the LORD had not yet been revealed to him. (1 Samuel 3:7)

Have you ever seen a Matryoshka Doll, sometimes called a nesting doll, from Russia? The dolls, normally hand carved and painted, were originally produced as toys. The toys created for children were painted in vibrant colors, always told a story or fable, and to the children's surprise, each opened to reveal another doll and part of the story. The one I saw had a total of nine dolls, from about a quart size jar to peanut size, one within the other. They told the story of Snow White. The dolls came in various sizes with brightly painted caricatures on the outside primarily portraying Old Russian peasant women. Each doll had an insignia which told the story. The dolls told the tale through these insignias starting with the largest and going to the smallest. As each doll is revealed, another part of the story is told until the marvelous tale is complete. Remarkably, no one would know the whole story from looking at the first doll nor would they know that within the first doll were more dolls telling a wonderful tale.

God's Holy Word is a lot like these dolls. To get to its true meaning and understand it, God unveils new revelations and insights each time we open it. God allows us to see only parts of His total truth and reveals it to us a little at a time. Eventually, when we come into His Kingdom the whole story will be complete in a marvelous ending, eternal life.

___

___

___

May 5

"Rudy's Rules"

Scripture: To those who by persistence in doing good seek glory, honor and immortality, he will give eternal life. (Romans 2:7)

One of my favorite movies is Rudy. I watch it about four times per year, because I love the story. If you haven't seen it, I highly recommend it. The story is about a young man who loved Notre Dame football and vowed to go there and play. He struggled through many setbacks including the ridicule of his family, but in the end, Rudy overcame through prayer, dedication, and faith.

We can all learn a valuable lesson from this story. We can accomplish anything we choose to accomplish if our focus is right, if our motives are sincere, and if we persist. Rudy teaches us that lesson and much more. We need to work for what we want, but we must not forget the additional tools needed to get us there: prayer and faith.

I will challenge each of you, as Rudy was challenged by his family: Set your goals and dreams high, but realize that the only way to reach them is with God's help. Then, follow Rudy's rules of prayer, dedication, and faith and your goals and dreams will be yours.

May 6

"Without a Shot"

Scripture: Jesus knew their thoughts and said to them, "Every kingdom divided against itself will be ruined, and every city or household divided against itself will not stand. (Matthew 12:25)

The attack of 9/11 was a horrific event in this country. We had not seen that amount of loss since Pearl Harbor. But, even in the face of death a marvelous thing occurred. We saw a glimpse of one of our country's finest hours as we bound together in faith, prayer, and compassion to help the rescue workers, survivors, and their families. We gathered and prayed for our country in every corner of our nation. Even the halls of Congress, united and were not ashamed to show their faith in public. We were truly one nation, under God, indivisible.

We have been extremely fortunate since that time to have not had any additional attacks on this country. Is this because the government is providing outstanding protection? Is it because we are so vigilant that we can foil the threats? Or, are we being lulled into a trap set by our enemy? Think about it. Since 9/11, we have forgotten what pulled us together. We are back—separating God from everything—including our government. We are back bickering over whose fault the attacks were, whether we brought the attacks on ourselves, and whether we should or shouldn't be defending our country. We are becoming a nation divided all over again. We are dividing ourselves into segments governed by a few without regard for their constituents, a court system that is intent on making law not upholding it, and a whole segment of our population who has no use for God at all. Our enemy knows that a nation divided will fall. It did in Russia and with the divisiveness in our land, it can happen here. Our enemy can wait and take us without a shot.

Pray that our country, our leaders, and ourselves go back to what our forefathers intended—One Nation, Under God, Indivisible!

May 7

"Obedience"

Scripture: The reason I wrote you was to see if you would stand the test and be obedient in everything. (2 Corinthians 2:9)

Boy, oh boy do I have a story to tell you. The story is about being obedient to God's leading and being able to take action on what God says.

I have been a Christian for about 39 years, however, like most I have drifted from the faith several times. It wasn't until about seven years ago that God really got my attention. I thought I was doing everything I should in a business venture only to find out that I was actually broke. I was not only broke financially, but found that I was broke spiritually as well. I received a wake-up call, losing everything showed me just how foolish I was. I had really thought I was in control. Anyway, from that point forward my life changed significantly. God is now the center of my life and I seek him for everything. He has blessed me because of that obedience and that is what I want to share.

The devotional you are reading is a direct result of my being obedient. God told me back in 1999 to start writing. I didn't know why or for what purpose, but I have learned that if God speaks I had better act. I wrote for several weeks and God then revealed his plan for my writing. As I continued writing longhand (and then via computer) more and more was given to me until this year. In May God told me to finish by August 31st. That was a challenge, but I stayed obedient. I finished the devotional on September 2nd. Upon finishing the last page, God opened the door to a Christian publisher and then to the publishing of this book.

God is faithful, if we are faithful and obedient. I do not know what God has told you to do, but I can tell you that obedience comes with many blessings. All I can say is this: Don't hesitate, don't wait, and step out in obedience and faith and let God guide the way.

May 8

"Skipping Stones"

Scripture: For in Scripture it says: "See, I lay a stone in Zion, a chosen and precious cornerstone, the one who trusts in him never be put to shame." (1 Peter 2:6)

I love to go to the creek or pond. Upon my arrival, I look for the best skipping stones I can find and then, I let 'em rip. I love how the stones seem to glide across the water until they run out of steam and sink. The stones leave behind a wake which radiates from each point they touched in the water. The ripples flow out from those points, overlap other points, and yet continue until they reach the edge.

Thinking about the stones and how the ripples radiate from the rocks' points of contact reminds me of the Gospel. We cast the stone of Jesus out into a sea of hopelessness (this world) and every time it touches someone, it makes a ripple. The ripple of God's love changes whatever it touches. The more it touches, the more it radiates from the point of origin and overlaps with other stones cast. The Gospel is spread to many and will continue to spread until Jesus comes again.

Let the next stone you throw be a stone of love, compassion, mercy, and grace that comes from the most precious stone of all—Jesus.

May 9

"Grateful Praise"

Scripture: I will praise you with the harp for your faithfulness, O my God; I will sing praise to you with the lyre, O Holy One of Israel. (Psalm 71:22)

Our church often sings a doxology at the time we collect our offering. The doxology goes like this:

"Praise God from whom all blessings flow, praise Him all creatures here below, praise Him above the heavenly hosts, praise Father, Son, and Holy Ghost."

The reason I mention this doxology is I was amazed when I heard it at my daughter's band competition. We have all been schooled about being politically correct, especially when it comes to the separation of church and state and the rules regarding religion in schools. The band competition was for the Indiana State School Marching Band Association and my daughter's band won the competition for the fourth year in a row. Needless to say, everyone was excited and after the awards ceremony the bands exited the stadium in order of their placement with the champion going last. It came down to my daughter's band and before they exited they played this doxology. They felt honored that God had blessed them with the talent and the ability to win the competition. With humility they played and it silenced the stadium. Upon completion of the song the crowd burst in applause, knowing God had truly been honored.

I am thankful that there are Christians in our schools and that they are not afraid to be grateful for God's blessings.

May 10

"Master Storyteller"

Scripture: And he told them this parable: "The ground of a certain rich man produced a good crop.

Then he told this parable: "A man had a fig tree, planted in his vineyard, and he went to look for fruit on it, but did not find any. (Luke 12:16, 13:6)

Jesus was a master storyteller. He made sure he had a connection with His audience and that He spoke in terms of their day. He wove a story around concepts they could grasp and related those to God's Kingdom and teachings from God's Word. His sincerity, truth, and emphasis captivated the people. Most were able to hear the words and grasp the concept of a relationship with God, but some did not understand, because their hearts were not right.

Jesus is speaking to each of us everyday. He talks to us in prayer, in devotion, through worship, and even through the words of a friend. Even though Jesus does not always speak to us directly, He does speak to us through His Spirit. Jesus speaks with the same truth, with the same sincerity, and with the same emphasis He had when He walked the earth and He solidifies His message with God's Word.

Jesus has many things to say, so pick up your Bible and read a story from the greatest story teller of all.

May 11

"Optimist or Pessimist"

Scripture: Aware of their discussion, Jesus asked them: "Why are you talking about having no bread? Do you still not see or understand? Are your hearts hardened? Do you have eyes but fail to see, and ears but fail to hear? And don't you remember? When I broke the five loaves for the five thousand, how many basketfuls of pieces did you pick up?" "Twelve," they replied. (Mark 8:17–19)

We all have a tendency to look at the pessimistic side of an issue rather than thinking optimistically. When we look at our finances, we tend to see how little we have. When we look at our health, we tend to see only pain and suffering. When we look at our faith, we tend to see only our shortcomings.

Jesus knows the difficulty we have with seeing the positive in things, because He dealt with His disciples who struggled with the same thoughts and feelings. Jesus had to remind them time and time again, just as He does us, that He is the provider of our needs. The sooner we can learn to trust and rely on Him to take care of us the sooner we will have joy.

Which are you, an optimist or pessimist? If you are a pessimist and see your glass half empty instead of half full, let Jesus show you how full your glass really is and you will live a life of optimism from then on.

___

___

___

May 12

"True Worshipers"

Scripture: Jesus declared, "Believe me, woman, a time is coming when you will worship the Father neither on this mountain nor in Jerusalem. You Samaritans worship what you do not know; we worship what we do know, for salvation is from the Jews. Yet a time is coming and has now come when the true worshipers will worship the Father in spirit and truth, for they are the kind of worshipers the Father seeks. 24God is spirit, and his worshipers must worship in spirit and in truth." (John 4:21–24)

There are always discussions in our church about the type of worship service we should have. We struggle with the ideas of being contemporary, traditional, or blended. Our church seems to be divided on the type of worship they feel is most meaningful. Therefore, our pastors, our worship committees, and our worship planning teams have a difficult time providing the congregation what it wants.

Worship is an important part of our relationship with God. We must come together to praise and to be blessed both individually and as a community. But, as it is in our church, our community is segmented. It is as if we have two churches in one building. Our struggle is in maintaining our identity as one body.

God knew the struggle that worship would be in different cultures. Each brought their own set of rituals, heritage, and feel to the worship experience. Therefore, as Paul found, there was a constant need to focus each church that God established on what was truly important—Jesus' life, death, and resurrection.

The truth is that God only seeks two things for us in worship. The first is that we worship in spirit. We must allow the Holy Spirit to fill our hearts, mind, and body, so that true worship can be obtained. And, second we must worship God in truth. We must accept the Bible as God's infallible word and must trust it with all our hearts to teach, preach, and guide everything we do.

I don't know what type of worship you enjoy, but know this: worship is not worship without spirit and truth.

May 13

"Productive"

Scripture: For this very reason, make every effort to add to your faith goodness; and to goodness, knowledge; and to knowledge, self-control; and to self-control, perseverance; and to perseverance, godliness; and to godliness, brotherly kindness; and to brotherly kindness, love. For if you possess these qualities in increasing measure, they will keep you from being ineffective and unproductive in your knowledge of our Lord Jesus Christ. (2 Peter 1:5–8)

As a society, we are always pressured to be more productive. Our employers are always evaluating our productivity and our efficiency to make sure our companies can increase profit. We look at our own goals and ambition to see how we can accomplish more and more. We allow technology to infect our lives as a way to help us in these endeavors to be more productive. And as Christians we are always asking ourselves, "Are we making any strides in our faith and for God?"

There are some relatively easy ways to become more productive and efficient for ourselves, our employer, and our God. The key is to seek to be filled with the fruits of the spirit. The fruits will put us in harmony with God and God will grant us the ability to get more done. I have seen this in my own life in one particular way. I often thought that getting involved with God's purpose would detract from what I wanted to accomplish. For example, writing this devotional, praying, and serving God caused me to have concern that I would be hindered from doing a good job at work, would be hindered from having more family time and also, would be hindered from having time for myself. What I found was just the opposite. The more I gave to God the more I got done, the greater the peace I enjoyed, and the more productive I became.

If you want to be productive, then work on the fruits of the Spirit and see how efficient you become.

May 14

“Obedience”

Scripture: In everything that he undertook in the service of God’s temple and in obedience to the law and the commands, he sought his God and worked wholeheartedly. And so he prospered. (1 Chronicles 31:21)

Growing up in a large family of nine people and living in a small, 48’ long mobile home, my mother and father demanded discipline from us kids. They required us to be obedient to their direction because of the confined quarters in which we lived. We all soon learned that living as they directed created harmony, peace, and joy within the family.

As a part of God’s family, we too must learn obedience and discipline. God gives us directives and commands not to inhibit us, but rather to protect and guide us. He knows the pitfalls of the world and if He can get us to live in obedience, then our lives will be filled with the same principles I learned living in a small, 48’ long mobile home: harmony, peace, and joy.

I have also learned to apply these same principles to my Christian and business life. It wasn’t all that many years ago that I tried living my life my way. Every way I turned and everything I did was met with disaster. I couldn’t get ahead under any circumstances. One day I decided to let God direct me and that I would be obedient to His leading. From that day on everything has changed. I now live in the house of my dreams, I have a job that provides an income level that I never thought possible, and I have been given an opportunity to share my faith with others through this devotional. God knows and understands our hearts’ desires and, as a loving Father, He wants us to have them. Of course these things can only come when we decide to be obedient and walk in His way.

May 15

"God Bless America"

Scripture: Abraham will surely become a great and powerful nation, and all nations on earth will be blessed through him. (Genesis 18:18)

Being middle-aged, I grew up in a period of social unrest. During my beginning years of college, our country was in the middle of the Vietnam War. Body counts were broadcast daily. We faced a lottery draft, and we knew if our number was low, death could be waiting for us overseas. The love and peace contingent of the day seemed to have a total disregard for authority and the established government. A whole segment of the peace movement had a number of radical factions demonstrating on campuses, in Washington D.C., and anywhere they felt the government was demanding everyone to abide by the laws of the land. Other radical groups burned their draft cards and the U.S. flag. Some even denounced citizenship and went to Canada. It seemed that patriotism and being a good citizen took a back seat to love, peace, rock 'n' roll, and drugs. It was the worst time ever to side with the U.S. in anyway. It was hard to fathom that any good could come.

The good news is that God never removed His hand of blessing from our nation. He continued to grow and prosper America. God gave us a charge to remove the regimes of tyranny and oppression from many lands. He showed Godly leaders how to free people everywhere and how to stand for truth and justice. He gave us wealth and power like no other nation and out of this prosperity, He gave us the great ability to fund and field missionaries all over the globe. And today, God has blessed us with the technology to teach and preach His Word in nearly every language, and in every part of the world. God has truly blessed our land.

God Bless America!

May 16

"Don't Despair"

Scripture: But we have this treasure in jars of clay to show that this all-surpassing power is from God and not from us. We are hard pressed on every side, but not crushed; perplexed, but not in despair; persecuted, but not abandoned; struck down, but not destroyed. (2 Corinthians 4:7–9)

I am a fairly large man—I stand 6'2" tall and weigh around 220 pounds. I have been athletic most of my life and have always been reasonably strong. I very seldom become afraid of anything. I am not a quitter and I have difficulty giving up even when I know the odds are against me. Despair is typically the last feeling that comes to me in situations that seem hopeless.

Therefore, in those seemingly hopeless cases when despair does creep its way into my spirit, I typically become immediately overwhelmed. The best way for me to describe it is to say that it's like being in the ocean, swimming in water over your head with a 50-pound weight on your back. You struggle to keep your head above water, but you know eventually your strength will give out and you will go under. Despair is a horrible emotion and from articles I have read, can lead to severe mental problems and even suicide.

My advice is to deal with despair at the onset. Cry out to God in prayer, ask for His spirit to fill you, and release the issue that created the despair to Him. God will hear your cry and will come to your aid. He will give you peace and comfort and will lift your burden. Despair will lift and God will lead you to a sense of peace that surpasses all understanding.

Don't despair, cry out and be saved.

May 17

"God's Adventure"

Scripture: They did not ask, 'Where is the LORD, who brought us up out of Egypt who led us through the barren wilderness, through a land of deserts and rifts, a land of drought and darkness, a land where no one travels and no one lives?' (Jeremiah 2:6)

I do not know about you, but I really enjoy stories of adventure and intrigue. I love a story that has suspense and mystery. I get enthused as I watch or read and try to figure out what is going to happen next. I especially like watching a movie with these elements and then re-watching it to try to see details that I missed earlier that reveal the plot of the story. It makes it exhilarating and enjoyable.

Living life for God is also an adventure. He leads and directs our lives in unique ways. He opens and closes doors of opportunity, He allows us to participate in the plot with our free will, and He keeps each day exciting, fresh, and new. I love living my life that way and seeing how God is going to take what seems to be the impossible and make it happen.

He navigates us through uncharted waters and leads us through the deserts, over the hills and through the valleys. God provides protection, instruction, and comfort every step of the way. He picks us up if we fall and sets us back on the path if we wander. Living for God is definitely the best adventure of all.

May 18

"A Vast Universe"

Scripture: In the beginning God created the heavens and the earth. Now the earth was formless and empty, darkness was over the surface of the deep, and the Spirit of God was hovering over the waters. (Genesis 1:1–2)

Our family enjoys sitting outside by the campfire. We try to have several outings of this kind during the summer and fall. We are pretty fortunate to live away from the city, so the lights from the city don't interfere with the visibility of the stars, the moon, and the planets. While enjoying the campfire, we watch the sky and try to identify the major constellations as well as catch a glimpse of a shooting star or a passing satellite.

God truly created a vast universe. The infinite number of stars, the distance the light has to travel to reach us, and the beauty of the moon is awe-inspiring. While we sit by the campfire, I feel a sense of gratitude. I am truly thankful for the heavens and earth God created and the beauty of being able to enjoy it.

A vast universe indeed, thanks God!

____

____

____

May 19

"Sink or Swim"

Scripture: The disciples went and woke him, saying, "Lord, save us! We're going to drown!" (Matthew 8:25)

In June of 1998, my family was in Florida for a vacation. We stayed in a wonderful area with white sand beaches and an azure blue ocean. The whole area was gorgeous and a sight to behold. My children especially loved the ocean, because they could wade out a long way before the water got too deep.

One day we saw a number of people out on a sand bar fifty yards or so from the beach. My youngest son expressed a desire to go out to play on the sand bar, because it appeared as though the water came up only as high as the swimmers' knees. After some prodding, I agreed to take him out. He was only ten at the time and wanted me to put him on my back to take him out to the sand bar.

I thought the task would be relatively simple, so I put him on my back and started out. We got within about fifteen yards of the sand bar, when suddenly there was no bottom. His added weight on my back forced me under, even though I kept him above water. Uncertain of his ability to swim the ocean, fear attacked me. I struggled to keep him above water and tried to turn back to the shallow waters that we had just left, but I felt myself tiring and unable to get enough breath to keep going.

I had to make a decision: Either shove him off my back and tell him to swim towards shore or keep struggling, potentially putting us both in a panic that could cause us to drown. Off he went while I shouted, "Swim to shore!"

I prayed a silent prayer and struggled to get my breath and continue. I was extremely tired from my efforts to keep him above water and had ingested some salt water. It took all the strength I had to stay calm and urge my son to keep swimming. Shortly the sandy bottom was beneath my feet and I stood up exhausted, just in time to see my son running onto the beach. We were saved. My prayers were answered.

We all face circumstances where we are in over our heads. We are overwhelmed and struggling to keep afloat in a difficult world. It is frightening and uncertain. We know that we must keep going, keep trying to make it, and we murmur a small prayer, "God save us." And, sure enough he answers our prayers, calms the water, and saves us indeed.

May 20

"Sleep On It"

Scripture: I rise before dawn and cry for help; I have put my hope in your word. (Psalm 119:147)

We all face decisions that are of serious consequence on occasion. We seek to make the right decision and in that effort, we ask God to help. We feel a little insecure, because no clear direction has developed from our prayer. We know the answer will come in time, and so in frustration, we decide to sleep on it.

Sleeping on it shows God we are willing to be patient. It also allows God to go to work by removing the clutter from our mind, allows His spirit to enter our thoughts, and eventually allows God to reveal the answers we need. We often think of sleep as inaction, but God uses sleep to gives us dreams, visions, and to establish hope within us. It seems with every dawning day there is new hope on the horizon. The serious consequences we face seem less scary and more within reason after a refreshing sleep. This is because we have allowed God to be God as we experience a simple, renewal of body and mind through sleep.

Don't rush to make decisions. Instead, seek God and ask for his help. Then show God your willingness to be patient and sleep on it.

May 21

"Senses versus Senses"

Scripture: "Not long after that, the younger son got together all he had, set off for a distant country and there squandered his wealth in wild living. After he had spent everything, there was a severe famine in that whole country, and he began to be in need. So he went and hired himself out to a citizen of that country, who sent him to his fields to feed pigs. He longed to fill his stomach with the pods that the pigs were eating, but no one gave him anything. "When he came to his senses, he said, 'How many of my father's hired men have food to spare, and here I am starving to death! (Luke 15:13–17)

I don't know about you, but my senses are definitely active. It starts the first thing in the morning, when that first splash of hot water touches my body in the shower. It again reveals itself as a melody comes from the radio that touches my ears. My nose is awakened to the smell of freshly brewing coffee. Then to top it all off, I look outside and see a beautiful sunrise. All my senses are alert, alive, and well.

These fantastic early morning senses eventually start to yield to the world. The TV comes on and my eyes see the news and the shock of violence, death, and destruction. I walk outside and the appearance of the beautiful day turns to frigid cold that penetrates my body. My nose catches a whiff of the pungent odor of pigs or cows. On my drive to the airport, my ears move from the joy of a melody to the honking of car horns in a gesture of anxiety.

It doesn't stop there. I am walking through the airport when I catch a glimpse of a strikingly beautiful woman, my noses catches a whiff of her perfume, my body is stimulated and the senses that are normally a blessing become a curse in a lustful thought. My senses are at fever pitch, but not for what God had intended.

Immediately other senses take over. It is God's spirit convicting me of my thoughts. God knows how the devil can manipulate our senses for his purpose. He seeks to deceive us, but thank God, He brings us to our right senses. We recognize our deficiency and our weakness and run to Him for forgiveness. God is there and He welcomes us with open arms, a hug, and a kiss of grace.

___

___

___

May 22

"Give Without Judgment"

Scripture: "So when you give to the needy, do not announce it with trumpets, as the hypocrites do in the synagogues and on the streets, to be honored by men. I tell you the truth, they have received their reward in full. But when you give to the needy, do not let your left hand know what your right hand is doing, so that your giving may be in secret. Then your Father, who sees what is done in secret, will reward you. (Matthew 6:2–4)

I had to travel to Milwaukee and decided to drive instead of fly. Along the way, I had to stop for gas and breakfast. Upon leaving the gas station, I was caught at a stop light and was asked to donate some money to help start a church. The person who approached me had a wonderful smile, but my initial thought was to question whether his intentions were true and just. My thoughts started racing in a judgmental fashion. This person is just doing this to gain a windfall for himself. He is just going to buy liquor or drugs, I thought. As the judgmental thoughts filled my head, an additional thought came to mind. It was a statement my mother used to make about giving. My mother told me it was not our place to judge the receiver; we were to leave that to God. Those asking for money are responsible for the gifts they receive in God's name and will be judged for their stewardship. With that thought, I reached into my billfold and gave to the man's effort.

God knows that we may be duped or taken advantage of and that funds will be misused. God also knows if we judge everyone prior to giving, we can come up with many reasons to withhold offerings. God wants us to give to His Kingdom, to give cheerfully, and to give without judgment. In doing so, He will bless the giver and the receiver as He chooses.

May 23

"Hands of Protection"

Scripture: The Father loves the Son and has placed everything in his hands. (John 3:35)

Living today with the potential of terrorist attacks, driving in ever-increasing traffic, visiting cities with tremendous violence, and flying all over the country on airlines that are suffering from substantial financial losses, gives great cause for concern about one's safety and protection. The other day as I climbed into my car for a trip, a slogan from an insurance commercial came to mind. It was, "You're in good hands." The slogan summed up the thoughts I normally have of being in Jesus' protective hands. I always ask for His protection before I drive, before I board an airplane, and before I walk down the street.

God has placed all believers in Jesus' hands. Jesus' hands protect, guide, and discipline. He does these things because He loves us so much. I love the idea of being protected by Jesus' hands, and I certainly enjoy the comfort His hands offer.

May 24

"THY WILL OR MY WILL"

Scripture: Do not conform any longer to the pattern of this world, but be transformed by the renewing of your mind. Then you will be able to test and approve what God's will is—his good, pleasing and perfect will. (Romans 12:2)

I remember when my children were just learning how to walk. It seemed almost instinctive for them to take steps as they gained strength to hold onto fingers. It wasn't long before they were pulling themselves up at a chair or couch and stepping away. I was amazed at their persistence. Nothing would deter them from taking steps until they could manage walking from chair to couch. Their legs were shaky and uncertain at first, but it didn't matter how many times they fell, they were determined to walk. It wasn't long before they were taking off boldly with confidence. They soon exercised their will to go where they wanted when they wanted.

It doesn't matter how long we have been Christians we still have to deal with our will. We started out a little uncertain and shaky like a baby taking his first steps, so we relied on God for everything and held onto His hand. We sought His direction for every step we took. It wasn't long though before we had gained our confidence and we stepped out on our own. We realized we could not only walk, but could run towards those things we wanted and thought were good. We gave up seeking God and continued down our own path. We exercised our will to go where we wanted when we wanted, until we stumbled and fell and with shaken confidence headed back to grab the hand of God.

As you walk in a world of enticement and temptation, guard your will, rely on God, and seek His will. By doing so, you can walk in confidence all the days of your life without fear of stumbling.

God blessed each of us with free will, but God's intention was that we would choose to walk with Him and not on our own. It really comes to a very basic decision about our lives with God—thy will or my will.

May 25

"EPIPHANY"

Scripture: for the Mighty One has done great things for me—holy is his name. (Luke 1:49)

A couple of years ago there was a commercial talking about an epiphany in life. The idea was that if you owned or bought what they were selling, it would have life-altering consequences. It really didn't have much impact on me until recently. I was sharing some thoughts about my Christian life when I realized that even though I was saved at eight, I wasn't really saved until I had an epiphany from God about seven or eight years ago. It occurred during a very difficult time in my life. I was struggling financially and was seeking God continually. It wasn't until God broke down the barriers of my pride that my true salvation came. I realized I wasn't my own man, I could not live without God in my life, and I had to surrender everything to Him.

At that point and in the darkness of my closet, God and I came to terms. I gave up and He became the true hope and salvation of my life. I knew I was saved and my life was His thereafter.

We will all face God in different ways and at different times, but one thing is for sure the time will come for you to face Him and it will change your life forever.

It will be a true EPIPHANY!

May 26

"Scars of Sin"

Scripture: But he was pierced for our transgressions, he was crushed for our iniquities; the punishment that brought us peace was upon him, and by his wounds we are healed. (Isaiah 53:5)

I love woodworking. I enjoy taking wood and making something from it. It gives me great joy and satisfaction to create something with my own hands. Being a woodworker though, is not without peril. You are working with power tools and if they come in contact with skin, they are not very forgiving. A few years ago I was cutting a piece of wood on a table saw. Before I could react, a piece of wood kicked back and severed the end of my finger. I will spare you the gory details, but let me just say, the hospital had to sew my finger back on. Fortunate for me the hospital had a wonderful hand specialist and you can barely see a scar from the ordeal.

The scar on my finger reminds me of the scars that sin has left in my life. Even though I have received forgiveness a scar remains. I believe it is God's way of reminding us how perilous and deadly sin can be. I know that the scar on my finger reminds me to be extremely careful around a table saw, just like the scars of sin remind me of the suffering and pain Jesus endured on my behalf. I am glad to have scars from past sin to keep me cautious and alert when temptation comes near.

May 27

"Common Man, Extraordinary Purpose"

Scripture: Jesus went through all the towns and villages, teaching in their synagogues, preaching the good news of the kingdom and healing every disease and sickness. When he saw the crowds, he had compassion on them, because they were harassed and helpless, like sheep without a shepherd. Then he said to his disciples, "The harvest is plentiful but the workers are few. Ask the Lord of the harvest, therefore, to send out workers into his harvest field."(Matthew 9:35–38)

It is extraordinary how Jesus called each of His disciples to further His Father's Kingdom. He knew the task would be daunting and difficult. Jesus could have called and got the cream of the crop, the best of the best, and the ones with the right stuff, but instead He chose common men. Jesus knew that to reach the lost, common-ground relationships must be established and that He could not establish such relationships unless He did it with people who could relate to those on the street. As a result, Jesus called murderers, tax collectors, and fishermen to preach and teach salvation to the world. Jesus called the common men and gave them extraordinary ability.

This is good news for us. It does not matter our status in life, where we live, where we work, how much we make, or the level of our education. Jesus will use us to further His Father's Kingdom. Through His spirit He will give us a bold witness and will send us to reach the common people everywhere. Jesus provides the resource for common men and women to do His work until He comes again.

Step up and be extraordinary for the Kingdom of God.

May 28

"Tools"

Scripture: Now the earth was corrupt in God's sight and was full of violence. God saw how corrupt the earth had become, for all the people on earth had corrupted their ways. So God said to Noah, "I am going to put an end to all people, for the earth is filled with violence because of them. I am surely going to destroy both them and the earth. So make yourself an ark of cypress wood; make rooms in it and coat it with pitch inside and out. (Genesis 6:11–14)

The working world could not function properly without the right tools. We would never send a surgeon into an operating room with a chainsaw, give a carpenter a baseball bat to build a house, give a mechanic a sewing kit to fix a car, or give a housewife an eggbeater to clean the rugs. Tools can make the job easier and make the worker more efficient and productive. Can you imagine Noah's thought when God gave him the job of building the ark? He did not have any power tools, just the hand tools of the day and the spirit of God within him. He completed the job as God commanded and saved a remnant to start a new world.

God knows the importance of having the right tools. He provides His Word to equip us and give us the means to do His work. God knows that we will become proficient and capable the more we rely on Him and the Word of life. Get into His tool chest daily, improve your abilities, and become efficient for His Kingdom.

Now is the time to equip yourself with the right tools and go build a larger Kingdom for God.

May 29

"Harmony"

Scripture: Finally, all of you, live in harmony with one another; be sympathetic, love as brothers, be compassionate and humble. (1 Peter 3:8)

I have had the opportunity to sing in a choir and in a men's chorus. I have always enjoyed singing and listening to musical groups. I especially enjoy hearing groups sing a cappella. Singing without musical accompaniment reveals the harmony within the song. Everyone can hear the unity of the singers and how tight the harmony impacts the sound. One of the things I learned while singing was to listen. You must hear all of the other parts to accomplish the sound of fullness and true harmony.

As Christians we would do good to take some lessons from a chorus. We all have a song to sing, but it becomes sweeter, richer and fuller, when we sing with others. Reach out to others within the community of Christ; listen to their needs with compassion and sympathy and extend a hand of love. This is the song God wants us to sing in harmony with others in the world.

May 30

"Got Desire?"

Scripture: It does not, therefore, depend on man's desire or effort, but on God's mercy. (Romans 9:16)

One of the keys to life-changing effort is desire. Desire is the catalyst that makes everything possible and without it nothing can change. I believe with all of my heart that a drug addict, an alcoholic, and a sinner cannot be helped by God without the desire to change. God has given me this anagram to help us all have the desire to seek Him for change.

D–stands for the dedication and discipline necessary for change. We must have dedication to discipline ourselves for change to take place. We must make the commitment to change and when we do, God will be there.

E–stands for the emotional investment we have to make in order to take the steps toward change. The emotional investment requires surrender to God and His will for our lives.

S–stands for the systematic approach to effect change. It requires us to take one step at a time. As we take a step God will be there to catch us if we fall, and if we fall, He will put us back on our feet.

I–stands for the interdependence we must have on God. We must depend on God and God wants us to love Him with all of our hearts. It is this interdependence that provides our strength, our power, and our hope for the future.

R–stands for resolve. We must have the fortitude and persistence to see the change through to completion. God's spirit will provide the sustenance we need to help us endure all that is required of us for change.

E–stands for the enthusiasm needed to face each day. God is doing a good work and change is at hand, so know that it can be faced with joy.

Do you have something in your life you need to change? If so, ask God to help you have the DESIRE to do so and it will be done.

____

____

____

May 31

"Fruit Tree"

Scripture: "Make a tree good and its fruit will be good, or make a tree bad and its fruit will be bad, for a tree is recognized by its fruit. (Matthew 12:33)

Everyone wants to be famous or at least to be acknowledged or recognized for their effort. Recognition and acknowledgment are things we work for. In our job we work to receive a raise or a promotion, in sports we work to win the league or trophy, and in life we work to be successful. With each of these strivings, our real desire is to be recognized and appreciated. The truth is most people only see us as an associate, a neighbor, or a member of the church. They do not recognize the effort we put forth to be better, more complete, and stronger in these areas of our lives. So why do we strive so hard to receive this recognition?

The passage in Matthew says more than the words actually portray. God knows we are like a tree in the middle of the forest. We are the same height, same diameter, and have the same leaves as other trees. When we look at a clump of trees we do not really recognize the benefit of any single tree or the potential of any tree to provide anything useful. It isn't until we get into the trees that we recognize there are trees that produce fruit and trees that produce nuts. These particular trees can feed a starving person because of what they produce, yet from a distance all of the trees appear to be the same.

The lesson here is that we should not be concerned with what the world recognizes from a distance, but should instead strive to produce the fruit that God intended for our lives to produce. True recognition comes from staying rooted in God's Word, so that we might reach our limbs to Heaven and produce the eternal fruit that will reach the people. When our attitude is to do as God wills, then we will be recognized and acknowledged before the multitude in Heaven. God will call everyone together and say, "Well done, my good and faithful servant."

June

June 1

"Divine Milestones"

Scripture: "Unless you people see miraculous signs and wonders," Jesus told him, "you will never believe." (John 4:48)

I recently had a conversation with my sister-in-law. She asked about my devotional and how things were going. As is usual, when the opportunity to discuss God arises, I seized it and spent about twenty minutes sharing stories of faith with her. It was during those minutes that I realized how many times God has been there for me, how He has impacted the circumstances of my life, and how He has opened doors of opportunity for me. Immediately, I thought about the number of people who are touched by God daily and yet miss the whole event.

After the conversation, God's spirit touched me. A whisper of a voice said, "These are divine milestones." God gave them to me to share my faith walk with others, so here are just a few that may strike a chord in your heart.

I was saved at eight, but was never really saved. God used the following situations and circumstances to get my attention and show His mighty works.

I was fortunate to participate in a recording session of a gospel quartet. I was there in support of the group, which turned into a great weekend of fellowship and prayer. At the hotel we were all praying together and one member of the group said he had a word from God for me. He told me that God said, "Eat the whole loaf." It wasn't until years later that "eat the whole loaf" was a representation of the bread of life—Jesus. This was part of the total surrender I needed to be truly saved.

God provided a word of prophecy through a friend about a business failure. I was proud and headstrong believing that failure would never happen to me, but it did come to pass. This failure cost me everything, but gave me true salvation, so it was worth every penny.

I asked God about a job I held and why things felt so wrong. I asked God to provide a new opportunity for me after a very sordid meeting at work and I prayed for this new opportunity to arrive that day.

Sure enough, I received an offer within an hour for a job that paid more money and which offered me more time to spend with my family.

God has spoken to me to change jobs, to build a house, to write, and to do many other things as He has instructed. I really didn't see any of these as significant at the time, but in hindsight I recognize that every part of my life has been touched by "divine milestones".

June 2

"The Lord's Prayer"

Scripture: And it came to pass, that, as he was praying in a certain place, when he ceased, one of his disciples said unto him, Lord, teach us to pray, as John also taught his disciples. And he said unto them, When ye pray, say, Our Father which art in heaven, Hallowed be thy name. Thy kingdom come. Thy will be done, as in heaven, so in earth. 3Give us day by day our daily bread. 4And forgive us our sins; for we also forgive every one that is indebted to us. And lead us not into temptation; but deliver us from evil. (Luke 11:1–4 KJV)

God has opened me up to many revelations in His Word. I read Scripture with a new vision and with new understanding. It impacts my life in specific ways based on the circumstances I face.

One of those scriptures that recently touched me was the Lord's Prayer. One day I was driving and praying, which is often the case, when God's spirit overwhelmed me. In this case it was while I recited the Lord's Prayer and with each verse God opened my heart to new understanding, which I would like to share.

Our Father who art in heaven, Hallowed be thy name, sets the mood for our communion with God. We praise and exalt Him and He comes into our presence to be with us.

Thy kingdom come, thy will be done, is our commitment to total surrender. This is the complete surrender of our lives and our possessions on earth and our eternal souls.

Give us this day our daily bread causes us to recognize that God is in control and that He will provide all that we need.

Forgive our sins, as we forgive those who sin against us, reminds us that we must reconcile ourselves with our Father, so that He can do a miraculous work in our lives. It also reminds us to fulfill the command to love our neighbor, which cannot occur until we forgive them.

Lead us not into temptation, but deliver us from evil, reminds us that God does not tempt us, but He keeps us from going down the wrong path. He guides us along our way and provides the protection we need from the devil.

This showed me why Jesus taught the Lord's Prayer to His disciples, because He knew it is the ultimate of all prayers. So pray it today and everyday and receive God's full blessing from it.

June 3

"Investment 101"

Scripture: "Will a man rob God? Yet you rob me. "But you ask, 'How do we rob you?' "In tithes and offerings. You are under a curse—the whole nation of you—because you are robbing me. Bring the whole tithe into the storehouse, that there may be food in my house. Test me in this," says the LORD Almighty, "and see if I will not throw open the floodgates of heaven and pour out so much blessing that you will not have room enough for it." (Malachi 3:8–10)

I am amazed at the number of commercials there are about investing money these days. They announce that their brokerage firms can make money for you in the stock market and can provide for your future. All you have to do is give them control of your life savings. I am not saying that there aren't good advisers out there, and I'm not saying that there aren't any who are led by God to help God's people, but I think we all need a lesson in "Investment 101".

God is extremely clear about what He expects from us. He tells us that a tithe and offering is the catalyst to great blessing. He says that we are to give as He instructs and if we don't that we are robbing Him, and we are under a curse. When we give as directed, then He will open the floodgates of Heaven and pour out more blessing on us than we can possibly store.

Therefore, "Investment 101" is this: Give God your tithes and offerings. Then take the windfall blessing that God promises you and multiple it through the sources God dictates. By doing your investing in this manner, you not only lay up for yourself treasures in Heaven through your obedience, but you will also have an abundant life here on earth.

God is offering classes with immediate openings in "Investment 101". Care to join?

June 4

"Strong Evidence"

Scripture: Peter and the other apostles replied: "We must obey God rather than men! The God of our fathers raised Jesus from the dead—whom you had killed by hanging him on a tree. God exalted him to his own right hand as Prince and Savior that he might give repentance and forgiveness of sins to Israel. We are witnesses of these things, and so is the Holy Spirit, whom God has given to those who obey him." (Acts 5: 29–32)

One of my favorite television series is CSI. You can now watch the original series plus many spin-off series to go along with it. It is intriguing to see how each episode portrays a crime and then unfolds the truth about it as evidence is presented. The series works because each event only leaves a trail of evidence, whether it is blood, DNA, bullets, clothing fibers, or glass shards. The characters develop the evidence until it is irrefutable in a court of law. What you seldom see and is never provided is an eyewitness account of the crime. The reason for this is that there would be no crime to solve if someone had seen it firsthand.

Jesus is real and does exist. He was surrounded by devoted followers, who followed Him through His life, death, and resurrection. These followers were eyewitnesses to the events that occurred in His life and they recorded them for all to read. This evidence is strong and irrefutable. Jesus is alive and sits at the right hand of the Father. Evidence gathered, evidence submitted, and truth wins—Jesus is Lord.

June 5

"Love the Children"

Scripture: Jesus said, "Let the little children come to me, and do not hinder them, for the kingdom of heaven belongs to such as these." (Matthew 19:14)

Being a father is one of the most important jobs I have. It is my responsibility to love, guide, and teach my children about life, but most of all about God. If I truly love them, I will seek opportunities for them to see God and His grace through me.

When I think about my children and being a father, I wonder about children who do not have a father or have been abused by a father. Where do they go to be loved? How do they see their fathers? Do they see them as people who abandoned them or hurt them mentally or physically? If they see their fathers like this, then how will they be able to accept God the Father?

God knows each and every person and especially children. He has a very special place in His heart for them. Therefore as Christians, when we see children without a father or children suffering abuse, we must reach out to them in love. We may be the only ones who can reach these children. We may not break through, but we may plant a seed of affection that can grow and be harvested by someone else. Jesus loved the little children and so should we.

June 6

"In a Word"

Scripture: Then Jesus said to him, "Get up! Pick up you mat and walk."(John 5:8)

Jesus always uses unusual circumstances to touch people's lives. Even when our lives are a shamble and we are in the pit of despair, Jesus seizes the opportunity to teach us to be witnesses of love. He moves our focus from our self to God and from our self-pity to self-improvement. He doesn't do it by therapy or by self-help books, but by the sheer mention of the words–I love you!

Jesus has always used unusual circumstances of affliction and sickness as a witness of love. He spoke these words of love without a crowd and without drawing attention to himself. He spoke out of compassion to glorify his Father. Jesus merely said to be healed or for demons to come out and it was done. Jesus saw their pain and even though the afflicted seldom asked to be healed, He did it because His heart was filled with love. And through speaking a word in love, He bore witness to His Father's love to the world!

June 7

"Follow the Leader"

Scripture: So Joshua fought the Amalekites as Moses had ordered, and Moses, Aaron and Hur went to the top of the hill. As long as Moses held up his hands, the Israelites were winning, but whenever he lowered his hands, the Amalekites were winning. (Exodus 17:10–11)

Everyone wants to be a leader, but as we all know there are "plenty of chiefs, but not enough Indians." The truth is followers are important, too. Without followers the work would not get done. So if you are not the leader, be a good follower of God's glory.

Joshua was a good follower before God chose him to lead. Joshua followed Moses and Moses followed God. In watching and emulating how Moses sought God in every situation, Joshua came to know the true importance of following. Because of his following God and in following Moses footsteps, Joshua would get to lead his people into the Promised Land.

Be content to be a follower and let God do the leading always; and, someday God will call upon you to lead His people into the Promised Land of His salvation.

June 8

"DENOMINATIONS, SO MANY DENOMINATIONS"

Scripture: There is one body and one Spirit—just as you were called to one hope when you were called—one Lord, one faith, one baptism; one God and Father of all, who is over all and through all and in all. (Ephesians 4:4–6)

There are so many denominations of Christians in the world and each of them has their own rights and rituals. Each of these holds a special significance in the hearts of the people who belong to them and all are fine as long as they carry one common denominator—Jesus. Jesus must be at the center of all worship, because through Jesus all things will be judged.

The Scripture is clear that there is only one body and one Spirit brought together by the saving grace of our Lord, Jesus Christ. We are not slave or free, Jew or Greek, black or white, Methodist or Catholic, but we are all one in Christ Jesus, the Savior of all.

June 9

"Work unto the Lord"

Scripture: So we rebuilt the wall till all of it reached half its height, for the people worked with all their heart. (Nehemiah 4:6)

Work unto the Lord in all things. It seems simple doesn't it? The truth is though we often become overwhelmed by the job before us. We complain and grumble over the work we have to do.

Nehemiah and the tribes were given a monumental task: to rebuild the collapsed walls of Jerusalem. They could have complained and procrastinated, but the work of the Lord would not have been done and they would not have had God's protection and the protection of the walls. Instead they dedicated their work to the Lord and the walls were built. Even though their enemies sought to destroy them, God saw their effort and came to their aid giving them strength and perseverance.

God will do the same for us, if we dedicate our work to Him. We will succeed in the face of all adversity and triumph in peace and joy—"Work unto the Lord."

June 10

"MIRACLES, SIGNS, AND WONDERS"

Scripture: Immediately Jesus knew in his spirit that this was what they were thinking in their hearts, and he said to them, "Why are you thinking these things? 9 Which is easier: to say to the paralytic, 'Your sins are forgiven,' or to say, 'Get up, take your mat and walk'? 10 But that you may know that the Son of Man has authority on earth to forgive sins. . . ." He said to the paralytic, 11"I tell you, get up, take your mat and go home." (Mark 2:8–11)

Jesus found that he was suspect whenever he forgave someone his or her sins. The Scribes and Pharisees called it blasphemy, because none recognized Him for who He was, the Messiah. He connected with the people through many miracles, signs, and wonders—the miracle of healing being the most effective. He taught that all things are possible through His Father, who gave Him authority to heal as well as to forgive. And, forgive sins He did.

If Jesus were in our midst today, would we recognize Him? Well, he is in our midst, not in body, but in Spirit. He still performs the same miracles today as He did then and He still forgives our sins. Don't miss Him. Open your heart and soul to Him today. Be transformed; recognize the one and only Savior, Jesus, the power and authority over all earthly things.

June 11

"God is in Control"

Scripture: But his delight is in the law of the LORD, and on his law he meditates day and night. He is like a tree planted by streams of water, which yields its fruit in season and whose leaf does not wither. Whatever he does prospers. (Psalms 1:2–3)

It has taken me many years to realize that God is in control. He provides blessings great and small to those who do not live in sin. That's the tough part. I try daily not to sin, but I never seem to make it. I am always outside the boundaries, knowing I have committed a sin against God and my fellow man. I fail and fall out of God's blessing each and everyday. Did you pick up the subtlety in the last line? I fail and fall everyday. That means I have to be reconciled to God to fail and fall. And, that is truly one of God's great blessings. By the saving grace of God, he forgives my sins through my confession and repentance, and therefore, each day I qualify for His blessings, which He gloriously gives.

My experience is that God wants us to prosper, not by doing whatever we can in this world, but by allowing Him to provide for us. He will provide blessing after blessing, not just enough, but in abundance, so we can share God's glory with others.

God is definitely in control.

June 12

"HUNGRY?"

Scripture: Then Jesus declared, "I am the bread of life. He who comes to me will never go hungry, and he who believes in me will never be thirsty." (John 6:35)

There is a food commercial that asks, "What are you hungry for?" Many would respond, "A burger and fries, or maybe some chicken wings." Others throughout the world would say, "The scraps off your table or your garbage," because they haven't eaten in weeks. In a land of abundance, we take our lack of hunger for granted. The majority of us go to bed with a full stomach, but yet we are still starving. Not for food, but the true bread of life.

The body needs sustenance to survive and yet we face a starvation everyday. It is the spiritual starvation created by anger, bitterness, resentment, and being overcome by the world. We are starving, but yet we refuse to ask for the true bread.

Jesus is the bread of life. He is waiting to provide for you a feast of joy, peace, and prosperity. It is there for the taking. Come and be fed today!

June 13

"Fish or Bait?"

Scripture: Then Jesus said to Simon, "Don't be afraid; from now on you will catch men." So they pulled their boats up on shore, left everything and followed him. (Luke 5:10b-11)

What a great story. Jesus calls Simon, James, and John to stop fishing for fish and become fishers of men. I wonder how many of us have been called to be fishers of men. I think all of us have, that is, all who know and have accepted the Good News of Jesus.

Each one of us can be a witness to people who have not heard about Jesus. We may be the only Jesus anyone sees, so are we not even going to wet a line? Are we going to sit on the shore, while people drown in the world of despair and fear? I pray not. Make your cast. You may only get a nibble or you may only feed the fish, but someone, someday will reel in the catch.

Fishing is an act of faith. You go to the shore, cast your line, and wait hopefully for that nibble to come. Some days it does and some days it doesn't. But one thing is for sure; if you don't try, you don't even have a chance. It is the same way with witnessing; you have to have faith, you have to share it, and then let God fill your nets.

June 14

"God's Bidding"

Scripture: For I am already being poured out like a drink offering, and the time has come for my departure. I have fought the good fight, I have finished the race, I have kept the faith. Now there is in store for me the crown of righteousness, which the Lord, the righteous Judge, will award to me on that day—and not only to me, but also to all who have longed for his appearing. (2 Timothy 4:6–8)

I have always been concerned about doing God's will in my life. What does He want me to do? What does He want me to accomplish? What does He will for me? I have always wondered about the role I am to play in God's Kingdom.

As I read about Paul, he knew exactly what he was called to do. He was called by Jesus to preach the Gospel to the Gentiles. You can't get much clearer than that. But, we, as Timothy, have a less clear course. Our course is one constantly being challenged or changed by the world around us. So what are we to do?

Paul wrote Timothy to encourage him. He told Timothy to be always prepared and to endure whatever course was before him as Paul himself did. If we do, we will receive the reward that God himself will give to us upon his return. It is the crown of righteousness.

I am still not sure what God has for me to do, but I do know I can face it with this certainty: God will reveal it to me as He sees fit. So I must be prepared always to do God's bidding.

____

____

____

June 15

"Are You a Servant?"

Scripture: She said to her husband, "I know that this man who often comes our way is a holy man of God. Let's make a small room on the roof and put in it a bed and a table, a chair and a lamp for him. Then he can stay there whenever he comes to us."

One day when Elisha came, he went up to his room and lay down there. He said to his servant Gehazi, "Call the Shunammite." So he called her, and she stood before him. Elisha said to him, "Tell her, 'You have gone to all this trouble for us. Now what can be done for you? Can we speak on your behalf to the king or the commander of the army?'

"She replied, "I have a home among my own people."

"What can be done for her?" Elisha asked.

Gehazi said, "Well, she has no son and her husband is old."

Then Elisha said, "Call her." So he called her, and she stood in the doorway. "About this time next year," Elisha said, "you will hold a son in your arms." (2 Kings 4:9–16)

I sing in a men's chorus and we have sung a song called the "Servants Song." A verse in the song asks very simply how we can be a servant for God. Are we a servant? Are we looking to be of service to others and to our God?

In 2nd Kings, we read of a Shunammite woman who opened her house to Elisha whenever he passed through her town. She even made a more permanent place for him. She set up a room for him with a bed, a table, and a lamp. She fed him and attended to all his needs. She wanted to make sure that this man of God had everything he needed. And through it all, when Elisha asked what he could do for her she said, "Nothing sir." She wanted nothing in return; she just wanted to be of service. Elisha, however, felt something needed to be done, so he inquired and found that she did not have a son. He summoned her and told her she would be blessed for her service to him and she could not believe what he told her, but accepted the news graciously. She would receive her blessing and her heart's desire—a son.

We will be blessed too, if we choose to serve others. Do it without notice, because our Father in Heaven knows and will bless us. So do a random act of kindness and service today!

____

____

____

June 16

"Can We Sing Our Praises to God?"

Scripture: The LORD is my rock, my fortress and my deliverer; my God is my rock, in whom I take refuge. He is my shield and the horn of my salvation, my stronghold.

I call to the LORD, who is worthy of praise, and I am saved from my enemies. (Psalms 18:2–3)

My rock, my fortress, my refuge—is this how we truly see our God? I do. God has seen me through some very difficult times. He knows the attacks, the sufferings, and the turmoil. He has been there for every step. He has seen me through divorce, death, and through business failure. I got to the end of my rope and the knot was coming unraveled and He was there. Through these circumstances of life, He taught me to trust in Him even though I am a slow learner. It has taken me 47 years to get to that point of trust and knowing that He is there for me and will not steer me wrong. Why couldn't I have learned it sooner? The key is even though I learned it late; I learned it. I now trust in my God and in his ability to be there for my protection. I can trust the Lord and praise His holy name.

Don't face life's circumstances without the God of all creation. Seek Him, find Him, and praise Him; He will be there for you always. I know because He certainly has been there for me.

___

___

___

June 17

"Jordan's Prayer"

Scripture: Whatever you do, work at it with all your heart, as working for the Lord, not for men, since you know that you will receive an inheritance from the Lord as a reward. It is the Lord Christ you are serving. (Colossians 3:23–24)

Sometimes I get discouraged about working. It seems the harder I work the more behind I get. I work hard and make less. When I start feeling that way, I stop and evaluate who it is that I am really working for and I typically find it is I. I am working for my personal gain and with focus only on my wants and my needs. When I realize this is happening, I get on my knees and pray for a change. I want to work for my God, the Lord of my life. In doing so, I receive a wonderful blessing. A blessing of great satisfaction, fulfillment, and joy knowing I am working for God's glory.

I pray this especially for my son, Jordan. He always tries to do enough just to get by. I pray he grasps the joy of doing a job well, as unto the Lord.

June 18

"Rejoice At What God Has Done"

Scripture: And God said, "Let the water teem with living creatures, and let birds fly above the earth across the expanse of the sky." So God created the great creatures of the sea and every living and moving thing with which the water teems, according to their kinds, and every winged bird according to its kind. And God saw that it was good. God blessed them and said, "Be fruitful and increase in number and fill the water in the seas, and let the birds increase on the earth." And there was evening, and there was morning—the fifth day.

And God said, "Let the land produce living creatures according to their kinds: livestock, creatures that move along the ground, and wild animals, each according to its kind." And it was so. God made the wild animals according to their kinds, the livestock according to their kinds, and all the creatures that move along the ground according to their kinds. And God saw that it was good. (Genesis 1:20–25)

Reading my devotional and the Bible today made me stop and realize how perfect God wanted things to be for his children. He created everything for our benefit, and yet we fail to enjoy and rejoice at what He has done.

We should take time each day to look at the sky with its rich, blue, color and puffy, white clouds, to watch the grace of the birds as they soar on the wind, to behold the beauty of a blooming flower, and to marvel at ourselves and how magnificently God put us together. God has created all of this for his children to enjoy, so do it today!

God created it all! How great is our God?

June 19

"Us or Him"

Scripture: Pilate called together the chief priests, the rulers and the people, and said to them, "You brought me this man as one who was inciting the people to rebellion. I have examined him in your presence and have found no basis for your charges against him. Neither has Herod, for he sent him back to us; as you can see, he has done nothing to deserve death. Therefore, I will punish him and then release him."

With one voice they cried out, "Away with this man! Release Barabbas to us!" (Barabbas had been thrown into prison for an insurrection in the city, and for murder.)

Wanting to release Jesus, Pilate appealed to them again. [21] But they kept shouting, "Crucify him! Crucify him!" (Luke 23:13–20)

I do not think that the people of Jesus day are so different from us today. They saw Jesus as a threat. They saw a man who upset their current way of understanding. He knew the Scripture and yet he accused the system that had been established for generations. He spoke against the priest and the scribes condemning them before the people, who held them in high regard. They sensed He was right and yet He was turning their lives upside down. And for this He was crucified.

I believe we are capable of repeating the same atrocity today. If Jesus were here He would have his followers and believers, but I still think the people would gather not to worship him, but to mock and to ridicule him. They would even find a way to kill him for upsetting their current way of living.

In Pilate's court the crowd demanded that Jesus be crucified. Jesus was innocent. Pilate knew it and even the people knew it, yet they asked for Barabbas, a murderer, to be set free, so Jesus would be crucified instead.

Jesus knew this was to happen to fulfill the will of his Father and the scriptures, so He allowed himself to be mocked, scorned, and ridiculed. And to what end? Jesus did it so our sins would be forgiven. He paid the ultimate price: He gave his life for you and for me.

June 20

"Parenthood"

Scripture: O LORD, you have searched me and you know me.

You know when I sit and when I rise; you perceive my thoughts from afar.

You discern my going out and my lying down; you are familiar with all my ways.

Before a word is on my tongue you know it completely, O LORD.

You hem me in—behind and before; you have laid your hand upon me.

Such knowledge is too wonderful for me, too lofty for me to attain. (Psalms 139:1–6)

Have you ever wondered if you were a good father or mother? I know there have been times when I knew I wasn't, but wondered if my children sensed it. Did they realize their old Dad wasn't stacking up or doing what he should? I pray not.

I have learned one thing since Jesus has come into my life: You cannot be a good father without Him. Jesus teaches you how to be a good father or mother, a husband or wife, a friend or co-worker. He shows you how to love your children and take care of them. The truth is without Jesus, life is all just a shot in the dark.

I pray that as my children grow and eventually become parents themselves they will recognize the connection between God and parenting. All of life's answers are in His Word. I pray they rely on God in all circumstances, they trust Him, and they learn from Him.

June 21

"Try It and See"

Scripture: If there is a poor man among your brothers in any of the towns of the land that the LORD your God is giving you, do not be hard-hearted or tightfisted toward your poor brother. Rather be openhanded and freely lend him whatever he needs. Be careful not to harbor this wicked thought: "The seventh year, the year for canceling debts, is near," so that you do not show ill will toward your needy brother and give him nothing. He may then appeal to the LORD against you, and you will be found guilty of sin. Give generously to him and do so without a grudging heart; then because of this the LORD your God will bless you in all your work and in everything you put your hand to. There will always be poor people in the land. Therefore I command you to be openhanded toward your brothers and toward the poor and needy in your land. (Deuteronomy 15:7–11)

How do you react to someone in need? Are you willing to help? If he or she needs money, do you automatically think about how he or she will repay you or what you should charge in interest or are you willing to help that person even when you know he or she can't repay you?

My mother was a great teacher of being a helping hand in someone's time of need. I saw her many times, struggling to meet her own obligations, reach in her purse and grab a $20 or even a $100 bill and give it to someone in need. My brothers told me of times she did without dinner so someone else could eat. She truly knew how to be generous. She knew how to rely on God to provide for her and her family.

God said He will bless us if we are generous to the poor and the needy. Our blessing may come back to us as we gave it or in a way we least expect. Either way, we can trust that God is true to his word and will bless us, if we are willing to give to others. Try it and see!

June 22

"Read and Hear the Word"

Scripture: "Do not let your hearts be troubled. Trust in God ; trust also in me. In my Father's house are many rooms; if it were not so, I would have told you. I am going there to prepare a place for you. And if I go and prepare a place for you, I will come back and take you to be with me that you also may be where I am. You know the way to the place where I am going."

Thomas said to him, "Lord, we don't know where you are going, so how can we know the way?"

Jesus answered, "I am the way and the truth and the life. No one comes to the Father except through me. If you really knew me, you would know[n] *my Father as well. From now on, you do know him and have seen him."*

Philip said, "Lord, show us the Father and that will be enough for us."

Jesus answered: "Don't you know me, Philip, even after I have been among you such a long time? Anyone who has seen me has seen the Father. How can you say, 'Show us the Father'? Don't you believe that I am in the Father, and that the Father is in me? The words I say to you are not just my own. Rather, it is the Father, living in me, who is doing his work. Believe me when I say that I am in the Father and the Father is in me; or at least believe on the evidence of the miracles themselves. I tell you the truth, anyone who has faith in me will do what I have been doing. He will do even greater things than these, because I am going to the Father. And I will do whatever you ask in my name, so that the Son may bring glory to the Father. You may ask me for anything in my name, and I will do it (John 14:1–14).

"In my Father's house are many rooms and I go to prepare a place for you," Jesus said. How difficult it must have been for the disciples to grasp what Jesus meant, as He taught them during his ministry. It wasn't until Jesus was crucified, raised from the dead, and revealed himself to them again that they truly understood.

We are basically the same way. We read the words of Jesus and hear the words of Jesus, but we just don't get it. Then one day, just like the disciples, when we face a crisis, a trial, or an unbearable circumstance we are finally able to put the pieces together. We call upon what we have read and heard in God's Word, and draw upon it as taking a drink of satisfying water. If we don't read or hear the word, from where will our strength come?

Jesus will return for us someday. We may not know the day or the hour of his coming, but we will recognize the signs, if and only if we know his Word.

Read his Word today!

June 23

"Black Dot"

Scripture: "Do not judge, or you too will be judged. For in the same way you judge others, you will be judged, and with the measure you use, it will be measured to you.

"Why do you look at the speck of sawdust in your brother's eye and pay no attention to the plank in your own eye? How can you say to your brother, 'Let me take the speck out of your eye,' when all the time there is a plank in your own eye? You hypocrite, first take the plank out of your own eye, and then you will see clearly to remove the speck from your brother's eye. (Matthew 7:1–5)

I want to share this story I heard a few years ago. A woman showed another woman a piece of paper with a black dot on it. As the first woman handed the paper to the other woman she said, "What do you see?" In a quick response the second woman said, "A black dot." The first woman said, "Is that all you see?" "Yes," answered the other woman. Then the first woman replied, "What about the white space around the dot?"

The lesson of this story is not to judge what we think we see. We are all too willing to judge people on their appearance, what they drive, or where they live. We are quick to judge the flaws of others rather than get to know them. We tend to focus on the black spot of someone's character and miss all the good around them.

Be careful not to see just the black dot.

June 24

"God's Wings"

Scripture: He who dwells in the shelter of the Most High will rest in the shadow of the Almighty.

I will say n of the LORD, "He is my refuge and my fortress, my God, in whom I trust." (Psalm 91:1–4)

When I read the Psalms of David I realize what David is referencing in his experience with God. David knew God intimately. He knew God was his safe house in the storm.

Sometimes I think we get too busy living in this hectic world that we fail to stop and be still under our Lord's wings. We can gain needed rest and spiritual filling. We can be protected, not only from the forces of the world, but from our own sinful nature.

Take time today to get to know your Lord intimately, like David did. Stop and come into his presence and renew yourself. Come under his wings and rest.

June 25

"Christ in Us"

Scripture: Examine yourselves to see whether you are in the faith; test yourselves. DO you not realize that Christ Jesus is in you—-unless of course you fail the test. (2 Corinthians 13:5)

How do we know if Christ is in us? We may not feel him as we do a pain in our side or through some supernatural feeling, but nonetheless He is there.

Christ is that consciousness that prompts us to do right. He is the revelation we receive when we read or hear the Word. He is that joy that comes to our spirit, when we sing a song of praise. He is that ever-flowing peace in our time of trouble.

Christ is in us—can you feel Him?

June 26

"Prayer Power"

Scripture: For this reason I kneel before the Father, from whom his whole family in heaven and on earth derives its name. I pray that out of his glorious riches he may strengthen you with power through his Spirit in your inner being, so that Christ may dwell in your hearts through faith. And I pray that you, being rooted and established in love, may have power, together with all the saints, to grasp how wide and long and high and deep is the love of Christ, and to know this love that surpasses knowledge—that you may be filled to the measure of all the fullness of God.

Now to him who is able to do immeasurably more than all we ask or imagine, according to his power that is at work within us, to him be glory in the church and in Christ Jesus throughout all generations, for ever and ever! Amen. (Ephesians 3:14–21)

Sometimes we feel that our prayers have no power at all. We lift them up to God and don't see any answers. Why?

I think the key is that we are focused on our will and not God's will for our lives. He has an answer, but we want to ignore it, because it is not the answer we want. So the answer comes and goes without notice.

My recent experience of prayer has had a much different outcome. I have come to realize that prayer is like planting a seed. It takes time to grow, to develop, and to bear fruit before us. As a matter of fact, I have come to enjoy how God works to answer my prayers. Sometimes the answer is quick, sped up like a time-lapsed film and other times it takes months, even years for God to orchestrate all that is needed to answer my prayer. Regardless of the length of time it takes, my prayers are always answered—not in my time but God's.

Paul knew the power of prayer as he prayed over the Ephesians. He prayed to teach, to reach, and to encourage. He prayed that the Ephesians would be blessed and that they would come into the total fullness of the Lord and they were.

I pray that for you, my family and me as well. I also pray that we would all come to know God fully and completely, in Jesus' Name, Amen.

June 27

"Recognize the Sabbath"

Scripture: "'Observe the Sabbath, because it is holy to you. Anyone who desecrates it must be put to death; whoever does any work on that day must be cut off from his people. For six days, work is to be done, but the seventh day is a Sabbath of rest, holy to the LORD. Whoever does any work on the Sabbath day must be put to death. The Israelites are to observe the Sabbath, celebrating it for the generations to come as a lasting covenant. It will be a sign between me and the Israelites forever, for in six days the LORD made the heavens and the earth, and on the seventh day he abstained from work and rested.' " (Exodus 31:12–18)

I am one of the biggest violators of the Sabbath. I work, I recreate, and I do everything but what the Lord commanded. I recognize this fault in myself and seek God's forgiveness. I repent and ask for God to change me that I can break this chain of violation.

I pray for help and forgiveness as I write this word. But even as I put down this paper and pencil, I am off to work again. I know that God will be with me and has already started working on the change in my life, so I don't have to break this command again.

Forgive me Lord!

June 28

"I Did It My Way"

Scripture: Blessed is the man who finds wisdom, the man who gains understanding, for she is more profitable than silver and yields better returns than gold. She is more precious than rubies; nothing you desire can compare with her. Long life is in her right hand; in her left hand are riches and honor. Her ways are pleasant ways, and all her paths are peace. She is a tree of life to those who embrace her; those who lay hold of her will be blessed. (Proverbs 3:13–18)

Wisdom is very precious. How I wish that I would have gained wisdom at a much younger age. Then perhaps the pain and anguish I suffered would not have been part of my life. My bank account would be full, my life more meaningful, and my relationships stronger.

Of course the only way to gain such wisdom is through years and years of experience or through knowing God. My suggestion to you, after trying it my way, is to know God and to do things His way. He is all truth, wisdom, and understanding. He will guide you, direct you, and make you wise. He will give you wisdom, understanding, and discernment through the power of his Holy Spirit that dwells within you. Tap into God's knowledge today.

June 29

"Without a Word"

Scripture: I always thank my God as I remember you in my prayers, because I hear about your faith in the Lord Jesus and your love for all the saints. I pray that you may be active in sharing your faith, so that you will have a full understanding of every good thing we have in Christ. Your love has given me great joy and encouragement, because you, brother, have refreshed the hearts of the saints. (Philemon 1:4–7)

Encouragement—we all need it and in different doses. I have often felt encouraged, not because someone has spoken a word to me, but because of the things around me.

God has produced many beautiful things and all I need to do is open my eyes and heart to see them. As I look at this beauty of God's creation, I am encouraged. I see that I am part of something bigger and greater than myself. I know God is there, all around me and I am encouraged—without a word.

June 30

"ANGELS"

Scripture: For it is written: "'He will command his angels concerning you to guard you carefully; they will lift you up in their hands, so that you will not strike your foot against a stone.' "(Luke 4:10–11)

Lately there has been an increased interest in angels. People have developed TV programs about angels, movies about angels, songs about angels, and books about angels. So do you believe in angels?

In Luke 4:10, God assigns his angels as He wills and they are at his beckon call to minister to whomever he chooses. I myself believe in angels. I have experienced firsthand the intervening power of God's heavenly army. They have saved me from wrecks and other disasters that try to overcome me. I like angels, because they add to the hope I have in God's care and protection of my life.

So do you believe in angels?

____

____

____

July

July 1

"Fruit, Much Fruit"

Scripture: "I am the vine; you are the branches. If a man remains in me and I in him, he will bear much fruit; apart from me you can do nothing. If anyone does not remain in me, he is like a branch that is thrown away and withers; such branches are picked up, thrown into the fire and burned." (John 15:5–6)

Ever since I accepted Jesus as my personal Savior, I get great comfort in knowing that He abides in me. This confidence helps me realize that apart from him I can do nothing and that I must be hooked into His power. It is like a lamp with a cord. It is definitely a lamp, but without it being plugged in it provides no light and no benefit to anyone. Jesus is our source of power and the light that can shine through is His love. It can manifest itself in the love I have for my wife, my family, my friends and yes, even my enemy. I cannot accomplish any good work without his wisdom and knowledge provided by this power. And, I cannot be a true disciple without abiding in him.

The truth is, when I am grafted into Jesus I will flourish and if I am severed, I will surely die. Join me through the grace of Jesus to be grafted into his vine, so we can bear fruit much fruit for him.

July 2

"Thoughts"

Scripture: For where your treasure is, there your heart will be also.

The eye is the lamp of the body. If your eyes are good, your whole body will be full of light. But if your eyes are bad, your whole body will be full of darkness. If then the light within you is darkness, how great is that darkness! (Matthew 6:21–23)

Thoughts? Does anyone struggle with undesirable thoughts? I know my mind has conjured up some horrible thoughts over the years. Thoughts that are inconsistent with God's leading and teaching and love.

These thoughts, if gone unchecked, could turn into unspeakable acts that could lead to death and destruction. This death and destruction I refer to may not be physical, but it is the death of my spirit and the destruction of trust of the others around me.

God's spirit is the only true way to control our thoughts. Everyone has heard the cliché about computers, "Garbage in, garbage out." So too it is with our minds. If we fill our minds with filth and corruption, filth and corruption will manifest themselves in our actions. Therefore, we must read the Word to keep the Holy Spirit strong within us. And, when undesirable thoughts come, God's spirit will chase them away. So guard your thoughts as you would the greatest of treasure, because they are the only thing of real lasting value.

July 3

"All Gone, Great Gain"

Scripture: We ought always to thank God for you, brothers, and rightly so, because your faith is growing more and more, and the love every one of you has for each other is increasing. Therefore, among God's churches we boast about your perseverance and faith in all the persecutions and trials you are enduring.

All this is evidence that God's judgment is right, and as a result you will be counted worthy of the kingdom of God, for which you are suffering. (2 Thessalonians 1:3–5)

Have you endured trials as a result of having God's presence in your life? I know from experience that when the things of this world that I thought were important collapsed around me, God was ever present. He was there and I didn't even know it, but He was there nonetheless. All I had to do was acknowledge Him and He began to strengthen me for a battle that lasted five years during the failure of my business. Without God's presence and faith which He instilled within me, I would have surely perished. He saw me through. He gave me strength, endurance, knowledge, and understanding. And, even though I lost every material possession I worked for, I gained much, much more. I gained the Kingdom of Heaven. Thanks be to God.

July 4

"Independence Day–Today"

Scripture: It is for freedom that Christ has set us free. Stand firm, then, and do not let yourselves be burdened again by a yoke of slavery. (Galatians 5:1)

Independence Day—July 4th, the day we declared our independence from British dominance. We as a people want our independence and our freedom. To truly seek independence, we need dependency. In declaring our independence from the British, we found that we had to be dependent on each other. We had to form a union and bond together to overcome the domination of British rule.

Today, we all seek to be free, to be independent. We want to make our own choices, to do what we want and to live as we wish. I have found that to really achieve this freedom, it requires dependence. I have to be dependent on God. He and only He can give me true freedom. He gives me freedom from fear, freedom from despair, and freedom from eternal condemnation; and He can do that for you too.

Declare your independence day today. Accept Jesus as your personal Savior and get a lifetime of freedom.

July 5

"God's Dwelling"

Scripture: For in the day of trouble he will keep me safe in his dwelling; he will hide me in the shelter of his tabernacle and set me high upon a rock. (Psalm 27:5)

The Psalms of David tell us vivid stories about his relationship with God. They tell of his joy, his anguish, his sorrow, his victory, and his love through knowing God. They describe his encounters with the world and how God made each of them bearable or more bountiful by being part of his life. God guided David through every situation. God made each experience better. God made his joy greater, removed his anguish, made his sorrow less, his victories sweeter, and his love more complete. David faced a lot, but without God, his life would not have been fulfilled.

We can all experience what David had with God, the Lord of his life. Like David, to receive such fulfillment, we must give God a dwelling place. Open your heart today and let God take up residence to see you through what the world has to dish out.

July 6

"To Do or Not to Do"

Scripture: But Moses said to God, "Who am I, that I should go to Pharaoh and bring the Israelites out of Egypt?" (Exodus 3:11)

Moses was asked by God to deliver His message to the Israelites. And when given this task, Moses had great concern. He was concerned about his ability to fulfill what God had asked and what God wanted him to do.

I sometimes feel much like Moses. I hear God ask and I want to do it, but doubt and concern creep into my spirit. I wonder how God can ask someone like me to carry out His will. Over the years, however, I have learned that God never puts more on me than I can handle. He equips me for the task and sometimes I don't even realize that I am equipped. He knows me better than I know myself. He knows my ability and sends me out knowing that I must rely on Him.

Our weakness is God's strength. He can do mighty things if and only if, we make ourselves available. All I can say, if God asks you to do it, don't doubt or be concerned. Proceed knowing that God always goes before you and prepares the way and will be there with you to see you through, even to the end.

___

___

___

July 7

"Namesake"

Scripture: Have I not commanded you? Be strong and courageous. Do not be terrified; do not be discouraged, for the LORD your God will be with you wherever you go." (Joshua1:9)

I often think about my son Joshua's name and how a dear friend told me what it means. My dear friend was a believer and his description of my son's name made me realize how perfect it was for my firstborn son.

In the Bible, Joshua was the one selected by God to lead his people to the Promised Land. Joshua had to be courageous, strong, and most of all, had to rely on God. His leadership came from learning to know and understand God's will. It was then and only then could he lead God's people into the land of milk and honey.

Step out, be bold, listen to God's command, and He will make you prosperous and successful in your endeavors. Joshua did and through his leadership he was blessed, God's people were blessed, and they learned that God would never forsake them and that He would be with them wherever they went.

I pray this for my son Joshua that he too may be blessed, wherever he goes.

____

____

____

July 8

"Holy Spirit within Us"

Scripture: You, however, are controlled not by the sinful nature but by the Spirit, if the Spirit of God lives in you. And if anyone does not have the Spirit of Christ, he does not belong to Christ. (Romans 8:9)

Paul wrote in Romans about his sinful nature and the struggle he had with it. He agonized over the issue and fought against it. He finally realized, however, the only way to totally remove the sinful nature within him was to replace it with something else: the Holy Spirit.

The Holy Spirit is given to us from God to keep evil spirits from dwelling in us. That is why Jesus said to his disciples he was sending them a Comforter, a Counselor, the living Spirit of God himself. The Holy Spirit is a powerful gift that God makes available to each and everyone of us. All we have to do is receive it.

Accept fully the Spirit of God today.

July 9

"Actions Speak Louder Than Words"

Scripture: But the man who looks intently into the perfect law that gives freedom, and continues to do this, not forgetting what he has heard, but doing it—he will be blessed in what he does.. (James 1:25)

Do we listen to God and read His word but then do nothing? Do we sit idly by and not take any action? It is important that we do take action. If a stream is blocked off and becomes stagnant it eventually cannot support life. It mosses over and chokes itself out. It is also true that God cannot do anything with someone who talks about doing his will, but then never takes the first step. God is ready, willing, and prepared to open doors, move mountains, and clear the paths for someone on the move for Him.

A positive, exciting relationship with God does not come from sitting on the sidelines, but rather from working to do what He instructs. For example, you cannot have a strong relationship with your spouse without giving it some effort. Lip service does not work. You cannot create a friend by sitting on the front porch and wishing for someone to appear next to you. You must get up and approach someone to make a friend.

A sound relationship with God means we must take action. We must read God's Word, pray in earnest, and then step out in faith. God does not want talk—He wants action.

My decision to write this daily devotional is a result of my acting upon God's leading and, in so doing; I have developed a stronger relationship with Him. Give God action not lip service!

July 10

"One Body in Christ"

Scripture: There is neither Jew nor Greek, slave nor free, male nor female, for you are all one in Christ Jesus. If you belong to Christ, then you are Abraham's seed, and heirs according to the promise. (Galatians 3:28)

I have always been amazed by some of the ethnic men I have come to know in the faith. One black man in particular seemed to have a sound and wonderful relationship with our Lord. I thought as I got to know him how marvelous his faith was and wished it for myself. Maybe, I thought, it was part of his heritage of trials and tribulations that gained him a greater understanding of the importance of putting God at the center of life. Maybe it was that he had learned life's lessons of getting close and staying close to the God of creation to strengthen his faith.

What finally struck me is that God does not see the color of a man's skin, but the condition of his heart. God seeks true worshipers. He does not care if you are white, black, yellow, or red, He only cares whether or not you seek Him. He wants and deserves one body in Christ Jesus forever and ever. He deserves a body of faith coming together for His glory.

____

____

____

July 11

"Enjoy the Journey"

Scripture: We wait in hope for the LORD; he is our help and our shield.

In him our hearts rejoice, for we trust in his holy name. (Psalm 33:20–21)

Are you amazed in today's society by how we want everything right now? We are not willing to wait for anything or anybody. We must have what we desire and we must have it right this minute. With this type of attitude, with this type of hurry and haste, we can miss out on some of God's very unique blessings.

God has waited on his people for thousands and thousands of years. He has waited on generation to generation from the beginning of time, but yet we have no patience. We want what we want and we want it yesterday. This includes God's blessings.

My life has taught me that the one of the true blessings can be in the waiting. God leads me on a journey. He lets me walk and rejoice in His very work and creation. He shows me and prepares me for my heart's desire. He helps me realize that everyday is a perfect and wonderful gift from him. He allows me to see blessing after blessing unfold before my very eyes. But just like speeding down a highway at 65 mph, we miss so much that the journey has to offer when we don't take time to slow down and spend time with God.

Slow down, enjoy the journey, and enjoy the time with God. He knows your destination. He knows what you desire. Maybe just maybe by slowing down to God's speed the blessings will be greater and grander than we can even imagine. Enjoy the journey, as God wants us to.

July 12

"Is God Real?"

Scripture: A righteous man may have many troubles, but the Lord delivers him from them all. (Psalm 34:19)

How can you be sure that there is a God and that He is real?

What a question! How can I answer that if my children, my wife, a co-worker or a friend ask it? I guess I would have to say that God is present in my life everyday. I know that His Spirit dwells within me, but how does that really answer the question? How does that answer the question for someone hurting or someone who only sees the suffering and pain in the world? What type of God allows that sort of thing to happen?

God gave all of us free will and with that comes some pretty awful stuff. People make choices, some good and some bad, and with those choices come the consequences associated with them. For example, if someone chooses to go to war, people die. When people choose to drink and drive, people die. When people choose to abandon their families, people suffer and the list goes on and on.

God knows about suffering. God, through His Son Jesus, came to earth and endured much more that we can ever imagine. He was ridiculed, beaten, and put to death. He even knew it was going to happen in advance, but chose to allow it to happen anyway. He took our sin and bore it unto death. And, he did this because he loves us so much. He did this in spite of ourselves knowing we would fail him over and over again. He loves us and endured the cross for us.

I know without doubt that if God is willing to do that He must be real, because I am a living testament to that fact.

July 13

"GOD–WORLD, WHAT A CHOICE!"

Scripture: Do not conform any longer to the pattern of this world, but be transformed by the renewing of your mind. Then you will be able to test and approve what God's will is—his good, pleasing and perfect will. (Romans 12:2)

Following God means I will have to give up all this worldly stuff?

Boy, I remember thinking that very thing when I rededicated my life to God. I thought Give up going out, getting drunk, chasing women, watching porn, and reading sex books? What kind of life will that be? Now that I am on the other side of that decision, I seek to do what God wants and not what I want. Through that, I no longer have hangovers from drinking; I have no worry about STD's, and I have no guilt about being a perverted man. My choice to serve God has saved me money and concern. I know now it was the best trade I could have made—God for the world.

Now I seek to let God rule in every part of my life. Does that mean I am not tempted? Not at all. The devil does not like to lose and is no pushover. He tugs at me all of the time, but when I think of the downside of what he offers, I run to the open arms of Jesus. Jesus will protect me and keep me from harm, and He will do the same for you—just run to Him.

Don't let the world control you anymore, let God.

July 14

"So Long or Goodbye"

Scripture: He answered, "While the child was still alive, I fasted and wept. I thought, 'Who knows? The LORD may be gracious to me and let the child live.' But now that he is dead, why should I fast? Can I bring him back again? I will go to him, but he will not return to me." (2 Samuel 12:22)

David grieved for Uriah's son who was dying. He fasted and prayed until the boy died. He knew that once the boy died he must go on, that there was nothing left for him to do. He knew that the boy was in God's hands.

Losing someone is a horrible thing. It puts a void in our lives that cannot be filled by anyone. But, the real void is found in our Spirit when we do not know whether that loved one accepted Christ or not. If he or she has we can say, "So long" knowing we will see him or her again in Heaven. If not, we will have to say "Goodbye" for all eternity.

It is our responsibility to make sure our family and friends have every opportunity to accept Christ. We cannot force it on them, but with gentle leading, fervent prayer, and God's divine intervention our chances are good.

Salvation is a gift from God. It must be received and accepted. The choice is yours, no one else's. Choose Jesus today, so your loved ones know when the time comes they can say, "So long" and not "Goodbye."

____

____

____

July 15

"Judge Not"

Scripture: "Do not judge, and you will not be judged. Do not condemn, and you will not be condemned. Forgive, and you will be forgiven." (Luke 6:37)

Why do we judge others?

I think we judge others because we think too highly of ourselves. Instead of seeing ourselves as God sees us, with all of our flaws, we see something different and better.

The next time you think about judging others; be it someone of another race, the kid with tattoos and piercing, or someone who says the wrong thing; stop and see what God sees. God sees someone to love and loves him or her unconditionally. He shows us that love through His Son, Jesus, who through that love died for our sins, our faults, and our transgressions. He did not judge us; He loved us even unto death.

God will judge each of us and ask us to give an account for our actions. Think about that the next time you want to judge someone.

July 16

"Winning and Losing"

Scripture: "You did not choose me, but I chose you and appointed you to go and bear fruit—fruit that will last. Then my Father will give you whatever you ask in my name." (John 15:16)

We all want to win. We want to win at life, at our careers, at competitions, or whatever we choose. We find great satisfaction and accomplishment in winning. We gain confidence and it shows, but how do we handle our defeats?

People often learn about us as Christians by how we act and react in life's situations. They seem to notice us more when we lose than when we win. Therefore, it is extremely important to handle our defeat and our winning with humility. Someone is always watching.

So how do we handle defeat? Keep in mind that in this world there is always winners and losers, but in God's Kingdom we are all winners. He doesn't care if we come in first or come in last. All He cares is that we finish the race.

Jesus has chosen us to be winners. He has chosen us and appointed us to bear fruit. Don't worry about how much, but step out and try. Remember we are all winners on Christ's team.

July 17

"Trust"

Scripture: May the God of hope fill you with all joy and peace as you trust in him, so that you may overflow with hope by the power of the Holy Spirit. (Romans 15:13)

Trust—a small word with a large impact. Without trust our marriages fail, our children live in fear, our employers are concerned, and our whole lives are frightening. We have all learned to trust people, some with good results and others with disappointment. People let us down. Not that they intend to do so, but they do just the same. And, yet we learn, if we don't trust people our lives are in shambles. It is important to trust. It gives us assurance and comfort, thus our tendency is to trust people.

Our God needs to be trusted the same way we trust people. The difference is that whereas people often let us down, God never will. He will always be there, waiting and watching to help us in any circumstance we face. He will never forsake us. He is our trust and salvation.

Trust the Lord today!

July 18

"The Spirit's House"

Scripture: Moses said to the whole Israelite community, "This is what the LORD has commanded: From what you have, take an offering for the LORD. Everyone who is willing is to bring to the LORD an offering of gold, silver and bronze; blue, purple and scarlet yarn and fine linen; goat hair; ram skins dyed red and hides of sea cows ; acacia wood; olive oil for the light; spices for the anointing oil and for the fragrant incense; and onyx stones and other gems to be mounted on the ephod and breastpiece. (Exodus 35:4–9)

The Lord commanded Moses to gather the materials for the tabernacle. He was to take an offering from all willing to give, but it was to be the finest materials: gold, silver, quality yarns, animal skins, and gems. God wanted His Spirit to have the best place to settle.

How do we house God's Spirit? There is no tabernacle just a dwelling place within us. Is it a place of glory? Do we keep it clean and pure?

If you are like me, I do not keep it the way I should or at least not all the time. I do things that I am sure cause God's Spirit to say: "What is this guy doing?" It is hard to keep holy and pure. We eat too much, we don't exercise, we smoke, we read or we watch the wrong things, and in general we keep a pretty messy house for God's Spirit. So how do we keep the Holy Spirit's house a place of glory? We clean it regularly like we do our own homes. We start in one room and move through the whole house cleaning and sweeping until everything is shining. Cleaning our spiritual dwelling is done by confession, repentance, and forgiveness. Each day we have to take out the trash or before long there is no place for the spirit to live.

Have you given the Holy Spirit a clean and pure place of glory? If not, clean it today.

July 19

"Supernatural Trust"

Scripture: Let the morning bring me word of your unfailing love, for I have put my trust in you. Show me the way I should go, for to you I lift up my soul. (Psalm 143:8)

Seek God in all things and trust in Him.

We often take this statement and speak it, but rarely do we live it. Trusting God to lead is something that David learned to do. He realized that he could never overcome his enemies without trusting God in a supernatural way and without God's divine direction.

Sometimes, I have difficulty trusting God. I try to take some situations and control them myself instead of allowing God to deal with them in his supernatural way and unfold results in His time.

My family and I recently built a new house and it was a direct result of God being God and our placing our trust in Him. Like many we have faced some horrible financial crises. Given our credit history from the business failure, we could have never qualified for a loan, especially to build a new house, but God proved differently. He removed obstacles, challenges, and opened doors. The only way we could build the house was to do a lot of the work ourselves, so He gave us strength to work full-time and to build the house as we could. Six months later, the house was complete. God made it possible through our trusting in His supernatural power.

I thank God for this wonderful miracle.

July 20

"Do You Believe This?"

Scripture: Jesus said to her, "I am the resurrection and the life. He who believes in me will live, even though he dies; and whoever lives and believes in me will never die. Do you believe this?" (John 11:25–26)

Sometimes as Christians we have this image that to explain salvation and eternal life it has to complicated or sophisticated. The simple truth is it is not complicated—the plan of salvation is simple.

Jesus described the Gospel when he went to Bethany to raise Lazarus from the dead. He said to Martha, "He who believes in me will live even though he dies, and whoever lives and believes in me will never die. Do you believe this?"

I guess we always try to make more of something than there really is. It comes from living life everyday and having to strive for everything. Nothing is free and everything has strings attached. It is no wonder that we cannot grasp this simple truth to believe in Jesus. That's it. It's that simple.

Do you believe this? Then salvation is yours!

July 21

"Know the Way and Trust"

Scripture: And a highway will be there; it will be called the Way of Holiness. The unclean will not journey on it; it will be for those who walk in that Way; wicked fools will not go about on it. (Isaiah 35:8)

I decided one day to take my two sons, Nathan and Jordan, with me on a business trip. We talked and planned the trip discussing what we needed to do to prepare and what things the boys would need to take along in order to keep themselves entertained. It was exciting for them and me to embark on a new journey.

Our relationship with God can be the same way—an exciting journey. God wants to take us places we have never been. He wants to show us things we have never seen. And, he wants us to experience things we never thought possible.

All we need to do is treat God as our children treat us when leaving for a journey - trust Him. Just as our children trust us to know the way, how to adjust for what we encounter along the way and then sit back and enjoy the adventure. We must trust that the Lord knows where He's taking us.

Are you ready for that type of journey? God's ready - let's go!

____

____

____

July 22

"The Truth . . . the Whole Truth"

Scripture: If we claim we have not sinned, we make him out to be a liar and his word has no place in our lives. (1 John 1:10)

Jesus always told the Jews, "I tell you the truth." I wonder if it was common to exaggerate or stretch the truth back then.

I sometimes think that if it was common for the truth to be stretched in Jesus' day that it's no surprise how common it is for the truth to be stretched today. I am in sales and I often find myself in situations where I can embellish or at least stretch the truth. It is a constant struggle knowing that my God does not want liars in His family. Therefore, each and every day the Holy Spirit convicts me not to commit this horrible sin. My prayer is that I continually be convicted of this and that I seek forgiveness for the times when I fail. I also pray that God grants me strength to overcome this horrible sin. It may be only a little white lie, but in God's eyes it is still a sin. I remember my mother telling me that liars will spend eternity in the fiery pits of hell. That scared me and has stuck with me all the days of my life. That is enough for me, so God continue to forgive me and help me not to lie.

July 23

"Money, the Root of All Kinds of Evil"

Scripture: For the love of money is a root of all kinds of evil. Some people, eager for money, have wandered from the faith and pierced themselves with many griefs. (1 Timothy 6:10)

I have learned many lessons over the years, but none has affected me more than the lesson Paul was trying to teach Timothy regarding worldly wealth.

There was a time in my life that I thought wealth or getting rich was the only goal worth attaining. It became a beacon on which I focused all of my time, energy, and ambition. In the end, however, I found my desire for money to be illusive and disastrous. I sought wealth to the detriment of my family, my God, and myself.

The good news, however, is that God never gives up on us. I sought and sought and sought and things started falling apart, but God was there proving to me that He was really all I needed. As He showed me, I accepted Him and my life was enriched far greater than any worldly wealth could have provided.

Don't fall into temptation to be rich above all else. It is a trap with many foolish and harmful desires, which plunges us into despair, ruin, and destruction, "For the love of money is the root of all kinds of evil."

I believe that God wants to bless us with the desires of our hearts, but our hearts needs to be right with God for it to happen.

July 24

"Peace? I'll take some"

Scripture: Peace I leave with you; my peace I give you. I do not give to you as the world gives. Do not let your hearts be troubled and do not be afraid. (John 14:27)

Peace. At one time, not too long ago, the meaning of the word eluded me. I was struggling so hard to survive a financial crisis from my ailing business that I felt drawn from all sides. The Devil sensed my situation and seized the opportunity to send a legion of demons to attack and constantly harass me. I felt so torn apart that I had no peace, and then Jesus came.

One day, after a horrible weekend that should have been a time of enjoyment and relaxation, I was a wreck. I remember being at such odds with the world and stretched to the limit that I retreated to a dark closet. I pleaded with God to give me peace and to renew my spirit. And, in the dark of the closet at the darkest hour of my life a miraculous thing happened: Jesus sent the Comforter. He sent the Holy Spirit to give me peace. Immediately, from that moment on, the Devil had no hold on me. His legion released me and fled and I had peace.

Several years have passed since that ordeal and God has never left my side. His Spirit dwells within me and I have peace.

July 25

"Great Peace"

Scripture: Finally, brothers, good-by. Aim for perfection, listen to my appeal, be of one mind, live in peace. And the God of love and peace will be with you. (2 Corinthians 13:11)

Do you and can you feel real peace, the peace that surpasses all understanding? The peace that sees you through trial and tribulation, the peace that lets you sleep comfortably and never creates a stressful moment in your life?

There is only one who can give you that kind of peace: Jesus. You can count on His love and the Holy Spirit to provide you with such peace. Paul knew this. Through all of his imprisonments and even to his death he knew this kind of peace. He had enough peace that he shared his heavenly blessing with others, so they could know it too. So the next time peace seems beyond your grasp and you are struggling, think of Paul, retreat to God, and let God's peace come in.

July 26

"Search Me and Know Me"

Scripture: O LORD, you have searched me and you know me. You know when I sit and when I rise; you perceive my thoughts from afar. You discern my going out and my lying down; you are familiar with all my ways. Before a word is on my tongue you know it completely, O LORD. (Psalm 139:1–4)

Has there ever been someone in your life with whom you felt really comfortable? You liked him/her, he/she liked you and you knew beyond a doubt that you could just be yourself around that person? No cover-ups, no pretenses, no guarding, no hiding; you could let your hair down and just be yourself. Can you remember that feeling you had around that person? You felt secure, loved, and confident that no matter what you said or did it was okay. What a feeling. It was great.

A good, quality relationship with Jesus is that same way. Jesus already knows everything about us. He knows our thoughts. He knows our actions. He knows every hair on our head—everything. Knowing and accepting the fact that Jesus knows us that well, makes him a trustworthy friend. No apologies, no criticisms, no judging, just acceptance.

If you do not know Jesus as a friend in that way, give him a chance. He will not disappoint you.

July 27

"If you can't find the Lord, Praise Him"

Scripture: Sing joyfully to the LORD, you righteous; it is fitting for the upright to praise him. Praise the LORD with the harp; make music to him on the ten-stringed lyre. Sing to him a new song; play skillfully, and shout for joy. (Psalm 33:1–3)

"Praise the Lord," what a phrase. I think sometimes that we do not really know the term. Praise is a very important part of my life and being. I enjoy praying and praising the Lord. I start each day, as I am driving to work, praying to the Lord. That praying eventually turns to thanksgiving and that thanksgiving turns to praise. Before long, my praise turns to songs of joy, which I sing at the top of my lungs. My troubles disappear, my Spirit is renewed, and I soon feel the presence of God right there with me.

Praising God is not an action, but an attitude. It is an attitude of worship that comes from wanting God to join you. Do you want His Spirit to overwhelm you with peace and joy? Then worship God. He will come to be with you and to take part in this joyous act of praise and worship.

I have heard people say that they can't find God. If you can't find God, then stop what you are doing- praise Him, worship Him, and He will find you.

____

____

____

July 28

"Reflecting Jesus"

Scripture: For this reason, since the day we heard about you, we have not stopped praying for you and asking God to fill you with the knowledge of his will through all spiritual wisdom and understanding. And we pray this in order that you may live a life worthy of the Lord and may please him in every way: bearing fruit in every good work, growing in the knowledge of God, (Colossians 1:9–10)

Can people see Jesus in me? Do I act and conduct myself in the way Jesus expects? Do I reflect the fruits of the spirit in my daily life?

Asking these questions of myself helps me evaluate God's presence in my life. I can see some differences occurring and know that my walk with the Lord is improving my life. I know the journey is long and that I have not fully matured, but I am still in the molding stage and God still has much work to do.

This came to mind as I read my devotion. It had a great illustration of some folks out on a lake very early one morning. The water was like a mirror reflecting everything near the water. It was so calm it reflected every detail—nothing was missed. Our lives should reflect Jesus in the same way. We should reflect Jesus' love, compassion, and all of his attributes the same way the lake reflected everything near it. The key word is near. If we are near to Jesus in study and prayer, then He will start reflecting himself through us.

____

____

____

July 29

"Believe It or Not"

Scripture: Immediately the boy's father exclaimed, "I do believe; help me overcome my unbelief!" (Mark 9:24)

All things are possible to those who believe in God. What a dramatic statement and yet the only way for it to happen is to believe. How do you do that? To believe in something or someone not seen is an incredible act of faith. You cannot say to yourself, "I am going to believe" and make it possible.

Have you ever had such confidence in something that you knew without a doubt it would happen? Did you have an undeniable trust and faith that it would come to pass? That is the belief that God talks about. In Jesus day, belief and faith were the catalysts that made everything happen. They made the blind see, the lame walk, the weak become strong, and most of all, the sinner saved. If you think it, believe it with all of your heart, and put it in God's hands, it will come to pass.

Believe it or not!

July 30

"Saved, Is that Enough?"

Scripture: "Then he will say to those on his left, 'Depart from me, you who are cursed, into the eternal fire prepared for the devil and his angels. For I was hungry and you gave me nothing to eat, I was thirsty and you gave me nothing to drink, I was a stranger and you did not invite me in, I needed clothes and you did not clothe me, I was sick and in prison and you did not look after me.' "They also will answer, 'Lord, when did we see you hungry or thirsty or a stranger or needing clothes or sick or in prison, and did not help you?' "He will reply, 'I tell you the truth, whatever you did not do for one of the least of these, you did not do for me.' (Matthew 25:41–45)

Is being saved enough to get into Heaven? We have been told and read that we have been saved by grace through Jesus, so what else do we need to do? Scripture makes it clear that Jesus is just the door to eternal life and accepting that comes at a price. Just as Jesus paid a price for our sin, He expects us to pay a price as well. Jesus wants each of us to put our Christianity into action. He no longer wants us sitting on the sideline, but rather wants us to get in the game. We have all made some attempt by attending church and giving money and that surely those things are enough. They are a start, but there is much more to be done. Jesus wants us to feed the poor, needy, hungry, and thirsty of the world. Not with food alone, but with the bread of life. And, do it only out of love.

Jesus, in His word, gave us an account of what judgment will be like when we get to Heaven. He and His Father will look at every decision we made. Not just the decision to believe in Jesus, but what decision we made to take action. So being saved by grace is important, but it is not enough.

July 31

"Rely on God"

Scripture: Hear, O LORD, and answer me, for I am poor and needy. Guard my life, for I am devoted to you. You are my God; save your servant who trusts in you. Have mercy on me, O Lord, for I call to you all day long. Bring joy to your servant, for to you, O Lord, I lift up my soul. (Psalm 86:1–4)

The book of Psalms is a remarkably unique collection of writings by David. His writings reveal his pleadings, his praise, and his search for God's intervention. In other words, David relied on God for his every need. He sought God's counsel in every situation and in every instance. We would do good to seek the Lord in the same way, seeking His counsel, knowing and believing that God will provide.

I guess I am weak in this area, too. I know that I need to, should, and want to, but sometimes that is as far as it gets, the woulda's, shoulda's, coulda's.

The Lord has all of the answers and sometimes His guidance occurs without our even asking. A recent instance, even though trivial, occurred while putting the stairs in our new house. My wife wanted to install the stairs in such a way that we would have a landing with two levels. My construction experience had given me an uncertainty, but I obliged her wishes. After completing the stairs, we thanked God for his guidance for having us do it that way. If we had not, we would have had to do the work over; we would not have passed code for head clearance between a beam and the steps. It was a marvelous lesson to receive simple guidance and instruction from the Lord of Lords through my wife.

God is there for each of us to call upon. He is a loving Father who cares and wants to guide us through the difficulties of life. Pray this Psalm written by David and learn to rely on God.

August

August 1

"Children of God"

Scripture: How great is the love the Father has lavished on us, that we should be called children of God. (1 John 3:1)

Did you know that God always has something wonderful for us? He knows everything we face and can and will provide something good for each one of us. And why shouldn't He? He is our Father and we are His children. Every Father wants to provide a life for their children, which is better than theirs. He wants to give His children the desires of their hearts, and wants to provide everything perfect, not only for this life, but for life eternal. In the same way, God wants us to be blessed and to receive from Him what He has in store for each of us.

The most perfect gift God has provided for us is His Son, Jesus. He gave him up to suffer and die for our sins. He gave him as sacrifice, so we would not have to suffer the wrath of sin for eternity. He wanted to provide a bridge, through Christ, for us to become His children and for us to be welcomed into His family. And, this having been done for us, makes us children of God.

August 2

"Why Tell About God?"

Scripture: I will exalt you, my God the King; will praise your name for ever and ever.

Everyday I will praise you extol your name for ever and ever. [3]Great is the LORD and most worthy of praise; greatness no one can fathom. One generation will commend your works to another; will tell of your mighty acts. (Psalm 145:1–4)

At this point, if you're reading through what I have written, you may have wondered why? Why would someone, especially not a pastor or theologian, take the time to write a devotional? Well, the Scripture above says it all. I want anyone who reads this to come to know God in a different way. Not from words of a well-known author or evangelist, but from a common Joe. I want them to come to know God as I have, as a friend and a companion. Throughout life we will face many things and the key, as I have found, is knowing where to go—God. We must learn to listen and communicate with God in a common way, as we would a close friend. We must learn to just be comfortable with Him, to just be ourselves without fear and concern about being revealed. In doing so, we will learn to be loved in the way only God can love—unconditionally.

God has instructed me to write this book of devotions. I hope you enjoy it, that it blesses you, and that you will share your thoughts about God with another generation.

August 3

"Enemies"

Scripture: "Do not kill them," he answered. "Would you kill men you have captured with your own sword or bow? Set food and water before them so that they may eat and drink and then go back to their master." So he prepared a great feast for them, and after they had finished eating and drinking, he sent them away, and they returned to their master. So the bands from Aram stopped raiding Israel's territory. (2 Kings 6:22–23)

Do you feel in your heart that you have enemies? It is hard for me to think in those terms. I can't imagine such a thing, but as I watch the news I see children and adults all over the world who have enemies who threaten their lives daily. I wonder if I could cope with such a threat. What would I do? How would my faith hold up under such a threat? Would my Christianity falter?

I hope and pray that I will never have to find out. But, if I am confronted, I believe I can handle the situation with God's instruction. I hope I can follow God's leading to pray for my enemies to be saved so that they may become my brothers in Christ. I pray that I can place a feast before them and let them leave knowing that I am a friend through Christ.

Enemies will come and go, but God lasts forever. Call upon him when you are threatened. He will be there.

___

___

___

August 4

"TRANSFORMED"

Scripture: Therefore, as God's chosen people, holy and dearly loved, clothe yourselves with compassion, kindness, humility, gentleness and patience. And whatever you do, whether in word or deed, do it all in the name of the Lord Jesus, giving thanks to God the Father through him. (Colossians 3:12, 17)

Over the years God has revealed to me many great truths. At one point He showed me how I was so headstrong, stubborn, and ambitious that I only thought of myself. He revealed that I would not allow anyone to get close to me, even Him, because it might keep me from doing what I wanted. And, when I did allow someone to enter my circle I imposed my thinking on them without consideration for their thoughts. Recently, He has shown me the grace of His wisdom.

By God's grace my life is different now. My priorities have shifted from what I want to what God wants. I have found that my wisdom comes from Him. He has transformed me from my old self to a new creation in Christ.

August 5

"Feeling Distressed and Alone"

Scripture: Save me, O God, the waters have come up to my neck. (Psalm 69:1)

I remember vividly the years after my father died. I had just turned sixteen—as a matter of fact he died the day after my sixteenth birthday. It was definitely a time of uncertainty. My mother especially felt very alone. Even though she had me around, she had lost her life companion. I found her sobbing in the middle of the day and night for years. She was alone and distressed, struggling to meet financial obligations, trying to raise a sixteen-year-old, and had no one to share the burden of what life had dealt her (or at least that is what I thought). It wasn't until years later, after my mother died and I received a book of poems she wrote and her personal Bible, that I discovered that my mother had not been as alone as I had thought. The poems and Bible revealed that although my mother truly missed my father greatly, she was never alone. God was with her always and she shared her burden with Him.

This taught me a very valuable lesson. When times are tough, when we think we are alone, when we are feeling distressed, and when we feel as though the tide of the world is going to overwhelm us, all we need to do is reach out to God. Reach out our hand and He will be there never leaving us alone.

August 6

"Comfortable Old Shoes"

Scripture: So from now on we regard no one from a worldly point of view. Though we once regarded Christ in this way, we do so no longer. Therefore, if anyone is in Christ, he is a new creation; the old has gone, the new has come! All this is from God, who reconciled us to himself through Christ and gave us the ministry of reconciliation: that God was reconciling the world to himself in Christ, not counting men's sins against them. And he has committed to us the message of reconciliation. (2 Corinthians 5:16–19)

As many times as I have read about God's amazing grace I have wondered how He could have accepted someone like me. Full of sin, He made provision for me. Before I was ever conceived, He made provision for me. He loved me and didn't even know me, but yet He made provision for me through Jesus.

Years later after accepting Christ, I still fell back into sin even though God was working in my life. How could He still love me? I wondered. 2 Corinthians 5:17 says it best, "Therefore if anyone is in Christ, he is a new creation; the old is gone, the new has come." Does this mean it is an immediate transformation? Maybe for some, but for me, my transformation is like a pot of chili. It's better the second day. I guess that is why God still allows me in his presence. He knows I will be better the second day, the third, and so on until I am totally reconciled to Him.

I look at this like a new pair of shoes. They are a little hard to walk in at first, but they get more and more comfortable each day you wear them—such is our relationship with Jesus.

August 7

"Do You Love Jesus?"

Scripture: The third time he said to him, "Simon son of John, do you love me?" Peter was hurt because Jesus asked him the third time, "Do you love me?" He said, "Lord, you know all things; you know that I love you." (John 21:17)

Do you really love Jesus? Think seriously about it, do you really love Jesus? Come on be honest, do you really, really love Jesus?

It is exasperating to be asked so many times, isn't it? Especially when you know that Jesus already knows. So why do you think Jesus asked Peter that question three times? Commentary says that first Peter was told he would deny Jesus three times before the cock crowed and the three questions of love erased the three denials. It makes sense, but what else did Jesus command Peter to do? "Feed my sheep," Jesus asked. With this statement, Jesus was commissioning Peter to minister to the people and to put Jesus' love into action. This would truly prove Peter's love for Jesus.

I recently heard a story about three children who always told their mother that they loved her. Two of the children would say, "Mother I love you" and then run off and play leaving their mother to do all of the chores. The third child also told the mother she loved her, but instead of running to play she swept the floor and picked up the house.

Who do you think loved the mother most?

Do you love Jesus? If so, put your love into action.

____

____

____

August 8

"Many Miles of Protection"

Scripture: He will not let your foot slip—who watches over you will not slumber; (Psalm 121:3)

I have driven many miles over the years for my job. It has taken me to many places from small towns to large cities and as driving does its exposes you to many perils. You tend to face the perils of weather, road construction, and other drivers. You find people on the road who are too preoccupied with other things to concentrate on their driving. Things such as fatigue, eating, and now the operation of cellular phones pose much risk for many drivers. Driving under these conditions can be just plain scary. I have been run off the road and had many near misses and each time that occurs I know that God is protecting me. I now start each trip by praying over my vehicle and me. To this day, God has protected me over the many miles I've traveled, not only the many miles of road, but also the many miles of life.

It does not matter what the situation, whether driving or living life, God protects.

August 9

"Christ's Return"

Scripture: "No one knows about that day or hour, not even the angels in heaven, nor the Son, but only the Father. Be on guard! Be alert! You do not know when that time will come. (Mark 13:32–33)

Are you ready for Christ's return? I must confess, when I am in a sinful situation or have violated God's commands, I would not want Christ to return. So what do we do to correct our ungodliness? As quickly as we sin, we need to run to God, ask for His forgiveness, and repent. We need to reconcile ourselves to God and let grace do the rest. The next step is to overcome that sin, so that we will always be ready for Christ's return. Sin is a struggle and it takes more than us to overcome it. Only God and the Holy Spirit can help us overcome the sinful nature within us. God will continue the work through the Spirit—then and only then will we truly be ready for Christ's return.

Dear God,

Forgive me of my sinful, lustful nature. My actions do speak louder than words, therefore, help me to overcome those times when my actions overtake what my heart knows is right. Accept me back into your arms and help me through your Spirit to be righteous before you.

In Jesus' Name,

Amen

August 10

"Hasty Prayers"

Scripture: Be still before the LORD and wait patiently for him; (Psalm 37:7)

Have you ever gone to the Lord in prayer only to become frustrated because nothing happened? You wanted it to happen, you prayed for it to happen and you wanted it to happen right then?

I have been there especially when things seem to go against my will. I get very impatient. I pray, seek God, and nothing.

The good news is, as God has granted me more wisdom, my prayers have always been answered, not in haste but in God's perfect timing. He always knows what is best for me and knows the proper time to fulfill my petition. I know that there are times that I entangle myself in such a mess that it takes God time to untangle it. It is like a fishing line that seems to get tangled easily; it takes time and patience to untangle it. So it is with God's answered prayer.

August 11

"Blessed Giving"

Scripture: "In everything I did, I showed you that by this kind of hard work we must help the weak, remembering the words the Lord Jesus himself said: 'It is more blessed to give than to receive.'" (Acts 20:35)

"It is more blessed to give than to receive," says the Scripture and it has proven itself to me time and time again. The most significant time was when my family and I were struggling financially. We could not make ends meet. We were behind on everything and wondered how we could survive. But, God in his infinite wisdom told me to give as the Bible instructed and to give sacrificially as I could, so I did. Every dollar I made I gave ten cents and as I knew someone who was in need I helped. As soon as I started giving as God instructed, doors started opening and money started flowing our way. We still struggled a while more, but God gave us peace and joy and we never worried about the outcome.

It is truly better to give than to receive!

August 12

"TV Preachers"

Scripture: "Not everyone who says to me, 'Lord, Lord,' will enter the kingdom of heaven, but only he who does the will of my Father who is in heaven. Many will say to me on that day, 'Lord, Lord, did we not prophesy in your name, and in your name drive out demons and perform many miracles?' Then I will tell them plainly, 'I never knew you. Away from me, you evildoers!' (Matthew 7:21–23)

I have heard many comments and complaints over the years about TV preachers. The rationale is that they only to seek to separate you from your money for their own personal gain. We have all seen them preach, seen some perform healing, and even heard some prophesy, yet how can we tell if it is all staged for TV?

Jesus told us to watch out for false prophets (Matt. 7:15) and I believe many TV evangelists have been judged and classified in that category. The truth is Jesus told us to recognize false prophets by their fruits. If the fruit they produce is good fruit it will be pleasing not only in your sight, but to God's as well. Examine yourself and refuse to be a judge of these. Instead, allow Jesus to judge all works on the day of His coming.

So the next time you are watching some TV preacher, check your Spirit. If it is telling you no, change the channel. If it says yes, partake of the good fruit.

August 13

"Tune In"

Scripture: Then David gave his son Solomon the plans for the portico of the temple, its buildings, its storerooms, its upper parts, its inner rooms and the place of atonement. He gave him the plans of all that the Spirit had put in his mind for the courts of the temple of the LORD and all the surrounding rooms, for the treasuries of the temple of God and for the treasuries for the dedicated things. (1 Chronicles 28:11–12)

How do we get our messages from God? As we go through our lives and walk with God, do we really get God's messages or do we pass them off as something else? If we are in tune with God He speaks to us all the time through His Spirit. We can be like a radio station tuned in to receive God or off station and receive static. Sometimes I feel off station and miss some important message God has for me. As I have gotten older, my antenna is more peaked to receive God's plan and I am more willing to put His plan in action. The next time you get something that seems to pop into your mind, don't just shrug it off, but meditate on it. It may be a message from God sending a signal for you to receive and all you need do is tune in to it.

August 14

"Where Have You Gleaned?"

Scripture: So Ruth gleaned in the field until evening. Then she threshed the barley she had gathered, and it amounted to about an ephah. She carried it back to town, and her mother-in-law saw how much she had gathered. Ruth also brought out and gave her what she had left over after she had eaten enough. Her mother-in-law asked her, "Where did you glean today? Where did you work? Blessed be the man who took notice of you!" (Ruth 2:17–19)

Today people are always looking for immediate gratification. They believe that a person's self worth is judged by the material possessions that he or she has accumulated. These people seem to get enormously depressed, if they don't get enough stuff.

I used to be just that way. Because of that foolishness, I lost everything. I lost my business, my house, my truck, and my income. I wondered what would happen and how others would judge me. Would I be branded a failure?

What really happened was truly a miracle. God used this circumstance of my life to get my total attention. He opened my eyes to a new set of priorities and helped me to gain a better focus. He showed me that true gratification does not come from stuff, but from doing the best job I can with what He has given me. Now, I enjoy everything I do whether I get paid or not, because I do it for God.

Where have you gleaned today? I hope it was for God.

August 15

"Planned Paths"

Scripture: This is what the LORD says: "When seventy years are completed for Babylon, I will come to you and fulfill my gracious promise to bring you back to this place. For I know the plans I have for you," declares the LORD, "plans to prosper you and not to harm you, plans to give you hope and a future. (Jeremiah 29:10–11)

Our lives often go down many paths. Some paths we choose and some are chosen for us by others. We often find ourselves in unfamiliar territory. We find ourselves facing unknowns, uncertainties, and even isolation. These things can put us in such disarray that we get discouraged and lose all joy from our lives.

Well hold on, there is some good news.

The people of Israel were given up to captivity in Babylon. They found themselves isolated from the land God had promised. They were afraid and wondered about their lives and what would happen to them. Then Jeremiah was told by God to deliver a message. God told them to stop sitting around complaining and wondering. God told them to build houses, plant gardens, and have children. He told them not to listen to dreamers and schemers, but to pray for peace and prosperity for the city, so that they would prosper too. God wanted this so they would have hope in tomorrow for He was going to deliver them back into the land He promised. He was going to set them on the right path and fulfill the promise He had made for these were His chosen people.

We are God's chosen people too and He has made plans for us. He has set a path before each of us and has given us each hope and a future—all we need to do is believe in God's plan for our lives.

August 16

"Jesus Returns, Who Cares?"

Scripture: But do not forget this one thing, dear friends: With the Lord a day is like a thousand years, and a thousand years are like a day. The Lord is not slow in keeping his promise, as some understand slowness. He is patient with you, not wanting anyone to perish, but everyone to come to repentance. (2 Peter 3:8–9)

I remember having many discussions about Jesus' return, especially facing a new millennium. Some said, as we approached a new millennium, "Jesus' return is at hand." Several purveyors of prophecy predicted how God had fulfilled His word and how Jesus was coming soon, even at the dawn of this new millennium.

I guess I don't care either way. I am prepared for Christ's return, but what about others? I would not want to see anyone perish.

I think God feels the same way. God has great patience and does not want to see anyone perish, either. He wants everyone to have an opportunity to receive the Good News and to have a chance to repent. God is the only one who knows the day of Jesus return, so let's all do our part to be prepared and help others do the same.

August 17

"Rising Waters and No Where to Go"

Scripture: But now, this is what the LORD says—he who created you, O Jacob, he who formed you, O Israel: "Fear not, for I have redeemed you; I have summoned you by name; you are mine. When you pass through the waters, I will be with you; and when you pass through the rivers, they will not sweep over you. When you walk through the fire, you will not be burned; the flames will not set you ablaze. For I am the LORD, your God, the Holy One of Israel, your Savior . . . (Isaiah 43:1–3)

Have you ever felt that you were in so much trouble, had so many things against you and had no hope in sight that it seemed there was no reason to go on? I have. I once experienced a horrible episode such as this in my life to the point that no matter how hard I tried nothing improved. I felt that I made such a mess of my life and I was in constant despair. It felt like I was in the middle of a flood. The waters were rising and increasing in intensity. I tried to climb higher, but the flood continued to rise even faster. Climb higher, climb higher I told myself only to find I was at the highest point with nowhere to go. When I reached that point, I knew it was over. The waters would soon overtake me, so I surrendered. In that surrender, in that very moment I gave up trying to save myself, I found that I had climbed into the arms of Jesus, my Savior. In the surrender, I was truly saved.

When the floodwaters of life threaten you don't rely on yourself, but surrender into Jesus' arms and be saved.

August 18

"Seek Before You Speak"

Scripture: But when they arrest you, do not worry about what to say or how to say it. At that time you will be given what to say, for it will not be you speaking, but the Spirit of your Father speaking through you. (Matthew 10:19–20)

I am in sales and am often asked to speak publicly on our company's behalf. I have also been blessed with numerous opportunities to deliver a message at our church. These situations have often been fraught with a certain amount of anxiety. Could I really say what was on my heart and mind? Would my nervousness cause me not to make my point? What would I do? - were the thoughts that would frequently run through my head.

Now, before speaking I pray for God's Spirit to come and speak through me. I ask for Him to speak His words not mine. In doing so, I end up saying the right thing at the right time without concern.

The next time you are faced with having to speak to someone or to a group, seek before you speak and God will see you through.

August 19

"God, Where Are You?"

Scripture: Hear my voice when I call, O LORD; be merciful to me and answer me. My heart says of you "Seek his face!" Your face, LORD, I will seek. (Psalm 27:7–8)

Being a Christian does not always mean I am in God's presence. I have to seek Him, because I have moved Him from my first priority somewhere to the back. I sometimes put Him behind work, family, sports, or other events. Then when trouble comes or I realize what I have done, I seek Him. "Where are you Lord?" I cry. What has happened to my Lord's presence? I wonder. At that moment, when I am desperate to find Him, I remember: The easiest way to find my Lord is to worship Him. If I worship Him, He will come find me. I will praise Him, sing songs to Him and truly worship my Lord. Sure enough, when I do that, the Lord comes. He reveals His presence, shows His love for me, and reminds me of my misled priorities.

So the next time you seek the Lord and do not know where to find Him, stop, worship Him, and He will find you.

August 20

"Contented"

Scripture: I know what it is to be in need, and I know what it is to have plenty. I have learned the secret of being content in any and every situation, whether well fed or hungry, whether living in plenty or in want. I can do everything through him who gives me strength. (Philippians 4:12–13)

Bombarded—that is what we are, bombarded. Each day of our lives we are faced with "Buy this! Buy that! You can't live without this! You have just got to have that." It is so overwhelming that many of us rush for more. In the not too distant past, I chased the very same thing. Nothing made me content. I pushed and shoved my way to get more and passed it off as ambition. It was so consuming I was totally discontented. Desperate to gain contentment through more and more, I lost it all and almost my family to boot.

One day, while searching for true contentment, I found Jesus. He rescued me and showed me that with Him I am truly rich. He showed me that He is the source of all contentment. Now that I realize that, my life has changed. He has restored everything I lost and much more. He has shown me that true riches come from the relationship I have with Him and with my family. And because of this, I have never been more content.

August 21

"Be Equipped"

Scripture: 10Finally, be strong in the Lord and in his mighty power. Put on the full armor of God so that you can take your stand against the devil's schemes. For our struggle is not against flesh and blood, but against the rulers, against the authorities, against the powers of this dark world and against the spiritual forces of evil in the heavenly realms. Therefore put on the full armor of God, so that when the day of evil comes, you may be able to stand your ground, and after you have done everything, to stand. Stand firm then, with the belt of truth buckled around your waist, with the breastplate of righteousness in place, and with your feet fitted with the readiness that comes from the gospel of peace. In addition to all this, take up the shield of faith, with which you can extinguish all the flaming arrows of the evil one. Take the helmet of salvation and the sword of the Spirit, which is the word of God. (Ephesians 6:10–17)

The world can be a very tough and intimidating place. Everyday the news shows lives being taken needlessly, people stealing from others, car accidents, and tragedies too numerous to mention. That is just the way it is today. So what are we to do?

We need to be equipped. A fireman does not go to a fire without the proper equipment. If he goes into a fire without his coat, helmet, gloves, respirator, and hose he can be overcome by the fire he is intending to fight. He must be properly equipped and trained for the battle. It is the same for us facing the battle each day. We must be prepared, trained, and equipped to fight. Equip yourself. Clothe yourself in God's armor, so that you can face whatever the world throws at you.

August 22

"Uphold the Law"

Scripture: Where, then, is boasting? It is excluded. On what principle? On that of observing the law? No, but on that of faith. For we maintain that a man is justified by faith apart from observing the law. Is God the God of Jews only? Is he not the God of Gentiles too? Yes, of Gentiles too, since there is only one God, who will justify the circumcised by faith and the uncircumcised through that same faith. Do we, then, nullify the law by this faith? Not at all! Rather, we uphold the law. (Romans 3:27–31)

I remember an acquaintance that accepted Jesus into his life. He was extremely excited about his new faith and newfound salvation. He loved to share his testimony with everyone. It was great to see this type enthusiasm for Christ.

One comment he made which set me back, however was, "If I sin it is okay, because I can go to Jesus for forgiveness." He felt that the Law of God was totally abolished by Jesus death and resurrection, and therefore felt that the Ten Commandments had no jurisdiction over him. I couldn't imagine that he thought he could do anything he wanted, whenever he wanted, and get forgiveness instantly. It didn't seem possible, so I did some research and found that when we are justified by faith through Jesus we should want to uphold the law. We should want to become righteous and strive to live by the commandments of God.

It is true that we have all sinned, will always sin, and will always need God's saving grace. We want, need, and gratefully accept God's atoning gift of His Son, Jesus. But, we must never forget to seek and uphold God's law.

August 23

"Cup Refilled"

Scripture: Do not cast me away when I am old; do not forsake me when my strength is gone. (Psalm 71:9)

I remember the time after my father's death very vividly. My mother was left alone to raise me, a sixteen-year-old teenage boy. She responded to the challenge admirably and was able to carry on even though she was lonely and even though she deeply missed her life companion, the person with whom she had shared her joy, sorrows, and thoughts. It was inspiring, now that I think back, how much she loved my father and what he truly meant to her. When he died, she was left alone to carry the burden of a sixteen-year-old, financially provide for our needs, and handle the day to day concerns every family faces.

I also remember my mother reading every night before bedtime. At first, I thought she was just reading a book for enjoyment, but she was actually reading her Bible. She was renewing her strength by reading and absorbing God's Word. None of this became evident to me until I received her Bible after she went to be with the Lord. It was well worn and underlined. It gave me comfort in knowing that she sought God's strength and refuge. And, she refilled her cup daily to meet the challenges of life.

August 24

"Spiritual Bread"

Scripture: Then Jesus declared, "I am the bread of life. He who comes to me will never go hungry, and he who believes in me will never be thirsty. But as I told you, you have seen me and still you do not believe. All that the Father gives me will come to me, and whoever comes to me I will never drive away. For I have come down from heaven not to do my will but to do the will of him who sent me. (John 6:35–38)

Recently the Dalai Lama visited our country. He came to speak of achieving peace in the world. As I watched the news clips of his trip, I saw literally hundreds and hundreds of people gathered to hear his words. I am not totally sure of why these people came to hear him, but I couldn't help wondering if they were seeking spiritual enlightenment or if they had come to partake of the spiritual bread he was offering.

The Bible makes it clear that Jesus and only Jesus is the bread of life. He came to feed the hungry and to give drink to those who thirst for righteousness. He and he alone will satisfy the spiritual yearning of each and every soul.

If you are seeking spiritual truth, are yearning to fill a void in your life, or have a deep hunger for something in your life, come to Jesus. He is the bread of life, life everlasting.

August 25

"Temptation"

Scripture: Then Jesus was led by the Spirit into the desert to be tempted by the devil. 2After fasting forty days and forty nights, he was hungry. The tempter came to him and said, "If you are the Son of God, tell these stones to become bread." Jesus answered, "It is written: 'Man does not live on bread alone, but on every word that comes from the mouth of God.'" Then the devil took him to the holy city and had him stand on the highest point of the temple. "If you are the Son of God," he said, "throw yourself down. For it is written: 'He will command his angels concerning you, and they will lift you up in their hands, so that you will not strike your foot against a stone.'" Jesus answered him, "It is also written: 'Do not put the Lord your God to the test.'" Again, the devil took him to a very high mountain and showed him all the kingdoms of the world and their splendor. "All this I will give you," he said, "if you will bow down and worship me." Jesus said to him, "Away from me, Satan! For it is written: 'Worship the Lord your God, and serve him only.'" (Matthew 4:1–10)

Temptation is a horrible thing. I know because I struggle with it every day. I see material things that draw me, I see sexy women that stimulate my lust, rage wants to take me over in traffic, and I seem to want whatever I know I shouldn't have. These temptations try to draw me away from what is right and push me toward the ways of the world.

I have to admit I sometimes yield to these temptations. They pull at me and try to lead me farther and farther from my God. Thankfully, God does not give up so easy. He tugs at my heart, convicts me of my sin, leads me to confession, and forgives me. He intervenes to help me reject the temptation. And, through His word He reminds me how Jesus himself rejected temptation.

We will always be faced with temptation and sometimes temptation will win the battle. But, remember that God is there; He knows what we face and has made provision for us through Jesus. We may lose the battle, but He will help us win the war.

August 26

"Wife Respect"

Scripture: 2Husbands, love your wives, just as Christ loved the church and gave himself up for her to make her holy, cleansing her by the washing with water through the word, and to present her to himself as a radiant church, without stain or wrinkle or any other blemish, but holy and blameless. In this same way, husbands ought to love their wives as their own bodies. He who loves his wife loves himself. After all, no one ever hated his own body, but he feeds and cares for it, just as Christ does the church—for we are members of his body. "For this reason a man will leave his father and mother and be united to his wife, and the two will become one flesh." This is a profound mystery—but I am talking about Christ and the church. However, each one of you also must love his wife as he loves himself, and the wife must respect her husband. (Ephesians 5:25–33)

My wife is a treasure to me. Even though I recognize that, I still do not always treat her as Christ would have me to. I take her for granted in many cases. I don't concern myself with her needs, but only mine. She sometimes has to do all of the household chores, even though she works. I, not thinking, allow the housework to fall on her shoulders. She is there to take care of the kids, have dinner ready, and wash my clothes; and, then I don't even have an ounce of appreciation, when she accomplishes it all. In spite of this, I still want her to be loving, caring, and to submit to my wants and needs.

When this happens, God reminds me of what she means in my life and that I should treat her with respect and as Christ did His church. He sacrificed himself for the church even unto death.

Ephesians puts it all into context by pointing out that as men we are to love our wives as we love ourselves. We would not treat ourselves that way. We would try to make it easier on ourselves, simplify our lives, and then pamper ourselves to boot. Why should we treat our wives any differently?

August 27

"Sue Crazy"

Scripture: (Now in earlier times in Israel, for the redemption and transfer of property to become final, one party took off his sandal and gave it to the other. This was the method of legalizing transactions in Israel.) (Ruth 4:7)

Sue crazy—the whole world is sue crazy. It seems as though people are constantly putting themselves in situations to sue someone. And, then to top it off, we have attorneys chasing cases to try and line their pockets.

Whatever happened to the belief that a man's word is his bond?

God intends for us to conduct our lives with truth and integrity. He expects us to honor what we say and to not look for loopholes. God has shown us the sincerity of a promise. A promise is to be kept and God has shown us this. He kept his promise to redeem our sins and He did so through Jesus.

The next time you make a pact, do it in truth, honor, and integrity.

____

____

____

August 28

"His Mighty Hand"

Scripture: Then the LORD said to Moses, "Now you will see what I will do to Pharaoh: Because of my mighty hand he will let them go; because of my mighty hand he will drive them out of his country." (Exodus 6:1)

Our family is truly blessed. We recently had the opportunity to build our dream house. This blessing is the result of God's fulfillment of a promise and the work of His mighty hand.

Back several years ago, a friend and brother in the Lord, gave me a prophetic word. He told me that the Lord said I would lose everything because of my business foolishness. When I first heard what the Lord had said, I could not even imagine such a thing happening to me. I knew God was a good God and thought surely He would not allow such a thing to happen to me. Well, I was wrong. I did lose everything: my house, my truck, all my sources of income, and even my pride. It was the most discouraging and frightening time of my life. There was only one word to describe it: devastating.

But, when things got to be their worst, God did His best. He showed his mighty hand and started putting everything back together, not overnight, but slowly and methodically opening doors of new opportunity. He showed His mighty hand in directing me and guiding me into His perfect will. And, now He has restored it all and has given us the house of our dreams.

August 29

"Are You Prepared?"

Scripture: But, dear friends, remember what the apostles of our Lord Jesus Christ foretold. They said to you, "In the last times there will be scoffers who will follow their own ungodly desires. These are the men who divide you, who follow mere natural instincts and do not have the Spirit. But you, dear friends, build yourselves up in your most holy faith and pray in the Holy Spirit. Keep yourselves in God's love as you wait for the mercy of our Lord Jesus Christ to bring you to eternal life. (Jude 1:17–21)

Everyone is trying to predict when Jesus will return. It seems especially so now with the difficulties of a new millennium. We all see signs that seem to point to the last days, but the truth is, no one on earth really knows when Jesus will return.

What we do know is that we need to take the signs seriously. We need to live each day to its fullest and make sure we are always prepared for Christ's return. We need to be careful not to be misled by the desires of the flesh and careful not to put off what we know we should do.

So today let's be sure our faith is strong, that we pray for our faith to increase, and that we pray for the love of Jesus to shine through us. In doing so, we will be prepared for Jesus' return and ready for the eternal life He has promised.

August 30

"Law of Protection"

Scripture: "Keep all my decrees and all my laws and follow them. I am the LORD." (Leviticus 19:37)

Laws are in the land and they govern us for our protection. They are not there to hinder us from doing what we want, but rather are there to protect us with a certain amount of restriction and restraint. For example, we have all learned about the law of gravity. If we jump off a building, we know without a doubt that we will fall and chances are good that we will get hurt. There are laws establishing limits for speed to minimize the chances for accidents. The police have learned that the faster we are allowed to go, the more chance there is for injury to occur to others and to ourselves.

The Old Testament shows us a set of laws that God gave Moses. God gave us these laws so we would not get hurt or cause hurt to anyone else. He loved us, so he gave us laws for protection, not for our salvation. So live by the law, not to be restricted in what you do, but for the protection God has offered.

August 31

"The Greatest Commandment—Love"

Scripture: It has given me great joy to find some of your children walking in the truth, just as the Father commanded us. And now, dear lady, I am not writing you a new command but one we have had from the beginning. I ask that we love one another. And this is love: that we walk in obedience to his commands. As you have heard from the beginning, his command is that you walk in love. (2 John 1:4–6)

God gave us his commandments and laws, because He loves us. He wants us to live blessed and fruitful lives though the obedience of living by His law. He also knew that gaining salvation by the law was beyond our ability, so God sent His Son to die for our sins and to save us from eternal damnation. He sent His Son to abolish the law, but not to abolish living by His law.

Our world today is subject to the laws of the world that have been established by man. Man also interprets these laws and if you have had legal dealings you know how difficult that really is. The commandments and laws God gave us are somewhat the same way. They are hard to uphold or interpret for living in today's world. Therefore, God has helped us. He has summed up all of His commandments in one word—LOVE. God knew if we loved one another then it would be impossible for us to transgress against each other. You cannot truly love someone and break a commandment.

Therefore, live by the greatest commandment, which encompasses all commandments, "Love One Another."

September

September 1

"Senses"

Scripture: Then the LORD opened Balaam's eyes, and he saw the angel of the LORD standing in the road with his sword drawn. So he bowed low and fell facedown. The angel of the LORD asked him, "Why have you beaten your donkey these three times? I have come here to oppose you because your path is a reckless one before me. The donkey saw me and turned away from me these three times. If she had not turned away, I would certainly have killed you by now, but I would have spared her." Balaam said to the angel of the LORD, "I have sinned. I did not realize you were standing in the road to oppose me. Now if you are displeased, I will go back." (Numbers 22:31–34)

I have seen and heard of stories about animals that sense danger. They seem to be able to instinctively realize that harm is approaching before it is seen. Humans on the other hand, seem to plunge into harms way without noticing the impending danger.

God is always trying to warn us of dangers in our lives. He does not want His children to harm even a hair on their head, however too often we miss His signs and continue to head our own way.

The next time you get a feeling, sense something unusual, or receive a sign that things are not what they should be, STOP! Stop and pray for God's guidance. Ask Him to help you discern what is about to unfold and then once He has, thank Him for revealing it. Use God sense, not your sense.

____

____

____

September 2

"Eye Witness Account"

Scripture: That which was from the beginning, which we have heard, which we have seen with our eyes, which we have looked at and our hands have touched—this we proclaim concerning the Word of life. The life appeared; we have seen it and testify to it, and we proclaim to you the eternal life, which was with the Father and has appeared to us. We proclaim to you what we have seen and heard, so that you also may have fellowship with us. And our fellowship is with the Father and with his Son, Jesus Christ. We write this to make our joy complete (1 John 1:1–4)

Have you ever watched a trial on TV, in a movie, or been involved in a court case yourself? The defense and prosecution work hard to make their cases and try to produce or eliminate doubt. Our laws are clear that a case must be proven beyond reasonable doubt. The jury then has to decide a verdict from the evidence presented, guilty or not guilty as it may be. But, in cases where there is an eyewitness to the account, there is no doubt, just truth.

The Word of God always seems to be on trial by some group or entity. These groups work hard to present their case that there is no God and that His Word is myth and mere conjecture. If the accusers, however, would read the Word they are trying to dismiss they will find an ironclad case. The Bible has many witnesses that testify to its truth. There is a total list of irrefutable evidence that proclaims that Jesus is Lord and that the Word of God is true beyond a reasonable doubt. Despite this there are people who still refuse the truth, and instead accept what they read in the newspaper or see on the news as the gospel—they fail to accept the written Word of God.

Believe the truth written by eyewitnesses: that Jesus is the Christ, the Son of a living, merciful God who was sacrificed for our sins.

September 3

"Blessing Upon Blessing"

Scripture: You will be blessed in the city and blessed in the country. The fruit of your womb will be blessed, and the crops of your land and the young of your livestock—the calves of your herds and the lambs of your flocks. Your basket and your kneading trough will be blessed. You will be blessed when you come in and blessed when you go out. (Deuteronomy 28:3–6)

Everyone wants to be blessed. We want to be blessed in every way and in everything, but if you are like me, I have been blessed in many ways and don't even recognize it. I sometimes think the word blessing gets mixed up with receiving stuff, material stuff. Blessings abound and I don't even see them.

God has blessed all who have accepted Jesus as Savior. God has blessed us with eternal life. God has blessed us with life itself and the free will to live life as we choose. He has blessed us with family, friends, and a legacy of memories. He has blessed us with the freedom to worship and to gather to praise Him. God has blessed us with the earth and the sky to brighten our days. And, He has blessed us by prospering us. All of this is made possible by our doing one thing: accepting Jesus as our Lord and Savior.

September 4

"What's the Benefit of being a Christian?"

Scripture: His divine power has given us everything we need for life and godliness through our knowledge of him who called us by his own glory and goodness. Through these he has given us his very great and precious promises, so that through them you may participate in the divine nature and escape the corruption in the world caused by evil desires. For this very reason, make every effort to add to your faith goodness; and to goodness, knowledge; and to knowledge, self-control; and to self-control, perseverance; and to perseverance, godliness; and to godliness, brotherly kindness; and to brotherly kindness, love. For if you possess these qualities in increasing measure, they will keep you from being ineffective and unproductive in your knowledge of our Lord Jesus Christ. But if anyone does not have them, he is nearsighted and blind, and has forgotten that he has been cleansed from his past sins. (2 Peter 1:3–9)

What benefit is there in being a Christian? What do we get from our faith, other than the knowledge of knowing where we will spend eternity?

I am sure many of us have wondered these things at times. We dedicate ourselves to worship, prayer, devotion, and service, but what benefit do we get?

It has taken me many years to see, feel, and be recognized as a Christian. Living by faith has produced many benefits in my life. God has helped me overcome evil desires—not to say I don't struggle with them occasionally, but overall He has made me victorious. He is continuing to develop in me the traits referred to in 2 Peter 1: goodness, knowledge, self-control, perseverance, godliness, and love. None of these qualities, in my eyes, were attainable without God.

The benefit of being a Christian is knowing that God can take a clay pot and make it a precious and useful vessel for His glory. And, by His hands make us effective and productive to fulfill His will of spreading the Gospel.

September 5

"Teamwork"

Scripture: "When the trumpets sounded, the people shouted, and at the sound of the trumpet, when the people gave a loud shout, the wall collapsed; so every man charged straight in, and they took the city." (Job 6:20)

I was a basketball referee for years and had the opportunity to see many talented players. Those individuals seemed to excel and many times helped their teams to victory. The most exciting times for me refereeing was seeing a team with lesser talent work together as a team and beat a team with an outstanding individual. With teamwork, the less talented team overcomes individual effort every time.

Teamwork in being a Christian is important too. We need to allow our Father in Heaven to work alongside us to accomplish great things. With God by our side, all things are possible. When you add His power to the multitude of other believers, great and wonderful things are accomplished.

The next time you face an insurmountable task or challenge, call upon the Lord. He and His legion of angels will be there to team up with you and the victory will be yours.

September 6

"Selfish Ambitions"

Scripture: 1Who is wise and understanding among you? Let him show it by his good life, by deeds done in the humility that comes from wisdom. But if you harbor bitter envy and selfish ambition in your hearts, do not boast about it or deny the truth. Such "wisdom" does not come down from heaven but is earthly, unspiritual, of the devil. For where you have envy and selfish ambition, there you find disorder and every evil practice. (James 3:13–16)

There was a period in my life when I was so consumed with ambition that it dictated every thought and every move I made. I was governed by a drive to be successful and to get rich at all costs.

Many employers and other entrepreneurs saw my ambition as an admirable trait that drove me to succeed. Even I admired my aggressiveness to get ahead and get the job done. Everything seemed to be going along great until my ambition overrode my wisdom. My decisions were driven by my need to get ahead rather than by what were right. People who got in my way got ran over and an insatiable hunger for power developed within me.

Well, as many of these stories turn out, my successes were temporal because of my lack of spiritual wisdom. My whole life was devastated and I started hurting the ones I loved. I sunk to depths where I thought even God himself could not reach me, but thank God I was wrong.

To have ambition and wisdom is fine, if such traits are spiritually directed. However, don't let yourself get out of control as I did. Seek God in all things and let Him govern your ambition.

September 7

"Peace and Joy"

Scripture: Praise be to the God and Father of our Lord Jesus Christ! In his great mercy he has given us new birth into a living hope through the resurrection of Jesus Christ from the dead, and into an inheritance that can never perish, spoil or fade—kept in heaven for you, who through faith are shielded by God's power until the coming of the salvation that is ready to be revealed in the last time. In this you greatly rejoice, though now for a little while you may have had to suffer grief in all kinds of trials. These have come so that your faith—of greater worth than gold, which perishes even though refined by fire—may be proved genuine and may result in praise, glory and honor when Jesus Christ is revealed. Though you have not seen him, you love him; and even though you do not see him now, you believe in him and are filled with an inexpressible and glorious joy, for you are receiving the goal of your faith, the salvation of your souls. (1 Peter 1:3–9)

I was driving across the countryside one day on business and looked out across the acres and acres of golden farm fields. I saw the preparation for harvest as farmers readied their combines and trucks. And, as I drove, I felt a great sense of joy and peace. It seemed as if I was in a wonderful dream and the cares of the world had stopped. It was if I had no worries, no concerns, no struggles, and no trials. I was in total awe of God's greatness, mercy, and salvation.

We are always going to face suffering and trials while in this world. The good news is that God is in Heaven preparing a safe place for us. It will be a place where we can have great feelings of peace and joy throughout all of eternity.

"Praise God from whom all blessings flow."

September 8

"Disappointment"

Scripture: The angel of the LORD went up from Gilgal to Bokim and said, "I brought you up out of Egypt and led you into the land that I swore to give to your forefathers." I said, "I will never break my covenant with you, and you shall not make a covenant with the people of this land, but you shall break down their altars." Yet you have disobeyed me. Why have you done this? (Judges 2:1–2)

It is an awesome chore to discipline and direct four children. They are all good children, but they often fail to comply with the rules. My wife and I assign duties and chores for them to perform only to find them not done. This lack of concern on their part creates a great disappointment for us as parents.

As I reflect on the disappointment with my children, it somehow makes it easier to understand how God must feel when we disappoint Him. We all sin and it must truly break His heart. We disobey His instructions and we follow our own will instead of His and it must make Him feel totally dejected.

As for me, I pray for God's forgiveness for the disrespect I show and I pray for Him to stir within me a determination to improve, so that I do not disappoint Him, my Father.

September 9

"Loyalty"

Scripture: But Ruth replied, "Don't urge me to leave you or to turn back from you. Where you go I will go, and where you stay I will stay. Your people will be my people and your God my God. Where you die I will die, and there I will be buried. May the LORD deal with me, be it ever so severely, if anything but death separates you and me." (Ruth 1:16–17)

Loyalty in today's society seems to be waning. Nobody has any loyalty. Everyone is looking for someway to get what he or she wants without concern for the people it may hurt. People seem only to see what is best for them and they are always looking for something or someone better just around the corner.

It seems the same way when people are trying to find a church. They search to find one that makes them feel good, but fail to make a commitment. It is as if, if they decide to commit, then they are tied down. So they stay on the fringe and don't allow themselves to get involved. They seem to be afraid or maybe deep down inside they do not want people to get to know them personally. In any case, they skate around having to be loyal and committed to one place.

Jesus was not afraid to be loyal. He was particularly loyal to God's will and His commitment to die for our sins. He chose, even before we existed, to take our place before the judgment seat of God. He took our punishment—you can't be more loyal than that.

September 10

"Repetitive Sin"

Scripture: It is impossible for those who have once been enlightened, who have tasted the heavenly gift, who have shared in the Holy Spirit, who have tasted the goodness of the word of God and the powers of the coming age, if they fall away, to be brought back to repentance, because to their loss they are crucifying the Son of God all over again and subjecting him to public disgrace. (Hebrews 6:4–6)

Christians should rejoice in the fact that we can receive forgiveness for our sins. After we have committed ourselves to Christ and then commit a sin, all we need to do is fall on our knees and ask God to forgive us. And, because of His graciousness and mercy, we will be forgiven.

It is wonderful to know that we can receive forgiveness for our sins, but what about repetitive sins? What about the sins we commit knowing that, 1) we have committed the same sin before and, 2) that our spirit tells us we shouldn't be committing it again? We know Jesus forgives, but how can He put up with it time and time again?

I did some research and through God's enlightening wisdom the answer was revealed. In the book of Hebrews it says that if we fall away "We are crucifying the Son of God all over again and subjecting Him to public disgrace." I don't know about you, but that makes me feel sick to my stomach. How or why would I subject Christ to that type of torture again? So I pray that the next time the world lures me and urges me to repeat a sin that I step back and think about Jesus going through the ridicule, disgrace, agony, pain, and death He did many years ago. And, maybe, just maybe, I will not fall.

September 11

"God Speaking, Do You Hear?"

Scripture: The LORD called Samuel a third time, and Samuel got up and went to Eli and said, "Here I am; you called me." Eli realized that the LORD was calling the boy. So Eli told Samuel, "Go and lie down, and if he calls you, say, 'Speak, LORD, for your servant is listening.'" So Samuel went and lay down in his place. The LORD came and stood there, calling as at the other times, "Samuel! Samuel!" Samuel said, "Speak, for your servant is listening." (1 Samuel 3:8–10)

Over the years the Lord has revealed many things to me. God, through His Holy Spirit, has spoken to me many times. The Lord has given me great wisdom in some areas of my life especially when I have been searching for an answer to a problem. God has often responded and provided me with the answer. God has also revealed to me how I am to serve Him. God seems to always be speaking, but my listening seems to be the problem. The old adage is that we have two ears and one mouth so we should listen more than we speak.

Are you listening to God?

In 1 Samuel, God is revealing Himself to Samuel for the first time. God calls to Samuel, but Samuel does not recognize God. Only when Eli, the High Priest, tells Samuel the Lord is speaking to him does he answer. Do we recognize God's call? If we do not, then we are not spending enough time in God's Word, in worship, and in prayer. God's calling, be still. Do you hear him? He is calling!

September 12

"Encourager"

Scripture: "Your love has given me great joy and encouragement, because you, brother, have refreshed the hearts of the saints." (Philippians 1:7)

I tend to be the optimist in my family. It doesn't matter what happens I strive to encourage others. Recently however, my wife has taken on that role. Her faith has grown and she has shown her faith to our family, to others, and to me.

A brother in Christ spoke a word from the Lord to me one day that my wife was a buried treasure. Over time God would reveal more and more of her treasure. I have begun to see, believe, and know that God has started the unearthing process and soon her rich treasure will be revealed.

I am truly in awe of her encouraging love for others and for me. I see God's treasure of an encourager, helper, companion, and wife. Thank you God for this beautiful spirit of encouragement you have given her.

____

____

____

September 13

"Godly Heritage"

Scripture: The LORD declares to you that the LORD himself will establish a house for you: When your days are over and you rest with your fathers, I will raise up your offspring to succeed you, who will come from your own body, and I will establish his kingdom. He is the one who will build a house for my Name, and I will establish the throne of his kingdom forever. I will be his father, and he will be my son. When he does wrong, I will punish him with the rod of men, with floggings inflicted by men. But my love will never be taken away from him, as I took it away from Saul, whom I removed from before you. Your house and your kingdom will endure forever before me ; your throne will be established forever. (2 Samuel 7:11–16)

I remember attending my brother-in-law's funeral and as was fitting, the preacher gave a brief summary of my brother-in-law's life. What penetrated my heart was the fact that his whole family had received Christ as their Savior because of his influence on them. He had left a heritage of believers. He went to his final rest knowing that his family would be in God's hands and under God's protection.

Fortunately, I am seeing the same heritage being built in my family. Each of my children has accepted Christ and is taking a position of service in God's Kingdom. As a father, there is no greater joy than knowing your children are under God's saving grace.

September 14

"Be Good"

Scripture: For the grace of God that brings salvation has appeared to all men. It teaches us to say "No" to ungodliness and worldly passions, and to live self-controlled, upright and godly lives in this present age, while we wait for the blessed hope—the glorious appearing of our great God and Savior, Jesus Christ, who gave himself for us to redeem us from all wickedness and to purify for himself a people that are his very own, eager to do what is good. (Titus 2:11–14)

Have you ever told someone to "be good"? I guess I have told my children at least a million times and I know I have told others the same thing, "I'll see you later, be good." I didn't realize what I was really saying until I read Paul's instruction to Titus.

Paul was instructing Titus in teaching the Crete on doing what is good. Paul knew and expressed to Titus that the only way for anyone to be good is to know Christ. Paul stated that we all have been, "foolish, disobedient, deceiving, and enslaved by all kinds of passions and pleasures. We live in malice and envy being hated and hating one another." There is no way for us to be good with all of this in us. We have to break down the walls of ungodliness and worldly passions. The only way to do that was to experience the saving grace and rebirth that God offers.

So the next time you tell someone to, "Be good" remember you are telling them to "Be in Christ."

September 15

"Discerning Heart"

Scripture: The Lord was pleased that Solomon had asked for this. So God said to him, "Since you have asked for this and not for long life or wealth for yourself, nor have asked for the death of your enemies but for discernment in administering justice, I will do what you have asked. I will give you a wise and discerning heart, so that there will never have been anyone like you, nor will there ever be. Moreover, I will give you what you have not asked for—both riches and honor—so that in your lifetime you will have no equal among kings. And if you walk in my ways and obey my statutes and commands as David your father did, I will give you a long life." (1 Kings 3:10–14)

I have given much thought about what I would ask for, if God would grant me anything I wished. My first thought was to be wealthy and have a lot of stuff and then I thought about world peace. The first two are normal thoughts for wish requests and the second very noble, but are they truly what is best?

God asked Solomon, when he had just taken the throne from his father David, "What do you want me to give you?" Solomon could have asked for anything, but he asked for a discerning heart.

Wow! What a powerful request: a discerning heart! I think that is really what I would ask for now after reading the Scripture. A discerning heart would give me the ability to handle any situation justly. It would give me the ability to say and react appropriately in all things. Yes, that is what I would ask for.

God is the purveyor of all wisdom and knowledge; therefore, we can all have a discerning heart. All we need to do is to tap into God's power and rely on Him before we do anything and He will instill in us a discerning spirit.

September 16

"Fight the Good Fight"

Scripture: In the presence of God and of Christ Jesus, who will judge the living and the dead, and in view of his appearing and his kingdom, I give you this charge: Preach the Word; be prepared in season and out of season; correct, rebuke and encourage—with great patience and careful instruction. For the time will come when men will not put up with sound doctrine. Instead, to suit their own desires, they will gather around them a great number of teachers to say what their itching ears want to hear. They will turn their ears away from the truth and turn aside to myths. But you, keep your head in all situations, endure hardship, do the work of an evangelist, discharge all the duties of your ministry. For I am already being poured out like a drink offering, and the time has come for my departure. I have fought the good fight, I have finished the race, I have kept the faith. (2 Timothy 4:1–7)

I can't stop thinking about the ending of the last millennium. I remember it stirred up a lot of concern, fear, and even the doomsayers. Most of the people I spoke with about the time felt uncertain about what was going to happen. The truth is everyone was thinking, "Is this the end of the world?"

I was not certain either of what was to unfold and truthfully I guess I had the attitude that it was in God's hands and there was nothing I could do. I believed that whatever his will was would be done and that there was nothing that was going to change that. But, as most, I kept a watchful eye on the signs of the coming and sought to prepare my family, my friends, and myself for Jesus' return. I helped to preach the gospel and to teach the scriptures and tried to fulfill God's great commission. I wanted to know that like Paul, "I fought the good fight."

September 17

"Financial Wisdom"

Scripture: The wife of a man from the company of the prophets cried out to Elisha, "Your servant my husband is dead, and you know that he revered the LORD. But now his creditor is coming to take my two boys as his slaves." Elisha replied to her, "How can I help you? Tell me, what do you have in your house?" "Your servant has nothing there at all," she said, "except a little oil." Elisha said, "Go around and ask all your neighbors for empty jars. Don't ask for just a few. Then go inside and shut the door behind you and your sons. Pour oil into all the jars, and as each is filled, put it to one side." She left him and afterward shut the door behind her and her sons. They brought the jars to her and she kept pouring. When all the jars were full, she said to her son, "Bring me another one." He replied, "There is not a jar left." Then the oil stopped flowing. She went and told the man of God, and he said, "Go, sell the oil and pay your debts. You and your sons can live on what is left." (2 Kings 4:1–7)

"Let us help you get out of debt," the newspaper read. "Got credit problems? We can consolidate your debt," the TV commercial said. "Are creditors hounding you? Bankruptcy counseling," the magazine beckoned. Today's society is the most debt-riddled, overextended society in history. The advertisements show that there is tremendous need for help. All of the ads claim to have the answer to the bill problems.

We have all made financial mistakes involving borrowing and overextending ourselves. The first thing we seem to do is try to borrow, seek credit counselors, or even file bankruptcy to find our way back into financial sanity, but in doing these things we often only make matters worse. The truth is the first thing we should do is run to God. We need to get down on our knees and pray for His wisdom. We need to take His wisdom, guidance, and instruction and, follow it step by step. Then, even though we have made a mess of our financial lives, He can put us back on the right track. If you have not experienced financial distress, go to God anyway and allow Him to direct your finances, so you will not face the credit bombshell.

September 18

"Contentment"

Scripture: But godliness with contentment is great gain. For we brought nothing into the world, and we can take nothing out of it. But if we have food and clothing, we will be content with that. People who want to get rich fall into temptation and a trap and into many foolish and harmful desires that plunge men into ruin and destruction. For the love of money is a root of all kinds of evil. Some people, eager for money, have wandered from the faith and pierced themselves with many griefs. (1 Timothy 6:6–10)

I once knew a man with a great eagerness to become rich. He viewed everything as a means to his ultimate goal—wealth. He wanted and accumulated all kinds of possessions. He was willing to sacrifice anything to get where he wanted to go. He worked hard and long to get to the top. He always wanted the latest and greatest and newest of everything. He was never ever content.

The man in this scenario is I. I suffered from all of these ailments only to find destruction and ruin as it says in 1 Timothy. I had created a house of cards, which came tumbling down. I lost everything.

Thank God that He had a better plan. Even though I lost every material possession I had, I gained Christ in return. I can tell you with certainty that finding Christ was worth it all, because it saved my family, my sanity, and most of all my soul.

In Jesus, I have found true contentment!

September 19

"SERVING THE LORD"

Scripture: "And you, my son Solomon, acknowledge the God of your father, and serve him with wholehearted devotion and with a willing mind, for the LORD searches every heart and understands every motive behind the thoughts. If you seek him, he will be found by you; but if you forsake him, he will reject you forever. 1Consider now, for the LORD has chosen you to build a temple as a sanctuary. Be strong and do the work."(1 Chronicles 28:9–10)

Serving the Lord is a great privilege and honor. It only requires one thing: willingness. Willingness to serve and willingness to make yourself available to God's leading. Willingness requires an open heart, mind, and soul. The obstacle that occurs in wanting to serve God is motive. Are we choosing to serve God for the right reasons? Sometimes people seem to take on positions of service in the church without first seeking God's counsel. They plunge right in knowing it is a visible position in the church, but without assessing the time required, talent needed, and the overall commitment necessary to be successful at the position. If we seek God first He searches our hearts and knows what will be required. God wants us to serve in capacities that have the greatest gain for His Kingdom. Therefore, if our motives are His motives, His Kingdom will be glorified.

So the next time you are asked to serve, ask God first!

September 20

"Stand Firm"

Scripture: But we ought always to thank God for you, brothers loved by the Lord, because from the beginning God chose you to be saved through the sanctifying work of the Spirit and through belief in the truth. He called you to this through our gospel, that you might share in the glory of our Lord Jesus Christ. So then, brothers, stand firm and hold to the teachings we passed on to you, whether by word of mouth or by letter. (2 Thessalonians 2:13–15)

Facing today's difficult world is sometimes frightening. It seems to get harder and harder to go out and keep the teachings of God, when so many disobey or ignore God's Word. How are we supposed to cope?

Paul was constantly being challenged by his converts. He fought fervently to ensure that the churches he established, by God's power, were not swayed by false teachings. He was always writing letters to encourage the church to grasp hold of the eternal hope through Jesus Christ. Most of all Paul wanted his church to stand firm in the faith, so they would not or could not be deterred from God's Word of truth.

We all have to face the world and we need to be willing to stand firm on what we believe. If we truly have faith in God, in Jesus' saving blood, and in the eternal hope of God's Kingdom, then we can face each day with the boldness of the Spirit to face whatever the world throws at us.

September 21

"Free Will—Gift or Curse?"

Scripture: For you know what instructions we gave you by the authority of the Lord Jesus. It is God's will that you should be sanctified: that you should avoid sexual immorality; that each of you should learn to control his own body in a way that is holy and honorable, 5not in passionate lust like the heathen, who do not know God; and that in this matter no one should wrong his brother or take advantage of him. The Lord will punish men for all such sins, as we have already told you and warned you. For God did not call us to be impure, but to live a holy life. Therefore, he who rejects this instruction does not reject man but God, who gives you his Holy Spirit. (1 Thessalonians 4:2–8)

"One of God's greatest gifts is free will," said the fallen angel in the movie "City of Angels."

What a statement! It really impacted my spirit. True enough free will is a great gift, but with the gift of free choice comes good ones and bad ones and the consequences that go along with them. Personally, my free will sometimes leads me down the path of misconduct. My intent is not to be tempted, but before I know it there I am in the wrong place at the wrong time.

I struggle with my free will constantly. I seek God for guidance, but He already knows my choice and leaves me to my own device. I do wrong, when He wants me to do right. It challenges me, so God in His wisdom has instilled in me His Holy Spirit to help me in those weak moments.

I thank God for His word, His wisdom, His Spirit, and the ability to come to Him when I choose wrong.

____

____

____

September 22

"True Repentance"

Scripture: While Ezra was praying and confessing, weeping and throwing himself down before the house of God, a large crowd of Israelites—men, women and children—gathered around him. They too wept bitterly. Then Shecaniah son of Jehiel, one of the descendants of Elam, said to Ezra, "We have been unfaithful to our God by marrying foreign women from the peoples around us. But in spite of this, there is still hope for Israel. Now let us make a covenant before our God to send away all these women and their children, in accordance with the counsel of my lord and of those who fear the commands of our God. Let it be done according to the Law. Rise up; this matter is in your hands. We will support you, so take courage and do it." (Ezra 10:1–4)

My wife and I have four children. Our house, like many, is always very active. Our children love each other, but it is not uncommon for one or more of them to tease or pick on the others. My wife and I issue orders for them to respect and treat each other as they want to be treated, but to no avail. They still continue to prod, tease, and fight. These actions greatly disappoint my wife and me. It breaks our hearts that they will not respect our wishes.

God must feel the same way when we disobey His will. We know He wants the best for us, yet we disregard His rules and disappoint Him with our actions. Sin is a horrible thing. It is a destroyer of lives and needs to be taken with great seriousness. We shouldn't take God's grace and mercy for granted by running to Him begging for forgiveness without humility and without true repentance. We need to fall on our faces knowing the serious dishonor we have brought to God, seek His forgiveness, and repent. We need to truly repent and we will want to put our sin away once and for all.

September 23

"Love as Christ Loved"

Scripture: Therefore, as God's chosen people, holy and dearly loved, clothe yourselves with compassion, kindness, humility, gentleness and patience. Bear with each other and forgive whatever grievances you may have against one another. Forgive as the Lord forgave you. And over all these virtues put on love, which binds them all together in perfect unity. (Colossians 3:12–14)

October 2nd is the date that my wife and I celebrate our anniversary. We have learned to really love each other over the years. When we first got married, we loved each other, but we didn't L-O-V-E each other as we do today. Maybe it's the years of trials, tribulations, joy, and children that have expanded our love, but one thing is for sure it could not have been done without Christ.

When He is Lord of our lives, Christ makes all things new. He takes the old desires and replaces them with Godly desires. He takes the lustful love of youth and makes it an enduring love of faith, trust, and respect. Therefore, husbands, if you want to love your wives like never before, let Christ take over. He will instill an attitude of compassion, kindness, humility, gentleness, and patience in you necessary to develop true love that we all seek. He will instill a love that will last throughout the ages into eternity.

September 24

"With God It Happens"

Scripture: When word came to Sanballat, Tobiah, Geshem the Arab and the rest of our enemies that I had rebuilt the wall and not a gap was left in it—though up to that time I had not set the doors in the gates—Sanballat and Geshem sent me this message: "Come, let us meet together in one of the villages on the plain of Ono." They were scheming to harm me; so I sent messengers to them with this reply: "I am carrying on a great project and cannot go down. Why should the work stop while I leave it and go down to you?" Four times they sent me the same message, and each time I gave them the same answer. (Nehemiah 6:1–4)

They say, "It will never be done" or "You will never accomplish that." Have you ever been involved in a project that received such responses and ridicule? Has a project you worked on ever failed to face criticism and comments of, "I told you so"? If you have been the recipient of such comments then you have probably worked on a project without seeking God's direction and guidance.

I personally have faced the disgrace and humiliation of failure. I had a business outside of God's direction and it failed. It caused me to face self-doubt, comments of being a failure, and the rejection of my peers. It cost me every material possession I had and yet it gained me all. God used the circumstance to teach me humility, perseverance, and reliance. He showed me that if I rely on Him all things are possible.

Losing all of the things I had worked for was tough, but it allowed me to see what God can do with desperation. He took a negative and made it a positive. He renewed what was lost with something better. The key is when God is in something nothing can put it down. No one or no circumstance can prevent it, because God glorifies His Kingdom by accomplishing the impossible and, if He is in it, it will not fail.

September 25

"In God's Service"

Scripture: If you have any encouragement from being united with Christ, if any comfort from his love, if any fellowship with the Spirit, if any tenderness and compassion, then make my joy complete by being like-minded, having the same love, being one in spirit and purpose. 3Do nothing out of selfish ambition or vain conceit, but in humility consider others better than yourselves. Each of you should look not only to your own interests, but also to the interests of others. (Philippians 2:1–4)

My oldest son has been fortunate to go on two mission trips. Both trips were to Mexico just across the border from Texas. The trips were dedicated to the building of wells, clinics, churches, and houses. He said it was a great deal of work in scorching heat, but more than the climate affected my son.

He never talked much about his experience, but it showed in his attitude. You could tell that something lasting and of great significance had happened to him. He seemed to grasp the principle of serving others and the blessings of joy that accompanies it.

Christ set an example for each and every one of us to serve others. We are not to do it out of our own selfishness, but rather out of humility. I know from experience what the impact of serving has had on my life and now it has impacted my son as well, in God's service.

September 26

"My Hero"

Scripture: Then Esther sent this reply to Mordecai: "Go and gather together all the Jews of Susa and fast for me. Do not eat or drink for three days, night or day. My maids and I will do the same. And then, though it is against the law, I will go in to see the king. If I must die, I am willing to die." So Mordecai went away and did as Esther told him. (Esther 4:15–17)

I love the movies. I especially love the ones with intrigue, suspense, and conspiracy. I recently watched the movie "Conspiracy Theory". The story told about a special agent who was brainwashed to assassinate an important government official. He did the job as he was programmed, but he somehow knew it was not the thing to do and finally figured the scheme was a government controlled conspiracy. Needless to say, the whole plot was exposed by the brainwashed agent and a beautiful girl who was the daughter of the assassinated official. It was exciting and thrilling, which is exactly what makes the movie interesting. The movie in this case had a hero and heroine.

I feel the same way about the stories in the Old Testament. One of my favorites is the story of Esther and Mordecai, heroine and hero of the story. The thing I like most is how God uses individuals to accomplish his purpose. God orchestrates the plot and the theme, positioning individuals to trust in Him. Through that trust, He does His good work and in this story of Esther and Mordecai He does just that.

I love a great movie and a great story, but most of all I love God. He is definitely my hero.

September 27

"Worldly Competition"

Scripture: Children, obey your parents because you belong to the Lord, for this is the right thing to do. "Honor your father and mother." This is the first of the Ten Commandments that ends with a promise. And this is the promise: If you honor your father and mother, "you will live a long life, full of blessing." (Ephesians 6:1–3)

If you are a parent you know that there is a lot of competition for our children's attention. Each of them is influenced by television, school, sports, and friends. Some of these influences are very positive and some are not. It is up to us to make sure our children have the right balance. The right balance means to have social and teaching influences that counter the worldly impact on their lives. The best way to accomplish this is to add church as one of their major activities. This influence will help them see the importance of God's impact on every aspect of their lives.

We have talked with our children over the years about God and His blessings. We have shared His commandments, especially the one about honoring parents. Not that we were seeking to orchestrate some type of grand scheme, but that they would understand obedience to God and the rewards that come from that obedience.

Children look for self-satisfaction. They want to know that following rules have consequences some good and some not, and with God those consequences are good. His commandments always have consequences, therefore it makes it easier for children to understand them and this will nullify some of the negative influences and the worldly competition in their lives.

September 28

"Atrocities"

Scripture: Job stood up and tore his robe in grief. Then he shaved his head and fell to the ground before God. He said, "I came naked from my mother's womb, and I will be stripped of everything when I die. The LORD gave me everything I had, and the LORD has taken it away. Praise the name of the LORD!" (Job 1:20–21)

There are many atrocities that occur all over the world. People are being persecuted, enslaved, and even destroyed. We see children singling out other children because they are different and even killing them because of this difference.

It makes me wonder about the acts of men being so cruel and vile against others. It also makes me wonder how God allows these atrocities to happen and why he takes no action in these matters. Why do some people stand and curse God for His lack of action and yet others praise Him in spite of these continued acts.

One of the best lessons to help us understand God better is the story of Job. Job was persecuted in front of his community and friends by the devil. He lost his family, his wealth, and even had his faith challenged. Even though he faced these horrific circumstances, he remained steadfast. Job loved God; therefore, he too sought answers to the why's that were occurring in his life. How could God allow this to happen? In spite of it all Job stayed focused on the only possession he had left, his faith. He praised and worshiped God continually in spite of his plight and in the end God blessed Job even more richly than before.

When we see or experience these atrocities in our own lives or watch them in others, we must remember to praise God and in doing so, God will renew our strength and further our understanding.

September 29

"Sin versus Spirit"

Scripture: But when the Holy Spirit controls our lives, he will produce this kind of fruit in us: love, joy, peace, patience, kindness, goodness, faithfulness, gentleness, and self-control. Here there is no conflict with the law. (Galatians 5:22–23)

I love to read about the fruits of the Spirit in Galatians. This is almost like a tally sheet for me. I read about the acts of the sinful nature and then the fruits of the Spirit; and then cross each of those sinful acts off as they are replaced by God's spiritual fruit in my life. It is great to monitor the progress I have made over the years replacing good for evil.

It is miraculous how God can take some people and give them an immediate transformation from their sinful acts, but as for me, I have struggled against sin all my life. I have to work on it constantly and work specifically to replace my sin with God's spiritual fruit. It has been a painstaking journey, but thanks to God He has supplied me with encouragement and hope. Someday soon He will have sufficiently supplied me with enough "spiritual fruit" that there will be no more room for the sinful nature to ever bother me again. Praise God for His faithfulness, His mercy, and His grace to see this to completion.

September 30

"Never Late"

Scripture: In times of trouble, may the LORD respond to your cry. May the God of Israel keep you safe from all harm. May he send you help from his sanctuary and strengthen you from Jerusalem. May he remember all your gifts and look favorably on your burnt offerings. (Psalm 20:1–3)

Several years ago my family and I struggled financially. I made some foolish decisions and mistakes in my business matters and experienced years of hardship, both financial and mental. It seemed that the harder I tried to rectify the situation the worse it got. During this time I was in continual petition to God for help yet it seemed nothing was improving. I was totally destroyed. My life as I knew it was over, my self-esteem was crushed, and my whole life was a failure. Even though God was there and I felt His presence, I felt like it was too late for Him to help me.

One night in a sound sleep God placed a Scripture in my spirit. It was Psalm 20. The next morning the Scripture was so foremost on my mind I could hardly get to the passage quick enough. Finally, I had my Bible open and read the Psalm. It was like Christmas morning when the anticipation of a child is at a fever pitch. I read the passage. I read it again and let the words flow over me like a wave. It was in that moment I knew everything would be okay. God was there as my rescuer and He would somehow straighten out the mess. God may not accomplish this in our time, but He is never late. He did answer my prayer.

Praise God who hears our prayers and answers our calls.

October

October 1

"Godly Wisdom"

Scripture: Blessed is the man who finds wisdom, the man who gains understanding,

for she is more profitable than silver and yields better returns than gold. She is more precious than rubies; nothing you desire can compare with her. Long life is in her right hand; in her left hand are riches and honor. Her ways are pleasant ways, and all her paths are peace. She is a tree of life to those who embrace her; those who lay hold of her will be blessed. . (Proverbs 3:13–18)

I have always been intrigued by the wisdom of my elders. Even though I have reached middle age, I am still in awe of those who have accumulated wisdom and understanding over many years. I am certain God's wisdom comes to us at different ages. My oldest son, compared to his years, is extremely wise. The main portion of his wisdom has come from being open to God and allowing God to fill him with a unique perspective and discernment. The rest, I believe, has come from his being exposed to my mistakes. I have never been afraid to share my failures and shortcomings. And knowing him, I am sure he has cataloged those discussions in his memory for future reference.

Parents don't be afraid to talk to your children. Share the experiences of your life, even the ones you are not proud of and let them know God is wiser than any man, any situation, and any mistake.

I am extremely proud of my son's knowledge and wisdom. I know God will bless him throughout his life. I hope and pray his brothers and sister will share in this same legacy—Godly wisdom.

___

___

___

October 2

"Spiritual Touch"

Scripture: Follow the way of love and eagerly desire spiritual gifts, especially the gift of prophecy. For anyone who speaks in a tongue does not speak to men but to God. Indeed, no one understands him; he utters mysteries with his spirit. But everyone who prophesies speaks to men for their strengthening, encouragement and comfort. (1 Corinthians 14:1–3)

I had a dear friend who taught me much about the Lord. He exposed me to many spiritual gifts and through my being exposed to them, he showed me how God uses those gifts for His purpose. He himself lived in the Lord and the Lord in him. God gave him these gifts to help others. In my circumstance, my friend was helping me through a very difficult, distressed business. He used his gift of prophecy to share with me God's outcome, not only for the business, but for my life. He shared the gift of tongues through the baptism of the Holy Spirit.

Even though my friend has gone to be with the Lord, his spirit lives on. He has continued to touch my life on countless occasions as I have drawn upon the cherished memories of his encouragement, praise to God, and the teaching of the Spirit he imparted in me.

God wants each and every one of us to gain spiritual gifts. He wants us to use those gifts to edify the church and not us. Seek and pray for those gifts, use them wisely and appropriately, and always praise the one who graciously gave them to you.

October 3

"Seasons of Life"

Scripture: There is a time for everything, a season for every activity under heaven: a time to be born and a time to die, time to plant and a time to uproot, a time to kill and a time to heal, time to tear down and a time to build, a time to weep and a time to laugh, time to mourn and a time to dance, a time to scatter stones and a time to gather them, time to embrace and a time to refrain, a time to search and a time to give up, time to keep and a time to throw away, a time to tear and a time to mend, time to be silent and a time to speak, a time to love and a time to hate, time for war and a time for peace. (Ecclesiastes 3:1–8)

The book of Ecclesiastes always reminds me of a song popular during my teenage years. When I first heard it, I liked it, but I did not know that it came from the Bible. (I probably wasn't the only teenager during that period to not know that fact.) The song came at a very pertinent time as we saw body counts from Vietnam posted everyday on TV and we watched riots in the streets of America. It seemed very evident that the writer of the song had captured the very meaning of what was occurring during this unsettled period. The song was "Turn, Turn, Turn" by the Byrds. The song brought reality to those of us who faced the draft knowing that life could be a fleeting moment. It helped us realize that it may be our time to die if we were sent to Vietnam and that facing uncertainties was part of the seasons of life.

Today, I know that the song was inspired from Ecclesiastes. I have experienced many seasons in life and realize that there is a time for everything. I know that as life moves forward there will be many more uncertainties. But now, unlike then, I know my God is there to see me through. He is there to help me through that time, that place, and that circumstance.

I don't know what season of life you are in, but I know that God makes every season worth living, when you accept Him as Lord and Savior and trust Him with every part of your life.

October 4

"Devil's List"

Scripture: No, in all these things we are more than conquerors through him who loved us. For I am convinced that neither death nor life, neither angels nor demons, neither the present nor the future, nor any powers, neither height nor depth, nor anything else in all creation, will be able to separate us from the love of God that is in Christ Jesus our Lord. (Romans 8:37–39)

Sometimes when I wake very early in the morning, just before I get out of bed, my mind starts projecting the activities of the day ahead. This is the time that the devil tries to rush in and confuse the issues. The devil tries to challenge each and everything I do including my motives behind them. He tries to expose my failures and shortcomings. He tries to terrify me with things that have not yet happened and cause me to fear the unknown. Most of all, he tries to challenge my love for God and my faith. He knows he can manipulate my doubts to be a good provider, father, and husband in a busy world by asking me "Where is your time for God? Where is your time for service? How could God love someone like you?"

The good news is, as soon as my conscience awakens to the new day and I get downstairs to my Bible and God's Word, the devil flees. The devil knows he is no match for the Lord of Lords and King of Kings. He realizes he can do nothing to separate me from my God, my faith, and my love for my Lord Jesus.

The Devil always has a list. He wants us to feel unloved, unwelcome and separated from God, but hold fast and stay the course—God will see you through.

____

____

____

October 5

"Love Taught"

Scripture: How beautiful you are, my darling! Oh, how beautiful! Your eyes are doves. How handsome you are, my lover! Oh, how charming! . . . (Song of Solomon 1:15–16)

In 1999 my wife and I were in the middle of building a new home. Our lives were very busy with work, children, and then on top of that we were doing most of the work on our house ourselves. During that period, we made it a point to have a standing date with one another, which was normally intertwined with doing some selection for the house, but which was a time when we could at least spend time together. We would walk, talk, and dream. We would discuss our past and our future. We would have lunch and enjoy each other's company.

God wants us to have someone to love and to share our lives with. He shows us this in His love for us and He demonstrated that love through the sacrificing of His Son, Jesus. He loves us unconditionally. He shows and teaches us that love by example, therefore, love your wife or husband the same way God loves you. Love him or her unconditionally, respectfully, and most of all forever.

October 6

"Your Call"

Scripture: As he neared Damascus on his journey, suddenly a light from heaven flashed around him. He fell to the ground and heard a voice say to him, "Saul, Saul, why do you persecute me?" "Who are you, Lord?" Saul asked. "I am Jesus, whom you are persecuting," he replied. "Now get up and go into the city, and you will be told what you must do." (Acts 9:3–6)

Do you remember when Jesus called you into God's family? Many people (including myself) share the story of experiencing a feeling of overwhelming guilt and sorrow which was so troubling that it became a burden too heavy to carry and too much to bear. We were touched one day by some music or message and we knew Jesus was calling. Opposite that however, are people who share a "Saul" experience. They were struck to their knees in a life-altering event and Jesus converted them immediately from their sinful life to a life in Jesus.

The key is, no matter whether God pulls on your heart strings over a period of time or changes you as fast as lightning strikes, a life changed for Jesus is the result. Make Him the Lord of your life today, because no one knows when life will end. Today is the day to decide—it's your call.

October 7

"SEND ME"

Scripture: Then I heard the voice of the Lord saying, "Whom shall I send? And who will go for us?" I said, "Here am I. Send me!" (Isaiah 6:8)

What is God's purpose for your life? Have you ever wondered this? I know I have. As a matter of fact, I remember having many discussions with a brother in Christ about this very thing. As we pondered this age-old question for ourselves, we could not come up with a complete and accurate answer. The only thing we could derive from our search was that God's purpose would be revealed to us in God's time, with God's reasoning, and with God in full control. With that in mind, we realized that our faith had to be strong, our resolve for God steady, and our willingness to readily respond to God fervent. We knew that walking with God and waiting for Him to reveal His purpose would be a true and wonderful adventure. We decided not to burden ourselves with the what, the where, and the why, but instead to just be excited about the adventure.

Now, several years later, I have seen more and more of God's purpose for my life unfold and with what I have seen I am willing to stand up and say " Here I am Lord, send me."

October 8

"Count On Jesus"

Scripture: Another of his disciples, Andrew, Simon Peter's brother, spoke up, "Here is a boy with five small barley loaves and two small fish, but how far will they go among so many?" Jesus said, "Have the people sit down." There was plenty of grass in that place, and the men sat down, about five thousand of them. Jesus then took the loaves, gave thanks, and distributed to those who were seated as much as they wanted. He did the same with the fish. When they had all had enough to eat, he said to his disciples, "Gather the pieces that are left over. Let nothing be wasted." So they gathered them and filled twelve baskets with the pieces of the five barley loaves left over by those who had eaten. (John 6:8–13)

Over the years I have faced many challenging situations that have tasked my resources financially, physically, and emotionally. Facing such situations tended to make me more of a pessimist than an optimist. I tended to see only limitations, road blocks, and insurmountable odds. I had no earthly idea how to face such circumstances let alone overcome them.

Today, I face a similar dilemma that seems to be totally overwhelming me. My job is on the fast track, I am trying to build a new home with my own two hands, I still face the demands of being a father and husband—you get the picture. The odds are against me and I have a sinking feeling. I am sure that Phillip felt the same way when Jesus asked him, "Where shall we buy bread to feed the five thousand?" He had to feel the same way I do: no time, not enough money, and a monumental task. Well Jesus, you worked things out for Phillip, so I trust you will do it for me now.

We will all continue to face overwhelming odds and will not always know what to do, but we must count on Jesus to see us through. Come on Jesus, I am counting on you!

October 9

"The Drought"

Scripture: "But blessed is the man who trusts in the LORD, whose confidence is in him.

He will be like a tree planted by the water that sends out its roots by the stream. It does not fear when heat comes; its leaves are always green. It has no worries in a year of drought and never fails to bear fruit." (Jeremiah 17:7–8)

This summer has been extremely dry. The meteorologist has declared it one of the worst droughts in the last 15–20 years. It has been so dry that fires have broken out everywhere, the water table has been significantly down causing well problems, and if we don't get precipitation in large doses, it could be devastating for the future.

Our lives with God are the same way. If we do not plant ourselves deeply and firmly in God's rich soil and if we face a prolonged period of drought, we could wither and die. It is our responsibility to keep well-rooted to God, to draw from His living waters, and to trust completely that even if tested by fire we will stand.

Facing droughts in our lives is certain, but don't let it be a drought from God. Get close to Him, stay close to Him, and refresh yourself with the everlasting water of life.

October 10

"Conversational Witness"

Scripture: While a large crowd was gathering and people were coming to Jesus from town after town, he told this parable: "A farmer went out to sow his seed. As he was scattering the seed, some fell along the path; it was trampled on, and the birds of the air ate it up. Some fell on rock, and when it came up, the plants withered because they had no moisture. Other seed fell among thorns, which grew up with it and choked the plants. Still other seed fell on good soil. It came up and yielded a crop, a hundred times more than was sown." (Luke 8:4–8)

In the office the other day a coworker asked me a question about her grandmother or at least that is what I thought until I replayed the question in my mind afterwards. Her question started, "Because of your faith, what would you do?" She was dealing with a quality of life issue involving her grandmother and had some feelings of guilt and remorse about putting her grandmother in a nursing home and she wanted to get my opinion.

We had spoken several times previously, but had only had minor discussions about faith and religion. She knew from those discussions that I was active in church and that I sang in a men's chorus, but most of our discussions had centered on family. I had never given my comments of faith and service much thought, but evidently they had stayed with her and at least on this occasion she felt comfortable enough to focus on faith more than family.

We never know when, where, or how our conversations may go, so we must weave our witness within them, because they may bear fruit just when we least expect it.

October 11

"God's Hope"

Scripture: I remember my affliction and my wandering, bitterness and the gall. I well remember them, my soul is downcast within me. Yet this I call to mind and therefore I have hope: Because of the Lord's great love we are not consumed, for his compassions never fail. 23They are new every morning; great is your faithfulness. I say to myself, "The Lord is my portion; therefore I will wait for him." (Lamentations 3:19–24)

There are people all over the world who face death and destruction everyday of their lives. There are countless examples of this in the news everyday. The old Soviet Union, through its break up has and is going through civil unrest. Kosovo is divided between Christians and Muslims fighting in the streets. Israel is faced with a constant threat of car bombs and bus explosions from their Palestinian neighbors. Even the U.S. population faces acts of terror that could occur at any time and any place. People all over the world have been persecuted, pillaged, and plundered. They face an uncertain world in an uncertain time and it is a horrific way to live.

Where is their hope?

As a Christian I have counted on the hope that comes from God. I have never had to face some of the atrocities that some in the world have had to face; I have never had to face death, fear, famine or persecution, but I do know God and trust in His salvation. I believe in God's hope, therefore, I can face today and tomorrow with confidence and a sense of peace. Today may be my last day, my last breath, the last time I see my family yet I know I can face it with God's hope.

October 12

"GOD'S HOUSE"

Scripture: "Have faith in God," Jesus answered. "I tell you the truth, if anyone says to this mountain, 'Go, throw yourself into the sea,' and does not doubt in his heart but believes that what he says will happen, it will be done for him." (Mark 11:22–23)

Let me tell you a story. A few years ago, my wife and I wanted to build a new house. Though this is what we wanted, we faced some huge issues. I had destroyed our finances and credit through a failed business venture. We had to relinquish our old home to the bank for outstanding debt and we were forced to rent a two bedroom condo for our family of six. It wasn't what we wanted and we believed in our hearts it was not what God wanted either.

We had lived there for about a year when my spirit became unsettled. God was working on me especially to get better and to do better for my family, so he placed in my spirit the desire to build a new home. I wondered how that would be possible but my wife and I felt compelled to try so we started looking for a lot, applied for a mortgage, and trusted God. We truly believed God was in our plans and that He would help make them happen. Shortly thereafter we were approved for a mortgage and found the lot of our dreams. All that was left to get was a construction loan. Even though we had a mortgage, a construction loan was tending to be more difficult.

We tried several banks with no positive results, but we still stood on faith. The next bank was different. The loan officer told me to have faith, to pray, and believe. One day the loan officer called and said, "Pray hard today," and that he would do the same as he was presenting our loan application to the loan committee. When I hung up the phone, my heart leaped because I just knew God would make it happen. Thirty days later it happened—all we needed was patience and faith in God.

Now we live in the house of our dreams and inscribed in the foundation is our commitment "As for me and my house we trust in God." This is God's house, but He is gracious enough to allow us to live here. Thank you Lord!

October 13

"The Lord Is There"

Scripture: "The distance all around will be 18,000 cubits. "And the name of the city from that time on will be: THE LORD IS THERE." (Ezekiel 48:35)

The last pages in the book of Ezekiel describe the vision God had given him of the temple. They describe the temple in great detail. The size, the gates, the altar, and the priest room down to every square cubit were revealed to Ezekiel. Ezekiel even received a vision of the city for the temple. Again in great detail, the city was described even down to the new name for which it would be known:

"THE LORD IS THERE."

This name would be inscribed on the gates and it was decreed to be that name forever.

Reading this passage in Ezekiel opened my mind to one major thought: My life, my word, and my deeds need to express the same sentiment as the name of the city:

"THE LORD IS THERE."

My hope and prayer is that people can see this same sign as they approach what is within me.

October 14

"Divorce"

Scripture: Jesus replied, "Moses permitted you to divorce your wives because your hearts were hard. But it was not this way from the beginning. I tell you that anyone who divorces his wife, except for marital unfaithfulness, and marries another woman commits adultery." (Matthew 19:8–9)

Many years ago I went through a divorce. I had a great struggle with the consequences of my action as it was presented in the Bible. I couldn't face the fact that I had sinned against my God who created the institution of marriage. It became such a burden that I sought counsel from a pastor who had been through a divorce. His circumstances were different from mine, but nonetheless he surely dealt with the same moral dilemma as I did.

I asked him if there was any Scripture to deal with this sin that would put my mind at ease. I guess what I really wanted was to find the proverbial "loophole" to justify what I had done. I wanted something that would allow the divorce and make it alright in the eyes of God. Much to my dismay, I found nothing. There were no scriptures to bail me out—just ones that condemned.

I did divorce and the issue haunted me until I decided to do one thing. I decided to go to the one who created the Scripture—God. I prayed fervently for forgiveness and for the answers I sought. God granted both. I felt the Spirit of God ease my concern and put a joy in my heart. I knew that He accepted my plea and forgave me. God gave me confirmation of His forgiveness by putting a new woman in my life and blessed me with four children.

It became obvious from that point on that I must work to follow the scriptures and to live by them day by day, but when I am faced with insurmountable sin, I must seek God. God has forgiven adulterers, murderers, and sins of all kinds, so He will surely forgive yours and mine.

October 15

"Tithing"

Scripture: "Bring the whole tithe into the storehouse, that there may be food in my house. Test me in this," says the Lord Almighty," and see if I will not throw open the floodgates of heaven and pour out so much blessing that you will not have room enough for it. (Malachi 3:10)

Where do you stand on tithing? Are you faithful with your tithe? Do you look forward to giving your tithe?

It seems people are tithing less these days due to a few bad apples that have ruined the whole bushel. Many people I have spoken to regarding tithing have a certain degree of mistrust when it comes to paying tithes. There have been several preachers and evangelists who have misappropriated funds and have not used them to glorify God. This misconduct has led to mistrust causing people to refuse or lessen their tithe.

My mother taught me a valuable lessen in regard to tithing. She said, "It is not for us to judge the use of the tithe—it is just ours to give. Those who receive it will have to answer for its use." I have never forgotten her comment. So now, when God lays on my heart to give, I give without concern. This allows me to get the full blessing and joy that comes from tithing.

October 16

"Forgive Me!"

Scripture: The more the priests increased, the more they sinned against me; they exchanged their Glory for something disgraceful. (Hosea 4:7)

Forgive me? These are two pretty simple words, but they are sometimes the most difficult to say.

I am sure, if you are like me, that you have done wrong to someone someplace who you need to ask for forgiveness from. I remember using some money given to me once as an investment for hiring an attorney. I diverted the money and used it for an unintended purpose. I knew it was wrong, because the money was given to me in good faith to be placed toward attorney fees and the only way to correct the wrong was to confess, to ask for forgiveness, and to repent my transgression. I needed to do this with God, but equally important was to correct the matter with the person who had given me the money. It was one of the most difficult things I ever had to do. The results were outstanding. The person forgave me and it released me from the burden of guilt and gave me true freedom and relief.

When we sin against God and others, it is a great burden. It eats at us through our conscience and we experience the conviction of the Holy Spirit until we get rid of it. The devil will try to keep it before us showing us how unworthy we are to be in God's family, but we don't have to let that happen. At the first sign of a troubled spirit, we must seek God. He will show us what needs to be corrected. God will grant us forgiveness, but we must not stop short. We must seek out the person whom we have wronged and ask for his or her forgiveness as well. God will accept our confession and graciously bestow a blessing upon us of full pardon and true freedom.

October 17

"Prophetic Salvation"

Scripture: "And I will pour out on the house of David and the inhabitants of Jerusalem a spirit of grace and supplication. They will look on me, the one they have pierced, and they will mourn for him as one mourns for an only child, and grieve bitterly for him as one grieves for a firstborn son. (Zechariah 12:10)

I have often wondered how prophets foretold Jesus coming and the salvation he was to bring to all people. For the first time, I read and understood prophecy that was given to Israel regarding the coming of the Messiah. This revelation came as I read Zechariah chapter 12, verses 10–14, which tell of how Jesus would be pierced and the weeping that will occur and still occurs today.

God has always worked in the lives of His people to ensure their salvation. He worked through prophets and then through His Son, Jesus. He wants us all to know Him and His mercy, so that we can have eternal life and truly understand all mysteries, which we have wondered about so long.

October 18

"Autumn's Splendor"

Scripture: Be glad, O people of Zion, rejoice in the LORD your God, for he has given you the autumn rains in righteousness. He sends you abundant showers, both autumn and spring rains, as before. The threshing floors will be filled with grain; the vats will overflow with new wine and oil. (Joel 2:23–24)

Autumn is a great time of year. Even though we know winter is just around the corner, it is still a wonderfully beautiful time. The leaves are in their most brilliant colors, the sky is the deepest blue and seems to go forever, the harvest grains are yellow gold, and the fall colors are spectacular. I rejoice in the Lord for providing such a colorful time.

Autumn reminds me of life itself. We struggle to grow and mature in the Lord, we face the stormy spring rains, we face the searing heat and drought of summer, and then, in the fall of our lives, we show our true color.

God has a miraculous way of knitting everything together. He has a lesson to teach us in everything He does. He shows us His glory in every way. So today when you see the beauty in God's land, rejoice for He is good.

October 19

"God's Makes Everything Possible"

Scripture: From this day on, from this twenty-fourth day of the ninth month, give careful thought to the day when the foundation of the LORD's temple was laid. Give careful thought: Is there yet any seed left in the barn? Until now, the vine and the fig tree, the pomegranate and the olive tree have not borne fruit.

"From this day on I will bless you." (Haggai 2:18–19)

I have been building a new house for many months and doing most of the work myself. It seems as the project draws closer to the end my strength and patience is wearing thin. All that has yet to be accomplished is almost totally overwhelming. It seems virtually impossible.

The house happening at all is only because of God. He wanted it. He orchestrated the lot, the financing, and my skill to see it to completion. I know with Him all things are possible. So when I feel weak and incapable of continuing, God steps in. He renews my strength to get me through. God has shown me that all I need to do is try and He will make things come together.

To God be the glory!

October 20

"Stuff More Stuff"

Scripture: Woe to you who are complacent in Zion, to you who feel secure on Mount Samaria, notable men of the foremost nation, whom the people of Israel come! Go to Calneh and look at it; from there to great Hamath, then go down to Gath in Philistia. they better off than your two kingdoms? their land larger than yours? You put off the evil day bring near a reign of terror. You lie on beds inlaid with ivory lounge on your couches. dine on choice lambs fattened calves. You strum away on your harps like David improvise on musical instruments. You drink wine by the bowlful use the finest lotions, you do not grieve over the ruin of Joseph. Therefore you will be among the first to go into exile; feasting and lounging will end. (Amos 6:1–7)

Our land and nation is very bountiful. We seem to have plenty of everything and yet we want more. The prevailing attitude is to have stuff and lots of it.

I, too, am the same way. I want the latest TV, stereo, car, and furnishings. I want a lot of money and power or a least I think I do. As I achieve these different levels of "stuff," I become more complacent in my walk with God. God is the one who provides these blessings and yet as blessings come my way I tend to forget from whom they come. My service to God lessens, my tithes get smaller, and I start taking the Lord for granted.

When this happens I pray:

"I recognize my complacency Lord, forgive me and be merciful to me, so I can remain in your presence." In Jesus' name, Amen

October 21

"Towards the Future"

Scripture: At that time I will gather you; at that time I will bring you home. I will give you honor and praise all the peoples of the earth I restore your fortunes your very eyes," the LORD (Zephaniah 3:20)

Everyone, to some degree, would like to know his or her future or at least the good parts. The future offers some fear, however. We are facing the unknown, which could bring hardships and trials too horrible to speak of, let alone live through. Yet the future also holds hope. We do not know what is before us; therefore, it will be better tomorrow. If we knew what good days lied ahead, then we would live each day to get to the good ones.

God's people have that hope. We know what lies ahead and can move toward the future living each day to the fullest. God promises an eternal Kingdom with no sorrow, no pain, no oppressors, no suffering, and no fear. What a glorious future we have before us.

October 22

"Golden Rule"

Scripture: "The day of the LORD is near all nations. You have done, it will be done to you; deeds will return upon your own head." (Obadiah 1:15)

The Golden Rule: "Do unto others as you would have others do unto you." It is a great rule and a rule that each one of us needs to take to heart. Not as the world sees it and twists it, but as God intended. The world sees it as an opportunity for revenge and a way to get even. Instead of putting the other person first they put themselves first, which is the not what the rule says. God's intention was to direct us to do good and kind acts for one another.

Keep this rule in mind the next time someone cuts you off in traffic or someone is rude to you in the grocery line. Just smile and be kind. You will find that your act is contagious and others will do the same.

October 23

"Attitude Adjustment"

Scripture: I heard and my heart pounded, my lips quivered at the sound; decay crept into my bones, and my legs trembled. I will wait patiently for the day of calamity come on the nation invading us. Though the fig tree does not bud and there are no grapes on the vines, the olive crop fails and the fields produce no food, though there are no sheep in the pen and no cattle in the stalls, yet I will rejoice in the LORD, I will be joyful in God my Savior. (Habakkuk 3:16–18)

What is your attitude? In the face of trial and tribulation, stress and distress, turmoil and chaos, and overall dismay, what is your attitude? Can you rejoice in all circumstances? Are you able to rejoice in all situations both good and bad?

If you can't, you need an attitude adjustment. This adjustment only comes from knowing the Lord. He alone can help you face these situations with a joyful heart. God brings great peace, removes all fear, and puts order to chaos. He knows each circumstance and can guide and direct your thoughts and actions to get you through. All you need to do is trust in Him.

Rejoice and be contented this day knowing that God is by your side.

October 24

"Grateful Heart"

Scripture: "When my life was ebbing away, I remembered you, LORD, my prayer rose to you, your holy temple." (Jonah 2:7)

There was a time in my life when I faced a horrible ordeal. I was losing my business and I thought God was leading me only to find my life falling apart around me. How could this business that God was a part of fall apart? I wondered. I had spent three years trying to build that business. I had worked hard and it seemed that everything was going my way. I felt I couldn't do anything wrong.

The key word is I. I relied on my own wisdom and knowledge only to wake up one day to financial turmoil. I struggled, but the ordeal got worse. I felt I had been swallowed up and didn't have a hope in the world.

One weekend my spirit was greatly disturbed and I felt that something or someone was trying to get my attention. Then it hit me: it was God. God was the one who was calling me. He showed me how I had messed everything up by not putting Him first. He told me that there would still be hurt and sorrow, but that He would be there through it and that He would make everything alright. I prayed fervently from that day on, primarily thanking God for not abandoning me and for not shoving me out to sink in my own trouble. He to this day has not forsaken me. My business is gone, but He is still there each and everyday.

October 25

"True Salvation"

Scripture: "You are the salt of the earth. But if the salt loses its saltiness, how can it be made salty again? It is no longer good for anything, except to be thrown out and trampled by men. "You are the light of the world. A city on a hill cannot be hidden.Neither do people light a lamp and put it under a bowl. Instead they put it on its stand, and it gives light to everyone in the house. (Matthew 5:13–15)

My walk as a Christian has had its ups and downs. I was saved and baptized at 8, but I did not have a church home and so I drifted from the faith. As a matter of fact, I stayed away from the faith for many years. It wasn't until my life became burdened with tragedies that I returned and even then it was not full dedication.

It actually took a series of many more tribulations for God to get me where he wanted me—on my face. It was through His totally breaking me that I was able to confess my sin totally and completely. It took many hours of prayer for my burdened soul to be lightened and for change to start taking place in my life. Finally, after days, weeks, and months people remarked at the change that occurred and with joy I shared my story. I guess when true salvation comes, it can't be hidden.

October 26

"End Time"

Scripture: As Jesus was sitting on the Mount of Olives opposite the temple, Peter, James, John and Andrew asked him privately, "Tell us, when will these things happen? And what will be the sign that they are all about to be fulfilled?" 5Jesus said to them: "Watch out that no one deceives you. Many will come in my name, claiming, 'I am he,' and will deceive many. When you hear of wars and rumors of wars, do not be alarmed. Such things must happen, but the end is still to come. Nation will rise against nation, and kingdom against kingdom. There will be earthquakes in various places, and famines. These are the beginning of birth pains.

"You must be on your guard. You will be handed over to the local councils and flogged in the synagogues. On account of me you will stand before governors and kings as witnesses to them. And the gospel must first be preached to all nations. Whenever you are arrested and brought to trial, do not worry beforehand about what to say. Just say whatever is given you at the time, for it is not you speaking, but the Holy Spirit. (Mark 13:3–11)

Over the years I have heard many speculations on the second coming of Christ. Some preachers have made it their life's work to interpret scriptures regarding the end of the age. I have tried to follow alongside them reading passage after passage to become more aware of what is to take place before Jesus' arrival. The only common thread I have found in Scripture that points to the end of the age is the preaching of the gospel to all nations and all people. Scripture says, "And the gospel first must be preached to all nations," Mark 13:10. Therefore, as the gospel is distributed through missionaries, electronic media, and the written word, the world is being reached like never before. More and more translations are being broadcast far and wide into nations never before approached, so keep a close eye—the end of the age is drawing near.

October 27

"Humility"

Scripture: The people were waiting expectantly and were all wondering in their hearts if John might possibly be the Christ. John answered them all, "I baptize you with water. But one more powerful than I will come, the thongs of whose sandals I am not worthy to untie. He will baptize you with the Holy Spirit and with fire. His winnowing fork is in his hand to clear his threshing floor and to gather the wheat into his barn, but he will burn up the chaff with unquenchable fire." And with many other words John exhorted the people and preached the good news to them. (Luke 3:15–18)

Humility is a very hard thing to achieve. We all want to be acknowledged and recognized for what we have done. We want to here accolades for our achievements and be noticed by everyone. So how do we overcome this need to expand our head with praise?

Being humble is not a frame of mind, but rather an attitude of the heart. Our hearts have to be dedicated to God and with God in us our accomplishments will not be of us, but of Him. He is the giver of all wisdom, knowledge, and understanding, therefore, when we achieve, God is glorified.

John the Baptist baptized many in his time. He was a great preacher of the gospel and had a great following. He could have had great power and wealth, because many thought of him as the Christ, but instead he accepted what God gave him to do and did it to God's glory. He was very humble and knew his true recognition would come from God.

October 28

"Unanswered Prayer"

Scripture: "So I say to you: Ask and it will be given to you; seek and you will find; knock and the door will be opened to you. 1For everyone who asks receives; he who seeks finds; and to him who knocks, the door will be opened." (Luke 11:9–10)

Have you ever prayed and prayed to not receive an answer? Have you sought God through prayer to find the result not clear? Well you are in good company, so have I. It has taken me many years to develop my prayer life and to gain a better understanding of God's answers. I believe sometimes we expect some miraculous sign or the answer to come immediately. I can tell you from experience it seldom happens that way. I am not saying miraculous requests of God aren't received, but sometimes we miss the answer, because it is not what we wanted or expected.

God answers prayers, all prayers. He never leaves any unanswered and never marks any "Return to sender." He listens intently and responds to every one. Our God is subtle and speaks in a whisper, so if you are not paying attention the answer may just pass you by. Don't give up though, keep asking and eventually you will see that God has answered your prayers.

___

___

___

October 29

"Whoever Believes"

Scripture: "For God so loved the world that he gave his one and only Son, that whoever believes in him shall not perish but have eternal life." (John 3:16)

One of the most famous passages in the world is John 3:16. We see it on trucks, on shirts, painted on bodies, on signs at sporting events, spray painted on municipal buildings, and we hear it in church. It has had an impact on many people's lives, but is that impact in seeing and hearing or really knowing and believing?

Nicodemus knew and heard similar words, but did he believe? Jesus told Nicodemus, "The way to enter the Kingdom of Heaven is to be born again, not of flesh and blood, but of water and spirit:" (paraphrased). The next time you see a man at a football game, in freezing temperatures, with John 3:16 on his chest remember God came to save us all and all we need to do is believe in His Son, Jesus.

Do you believe?

October 30

"Just Do It"

Scripture: Greet one another with a holy kiss. (2 Corinthians 13:12)

I had a friend who always greeted me with a hug whenever he saw me. It didn't matter where we were or what was going on he always greeted me that way. At first I was very uncomfortable with this, especially because we were men. I wasn't quite sure how to respond, but as time passed and his greeting continued I learned that his care, concern, and love were wrapped up in his hug. It was his way of saying, "I hope you're okay and I missed you"; and, to me that was a great encouragement.

Paul was a great encourager as well and he instructed others to be the same way. He, too, knew the power of a hug and how it could help lighten a brother's load. So the next time you see a brother struggling, don't hesitate, and don't hold back, don't worry about what people will think: pass on a hug—do as Michael Jordan said on the old Nike commercials, "Just Do It."

October 31

"Spontaneous Worship"

Scripture: Jesus declared, "Believe me, woman, a time is coming when you will worship the Father neither on this mountain nor in Jerusalem. You Samaritans worship what you do not know; we worship what we do know, for salvation is from the Jews. Yet a time is coming and has now come when the true worshipers will worship the Father in spirit and truth, for they are the kind of worshipers the Father seeks. God is spirit, and his worshipers must worship in spirit and in truth." (John 4:21–24)

Worship—many think the only time to worship God is on Sunday and at church. On the contrary, I have found that sometimes my best worship experience comes at times least expected, spontaneously. It seems worship comes when I need God the most.

I travel a lot and often when I am driving, I pop in a praise and worship tape. When I start to sing songs of praise, my whole mood changes, my attitude changes, and worship becomes the center of my being. The praise and worship I offer while driving beckons God's presence and He shows up. I feel His presence envelop the car and my spirit. It is a grand worship experience and it doesn't happen in church on Sunday with other worshipers. It is just me and my Lord.

Scripture says, "The Father seeks worshipers," so if you seek God and don't know where to find Him, worship Him and He will find you.

November

November 1

"Sacrificial Love"

Scripture: Greater love has no one than this, that he lay down his life for his friends. (John 15:13)

Veterans Day—we take so much for granted. Our freedom in this country is taken for granted everyday. Recent generations have never seen a war on this land. We have been attacked, but never have we seen war. We have always been fortunate to fight our wars elsewhere and not see the horror and devastation of it here. Our veterans have a much greater appreciation for our freedom. They chose to keep this land free from invasion and they were even willing to lay down their lives for us. They were willing to sacrifice themselves that we might live free from our oppressors.

Jesus did the same thing. He loves each and every one of us so much that he gave His life for us. He gave it willingly that we might live free from the oppression of sin. Jesus gave the ultimate sacrifice for our eternal freedom and all we need to do is accept and believe.

November 2

"Carefree"

Scripture: Therefore I tell you, do not worry about your life, what you will eat or drink; or about your body, what you will wear. Is not life more important than food, and the body more important than clothes? Look at the birds of the air; they do not sow or reap or store away in barns, and yet your heavenly Father feeds them. Are you not much more valuable than they? Who of you by worrying can add a single hour to his life? (Matthew 6:25–27)

Recently I was watching the birds flying in a beautiful blue sky over my house. They soared on the air in a carefree motion and glided effortlessly. The birds seemed to be enjoying a beautiful fall morning without a care in the world. I couldn't help thinking to myself how wonderful it would be to have a life that carefree.

We always seem to feel that way when our lives are filled with many issues and concerns. We are all faced with the issues of jobs, kids, spouses, houses to keep up, churches, and countless other things in our lives. I know I become overwhelmed and worry about how to get it all done.

Jesus gave us a valuable lesson in the birds of the air. He said, "Do not worry." He wants us to rely on Him as the birds do, so that we too can live carefree lives.

November 3

"God's House"

Scripture: Unless the LORD builds the house, builders labor in vain. (Psalm 127:1)

Building a new house is a daunting task, especially if you are doing most of the work yourself. It seems as if the house will never be completed. You toil and you know you are one step closer, but it still seems the end is a long way off. You ask yourself, "Is it worth it?"

Then one morning you walk into the house and you feel a familiar presence. It is the Lord. He has come to inspect. He has come sensing that your spirit needs peace and comfort and that your body needs renewed strength. God made this house possible and He wants it complete, so He can allow my family and me to live in it.

Thank you Lord for your graciousness!

"God made this house possible and He wants you to complete it so that He can allow your family to live in it."

"Trust in Him and He will see your house through to completion."

November 4

"Good Hymn"

Scripture: Sing joyfully to the LORD, you righteous; it is fitting for the upright to praise him. Praise the LORD with the harp; make music to him on the ten-stringed lyre.

Sing to him a new song; play skillfully, and shout for joy. (Psalm 33:1–3)

There is nothing more uplifting than a good hymn. It excites the spirit, soothes the soul, and brings joy to the heart. A hymn is the start to worship and praise. It is an expression of our love for God and it brings joy to Him as well.

A hymn that truly touches my spirit and puts me in worship mode is "He Touched Me." Of course as soon as I write the title down, another comes to mind and another until my mind is flooded with hymns. I guess that is what I mean by a good hymn or hymns are uplifting.

November 5

"True Church"

Scripture: They devoted themselves to the apostles' teaching and to the fellowship, to the breaking of bread and to prayer. Everyone was filled with awe, and many wonders and miraculous signs were done by the apostles. All the believers were together and had everything in common. Selling their possessions and goods, they gave to anyone as he had need. Everyday they continued to meet together in the temple courts. They broke bread in their homes and ate together with glad and sincere hearts, praising God and enjoying the favor of all the people. And the Lord added to their number daily those who were being saved. (Acts 2:42–47)

I have noticed something missing in my life over the last few months. I have had to work every Sunday, which has caused me to miss church. Missing church has left a void in my life. It is not that I simply miss old friends and being with our church family, but that I miss the corporate worship experience. I miss worshipping with other believers in a collective attitude, body, and spirit.

I remember my mother telling me how she missed her church after moving to Indianapolis. She tried several churches, but none felt like home. She told me to never stop going to worship and praise God with others, even though we didn't every Sunday. I guess she knew the significance of belonging to God's church and now I know too.

November 6

"DISCIPLINE OR CHAOS?"

Scripture: Discipline your son, and he will give you peace; he will bring delight to your soul. (Proverbs 29:17)

My second son has had difficulty with some of his school work here in recent years. He is very bright, outgoing, and fun to be around, but he has come home with some very low grades. We know he is smart enough and understands the material, be he still has struggled in a couple of important subjects.

As parents who love, care, and know he can do better, we have had to discipline him. We have had to take away privileges to force him to concentrate and take action to improve. It is hard to discipline your children, but as parents we must. We must stay true and be sure to follow through with our disciplinary action and word, because as God's Word is truthful and just, so must ours be.

Discipline is an act we must learn to administer and enforce as parents, because the opposite of discipline is chaos.

November 7

"Keep the Faith"

Scripture: By faith we understand that the universe was formed at God's command, so that what is seen was not made out of what was visible. (Hebrews 11:3)

Facing this world everyday is burdensome. It seems to pull at us from all directions. The things you seem to have control over, you actually find you don't. We catch glimpses of joy, peace, and happiness only to have them subdued by the worldly activities we face. Through it all, however, we keep going, keep trying and willingly face another day, so some say, "We are keeping the faith."

I guess faith is what truly drives each and every one of us. It is the hope of things not yet happened or seen, so it propels us to go on, to see what is around the next corner.

We Christians know the true hope. The hope that insures us that the days we labor here on earth are not in vain, but will lead us to eternal life in Christ. So the next time someone says, "Keep the faith," know that through Christ you truly are.

November 8

"Pride"

Scripture: If anyone thinks he is something when he is nothing, he deceives himself.

Each one should test his own actions. Then he can take pride in himself, without comparing himself to somebody else, or each one should carry his own load. (Galatians 6:3–5)

We have been taught as Christians to not be prideful. We need to walk in humble obedience to God and not boast of our accomplishments and for good reason—pride goes before a fall. Does that mean we cannot be satisfied and content with ourselves in our accomplishments? Is it possible that we take pride one step too far?

God is a loving and caring God. He wants the best for His children, so why wouldn't He want us to be proud of our accomplishments? Sure He wants us to be proud, but He does not want us to gloat in an outward fashion. He wants us to experience and be proud of a job well done in a humble fashion.

My Bible dictionary gives a positive and negative definition of pride. I guess that is what I am trying to say about pride—in a positive way it is healthy and satisfying and it pleases God.

November 9

"Burdens Lightened"

Scripture: "Come to me, all you who are weary and burdened, and I will give you rest. Take my yoke upon you and learn from me, for I am gentle and humble in heart, and you will find rest for your souls. For my yoke is easy and my burden is light." (Matthew 11:28–30)

My activity calendar seems to always be full: full of school activities, church activities, work activities, and the ever illusive free time. Oh how to handle it all! It seems increasingly difficult to handle the burden of living in this world.

Being a Christian, I know where to go to renew my energy and have my burden lightened. I am not sure how non-Christians handle it. I am not sure that they do handle it. They must feel like the proverbial camel with more and more straw added to them until it breaks their backs. If they only knew how God wants to lighten their worldly and spiritual burdens.

If you are carrying a heavy load, whether a worldly load or sin load, call on Jesus. He will remove your burden and give you joy, peace, and happiness in exchange.

November 10

"Focused Light"

Scripture: No one lights a lamp and puts it in a place where it will be hidden, or under a bowl. Instead he puts it on its stand, so that those who come in may see the light. (Luke 11:33)

Life has many distractions, some good and some bad. Our lives seem to be most fulfilled when we are focused and all of our energy is directed toward something specific. We can accomplish anything when we are intent on a goal.

Fresnel lenses were developed to take a very small light and magnify its intensity. The light magnified by these lenses were so intense that it was used in lighthouses to steer ships away from rocky shores. A tiny light would save ships and lives from disaster and it was all made possible by Augustine Fresnel and his lens.

We are the light of Jesus and if we allow God to focus us, we can shine as a beacon to the whole world. With the intensity of Jesus shining in our lives, we may never really know of all of the souls saved from the rocky shores of life.

November 11

"Two-ly Blessed"

Scripture: The body is a unit, though it is made up of many parts; and though all its parts are many, they form one body. So it is with Christ. (1 Corinthians 12:12)

I am truly a fortunate man. My wife is not only my best friend, she is also my partner. When she and I set our minds to a task, we are like two oxen yoked together. We work and pull together as one unit. If one gets tired, no one knows the difference, because we are a team.

God, through Jesus, is yoked to us. He works with us that we might accomplish our goals, further His Kingdom, and receive satisfaction from a job well done. He is our invisible teammate. When we are weary from the burden, He lightens our load. When we are worried, He removes our concern, and when we want to give up, He encourages us on.

I consider myself truly or two-ly blessed, because I have a great wife and an awesome God.

November 12

"Prayer Warriors"

Scripture: Be joyful always; pray continually; give thanks in all circumstances, for this is God's will for you in Christ Jesus. (1 Thessalonians 5:16–18)

Last weekend I spent many hours on my knees, not in prayer, but in laying ceramic tile. The hours of knee-busting work gave me a new sense of appreciation for those who are diligent prayer warriors. Spending hours and hours on their knees on behalf of others is truly a labor of love.

I personally don't know how my life would have turned out without prayer warriors. Their persistent petitions on my behalf surely made the difference between my being saved and my experiencing eternal death. I know through their dedication to pray that they had God's ear.

Thank God for these blessed folks who intercede for us and seek God for our every need.

November 13

"Big Hug"

Scripture: For the LORD is good and his love endures forever; his faithfulness continues through all generations. (Psalm 100:5)

One of the best things in the world, especially after a hard day, is to be welcomed home with a big hug. Yesterday was one of those days. I had a lot going on and too many things on my mind. I was rushing from appointment to appointment trying not to forget anything. It was extremely demanding, but all of that disappeared when I received a big hug from each of my kids when I walked through the door. Those hugs were just what I needed to soothe my weariness and to put everything at rest.

God is there as well waiting at the door to give you a big hug. He is there in your wife, your children, or a good friend. God knows exactly what you need and when you need it. Don't ever forget that God loves you and He is waiting to give you a hug that will last throughout eternity.

November 14

“Nation of Plenty”

Scripture: Now he who supplies seed to the sower and bread for food will also supply and increase your store of seed and will enlarge the harvest of your righteousness. You will be made rich in every way so that you can be generous on every occasion, and through us your generosity will result in thanksgiving to God. (2 Corinthians 9:10–11)

Sacrifice is a word we Americans know little about. We have plenty of everything. I know that some struggle to have enough money to eat and to pay bills, but the majority of the nation has plenty.

God wants us to have plenty; He is a God of abundance. He wants us to have more than enough and as we gain, God wants us to give it out with a cheerful heart. He wants us to sow seeds everywhere, so that those who do not have enough will have enough.

As we approach from Thanksgiving and move into Advent, let's do our part to make sure everyone is blessed. Give generously to those in need and most of all give the blessing of Christ, who is more than sufficient to meet all of our needs.

November 15

"Your Worth"

Scripture: Do not take along any gold or silver or copper in your belts; take no bag for the journey, or extra tunic, or sandals or a staff; for the worker is worth his keep. (Matthew 10:9–10)

What is our worth? We often ask ourselves this question. What are we worth to the world, ourselves, and to others? Our earning potential tells us what we are worth on the job, but what about in service to God? In God's Kingdom, how is our worth measured?

Jesus sent out twelve disciples with specific instructions and at the end He told them not to take anything along. He knew that what they offered should be met with reward, not as God gives, but to their keep. Jesus knew their worth and was confident of the outcome.

We may not know exactly what we are worth to God's Kingdom, but God knows and He is keeping track. He will provide our resources to further His Kingdom while we are here and will give us our reward, when we get to Heaven. Don't hold back if you are not sure you're worthy, but instead step out in faith and let God do the rest.

November 16

"Out of Weakness"

Scripture: But he said to me, "My grace is sufficient for you, for my power is made perfect in weakness." Therefore I will boast all the more gladly about my weaknesses, so that Christ's power may rest on me. (2 Corinthians 12:9)

Have you ever said, "There is nothing I can do" or "That is outside my control?" We often feel our hands are tied to do anything good. We either feel we are handicapped in some fashion or inadequate to make any impact at all, and we wonder what we can do for God's service.

The truth lies in recognizing that we are not in control, that we are weak and incapable without God. In doing this we give God the authority to take control. Out of our weakness He equips us with power, wisdom, knowledge, and His Spirit. He supercharges us to accomplish His will. As long as we rely on our own strength, we are useless to God.

Give up. Surrender and submit to God, put Him first in your life, trust Him, and He will perfect a good work in you.

November 17

"Time"

Scripture: So God said to Noah, "I am going to put an end to all people, for the earth is filled with violence because of them. I am surely going to destroy both them and the earth. So make yourself an ark of cypress wood; make rooms in it and coat it with pitch inside and out." (Genesis 6:13–14)

Time is a valuable commodity. Once it is spent it cannot be recovered and used again, therefore, our use of each and every minute is important.

How do we use our time? How should we use our time? Are we using our time in the best way possible?

These are all important questions. Corporations have spent enormous amounts of money to teach their people how to use their time productively. They teach them how to squeeze the most from every minute to the benefit of the company. God wants us to be productive. He wants us to accomplish the most we can for His glory and to be the best we can be. God wants us to be successful and to glorify Him. Truthfully, all of the money in the world, self-help books, PDA's, and calendars will not help. We need God to guide and direct our time. If we don't, we are like ships without navigators—lost. If Noah would have procrastinated and had not organized his time, where would we be? With God guiding and leading our time, who's to say how generations may be impacted in the future.

God is going to hold each and every one of us accountable for our time and how we spent it. Get organized, seek God, and impact God's Kingdom. There is no better time.

November 18

"God's Strength"

Scripture: He gives strength to the weary increases the power of the weak. Even youths grow tired and weary, young men stumble and fall; but those who hope in the LORD renew their strength; they will soar on wings like eagles; they will run and not grow weary, they will walk and not be faint. (Isaiah 40:29–31)

Over the last few months, I have burnt the candle at both ends. I have worked a full-time job and worked to finish a new house. The last few weeks have been even worse. I have put in as many as 50 hours on the house from Friday afternoon until Sunday night. I have pulled myself through the door and into bed in the wee hours of the morning to get up and do it again. The more tired I get the more I wonder how much more I can do, but since the house is a blessing from God, He gives me the strength to endure. When I am on my last step and ready to fail He renews me and encourages me to keep going.

I love God and all He has done for me in my life. I know when given a task too monumental for me, He will be there to see me through. God gives me the strength I need to do the work before me and He will do the same for you.

November 19

"Good News"

Scripture: And there were shepherds living out in the fields nearby, keeping watch over their flocks at night. An angel of the Lord appeared to them, and the glory of the Lord shone around them, and they were terrified. But the angel said to them, "Do not be afraid. I bring you good news of great joy that will be for all the people. Today in the town of David a Savior has been born to you; he is Christ the Lord. This will be a sign to you: You will find a baby wrapped in cloths and lying in a manger. Suddenly a great company of the heavenly host appeared with the angel, praising God and saying, "Glory to God in the highest, on earth peace to men on whom his favor rests." (Luke 2:8–14)

The Christmas season is an exciting time. It is great to visit family and friends, to give and receive gifts, and to just enjoy the season. Imagine how excited the shepherds were when the angel appeared to them proclaiming the birth of Jesus. They had heard the stories of a Messiah and the angels confirmed these stories. God selected these shepherds to pass on the word about this magnificent event, that God had sent a Savior for the world. This good news was given to these shepherds to announce and they, with the angels, rejoiced. Once the praise finished, the shepherds wanted to see for themselves the newborn Christ, so they went to Bethlehem and spread the word that the angel had told them.

I hope the season will fill you with the same excitement the shepherds experienced everyday. I hope that you, like them, want everyone to know that Christ is among us to save the world. Spread the Good News

November 20

"Got Wisdom?"

Scripture: My son, if you accept my words and store up my commands within you, turning your ear to wisdom and applying your heart to understanding, and if you call out for insight and cry aloud for understanding, and if you look for it as for silver and search for it as for hidden treasure, then you will understand the fear of the LORD and find the knowledge of God. For the LORD gives wisdom, and from his mouth come knowledge and understanding. He holds victory in store for the upright, he is a shield to those whose walk is blameless, for he guards the course of the just and protects the way of his faithful ones. (Proverbs 2:1–8)

I have often heard the expression, "You are wise beyond your years" or "Your wisdom comes from your life experiences." Wisdom seems to be held in high regard by most people. Wisdom is something everyone seeks, but not all find.

Wisdom comes from seeking truth, knowledge, and understanding. Solomon was wise because he sought the truth in every situation. He cherished wisdom and he became wise through his relationship with God.

We can all be wise if we put God first in our lives and allow His truth, knowledge, and understanding to come from Him and not from our worldly experience. God wants us to be wise and use our Godly wisdom to His glory.

You want wisdom? Seek God.

November 21

"God's Wrath"

Scripture: O LORD, do not rebuke me in your anger discipline me in your wrath. (Psalm 6:1)

Our dog ran out of the house this morning before anyone could react to get the door latched. As is customary for our dog when he gets loose, he runs and runs and runs. He visits all of the neighborhood dogs, he runs through the woods, and he totally refuses to obey our commands. When he gets free he enjoys it. His disobedience gets frustrating since we all have to be at work or school. This doesn't matter to him though because when he is having fun; he is not concerned with coming when he's called. Therefore, as the pressure builds within me and anger sets in, I vow to beat him within an inch of his life for his act of defiance.

Then in that moment my anger is interrupted and my spirit is summoned. It relays a message from God saying, "Now you know how I feel when you disobey and why I sent my Son rather than my wrath out to the world." In an instant, my anger disappears and my heart is repentant. My mind focuses on the Old Testament stories about God's wrath and anger with a better sense of understanding. Thank you God for loving us so much that you sent your Son rather than your wrath.

November 22

"Be Productive"

Scripture: But seek first his kingdom and his righteousness, and all these things will be given to you as well. Therefore do not worry about tomorrow, for tomorrow will worry about itself. Each day has enough trouble of its own. (Matthew 6:33–34)

What are your thoughts every morning when you first wake up? Do you start running down the list of things that have to get done: get the kids up and ready for school, get ready for work, attend that important meeting, don't forget the dentist appointment, etc? Our lives are filled with many things all of which are basically important, but all of which are temporal in trying to dominate our actions.

God can help you be more productive and happy with the busy life you lead. He is waiting for you to put Him first, not just somewhere on the list. Make God your first thought every morning and you will see how fruitful and organized your day will truly be.

November 23

"Encourager"

Scripture: Therefore encourage one another and build each other up, just as in fact you are doing. (1 Thessalonians 5:11)

Who is your encourager? We face a world of trials, tribulations, uncertainties, and difficult times. Who helps you persevere and keep the faith? There is surely someone through comment, action, or deed who helps you to overcome and finish the race.

Barnabas was that type person for the disciples. His name was originally Joseph, but he was such an encourager that his name was changed to Barnabas, meaning "encourager." He was always there with the right word or deed to motivate the people to move forward to the end. One of the disciples he encouraged was John Mark, who fell out of favor with Paul. Paul no longer wanted John Mark to accompany him on a mission. This devastated John Mark, but waiting in the wings was Barnabas with his ever present words of encouragement. John Mark overcame his devastation and went on to write the Gospel of Mark.

If you cannot identify an encourager in your life, do not fret, because Jesus is the encourager of all.

November 24

"Count Your Blessings"

Scripture: "because of your father's God, who helps you, because of the Almighty, who blesses you with blessings of the heavens above, blessings of the deep that lies below, blessings of the breast and womb." (Genesis 49:25)

Thanksgiving Day, as if there is only one day to give thanks, forces me to reflect more deeply on what God has done in my life. The process starts and a song from the movie White Christmas comes to mind–"Count your Blessings."

Like many people, I sometimes have difficulty falling asleep, so I count my blessings instead of sheep as the song says to do. I find the blessings to be not just a few, but a whole flock. They are too numerous to count and I often fall to sleep before I ever get to the end. So the next time you have difficulty falling asleep "count your blessings instead of sheep."

____

____

____

November 25

"Thanksgiving"

Scripture: God sets the lonely in families, he leads forth the prisoners with singing; but the rebellious live in a sun-scorched land. (Psalm 68:6)

Thanksgiving is a time for family and friends to get together, enjoy a great meal, and be thankful for God's blessings. During the day, if you are like me, you think of loved ones who are no longer around. It is in a recipe, a joke, a joyful laugh or just missing their presence that brings the person to mind. Whatever it is they seem to visit that day.

God knows the importance of family and when we accept Jesus, we become part of His family. We become joint heirs with Jesus himself and inherit the Kingdom of God.

Thank you Lord for making provision for everyone to enjoy family, it doesn't matter whether we are blessed with earthly mothers, fathers, sisters, brothers and children or whether we are simply a part of God's family in Jesus.

November 26

"The Day After Thanksgiving"

Scripture: But the angel said to them, "Do not be afraid. I bring you good news of great joy that will be for all the people. Today in the town of David a Savior has been born to you; he is Christ the Lord." (Luke 2:10–11)

The day after thanksgiving is the biggest shopping day of the year. People run around frantically searching for the right present. They try to find the perfect gift for their husband, father, wife, mother, son, daughter, aunt, uncle, or cousin. The day after thanksgiving is the start of the fast pace to Christmas.

It is true that the season is about gifts and presents, but it started with the greatest of all gifts—Jesus. This gift of Jesus is freely offered to everyone—all we must do is accept Him.

During the Christmas season stay with your shopping, your traditions, and your rituals, but take a little time to reflect on God's gift and reflect on God's love.

November 27

"Accountable"

Scripture: Now we know that whatever the law says, it says to those who are under the law, so that every mouth may be silenced and the whole world held accountable to God. (Romans 3:19)

Accountability for our actions in today's society is virtually non-existent. It seems that criminals or people who commit acts of immorality want to blame someone or something else for what they have done. It doesn't seem to matter if you're the President of the United States or a thug in the streets, everybody tries to blame others, skate around responsibility, or shift from being held accountable.

Someday we will all be held accountable for our actions. God has promised to judge each and every one of us. He will not allow us to shift blame or skirt the issue. He will judge us and we will have to pay for what we have done, unless, we have Jesus. Jesus alone can gain us pardon and have us freed, because He paid the price for our sin. Judgment and condemnation are certain and if you don't want to suffer the consequences, accept Jesus today and your pardon will be signed, sealed, and delivered.

November 28

"Sacrifice"

Scripture: God presented him as a sacrifice of atonement, through faith in his blood. He did this to demonstrate his justice, because in his forbearance he had left the sins committed beforehand unpunished—(Romans 3:25)

We are all ready, willing, and able to sacrifice for our families. We might even be willing to sacrifice for a friend or someone we know, but would we be willing to sacrifice for a stranger?

Jesus sacrificed His life for not only ones he knew, but for all generations. He didn't know us, but He gave willingly that we would not perish. He wanted us to live our lives without fear or concern and to live our lives abundantly. The only sacrifice we have to make in return is to give ourselves to Him. We need to acknowledge that He came to save us and then surrender our lives to His will. Although sacrifice normally means, "To give something up," God's blessings far outweigh our sacrifice. Sacrifice your life to Jesus today.

November 29

"SERVE TO BE SERVED"

Scripture: For even the Son of Man did not come to be served, but to serve, and to give his life as a ransom for many. (Mark 10:45)

Have you ever noticed how people in the service business treat you? It is not wholeheartedly, but they consider us privileged to be served by them. They are often short-tempered and rude. They act as if you have inconvenienced them by their having to wait on you.

Let's think about this for a minute. In today's economy there seems to be more jobs than people. It seems that management is asking people to do more because of this shortage of help and it has become increasingly difficult to staff the workplace. In this light, watch how the public treats these folks who are simply trying to do their job.

I am a believer in the old saying "You get what you give." If you are pleasant, people are pleasant back to you. If you try to brighten someone's day he or she will likely respond in kind. Remember to give each person you greet a little Jesus in your smile, your words, and your actions and, you just may spark an epidemic of goodwill and kindness—serve to be served.

November 30

"Attacked"

Scripture: Put on the full armor of God so that you can take your stand against the devil's schemes. For our struggle is not against flesh and blood, but against the rulers, against the authorities, against the powers of this dark world and against the spiritual forces of evil in the heavenly realms. Therefore put on the full armor of God, so that when the day of evil comes, you may be able to stand your ground, and after you have done everything, to stand. (Ephesians 6:11–13)

What do you do when the enemy attacks? I am not talking about a country or a person as an enemy, but I am talking about the legion of demons that is available to the devil. He sends his legion against us all in many forms and it does not normally come as a frontal assault. The devil attacks in the form of fear, misconception, confusion, resentment, prejudice, and discouragement. He uses our own flesh against us. He wants us to be in a constant state of doubt about ourselves, our surroundings, and our faith.

Jesus knows the devil's tricks and He will remain by your side. All Jesus asks is that you call upon Him to fight your battles and not rely on your own strength. Jesus wants to be your champion and He will be victorious. So the next time you feel attacked, call upon Jesus and He will crush Satan's plans and give you peace.

December

December 1

"Christmas Countdown"

Scripture: "For God so loved the world that he gave his one and only Son, that whoever believes in him shall not perish but have eternal life. For God did not send his Son into the world to condemn the world, but to save the world through him. Whoever believes in him is not condemned, but whoever does not believe stands condemned already because he has not believed in the name of God's one and only Son." (John 3:16–18)

December is upon us. Twenty-four days until Christmas, but what does that really mean? Does it mean twenty-four shopping days, parties, and programs to attend or does it mean we are counting the days until we celebrate the most important event of mankind? It is all of those, but as we endeavor to take in all that the holiday has to offer, let's do it with the right attitude and mindset.

Jesus needs to be at the center of the season. He needs to be the "reason for the season," to use a popular phrase. We need to keep in mind the greatest gift every given by God to each and every one of us: "God so loved us that he gave His one and only Son for us" and all we need to do is accept Him.

Enjoy the holidays and the joy of knowing Christ as your Savior!

December 2

"Distractions"

Scripture: Peace I leave with you; my peace I give you. I do not give to you as the world gives. Do not let your hearts be troubled and do not be afraid. (John 14:27)

Distractions, distractions! With Christmas around the corner, there are so many distractions: children's programs to attend, shopping to complete, parties to throw, Christmas cards to prepare, and holiday planning to do. While each of these things is fine and good, they can all create distractions from what is truly important this time of year.

I suggest you force yourself to take time and focus back on the first Christmas. They too were distracted from the most important event of all time. Everyone had to travel back to their hometown for a census. They had to pack, gather their children, and head out to their homeland. When they arrived at their destination, they had to worry about accommodations, about where to eat and sleep, and about taxes—how much they would owe and whether or not they had enough to even pay them.

Distractions occur in everyone's life, but the key is not to miss the important events. Don't miss Jesus' birth in your life. He has come to provide comfort and rest to a busy world, so don't be distracted; come and experience the peace of Christ.

December 3

"Blessed Event"

Scripture: At that time Mary got ready and hurried to a town in the hill country of Judea, where she entered Zechariah's home and greeted Elizabeth. When Elizabeth heard Mary's greeting, the baby leaped in her womb, and Elizabeth was filled with the Holy Spirit. In a loud voice she exclaimed: "Blessed are you among women, and blessed is the child you will bear! 43But why am I so favored, that the mother of my Lord should come to me? As soon as the sound of your greeting reached my ears, the baby in my womb leaped for joy. Blessed is she who has believed that what the Lord has said to her will be accomplished!" (Luke 1:39–45)

The times are exciting when new babies come into our lives. I remember the birth of my children. The excitement and anticipation was amazing, whether it was the first or the last. I noticed that same excitement spills over to grandparents, aunts, uncles, brothers, and even friends. There is a hope and joy that each of us experience as we wait patiently for the blessed day.

Mary, mother of Jesus, was the same way. She experienced excitement mixed with concern, so she retreated to a relative's house for a visit. Upon her arrival, her excitement grew more intense and her concerns diminished. She pondered the importance of this event in her life. Her relative, Elizabeth, sensed the excitement too. She helped Mary understand her role and gave her great encouragement, which removed all of Mary's doubts and fears.

At this time of year, we need to imitate Elizabeth. We need to sense the jubilation of a new child that has been born in our midst. We need to put away all of doubts and concerns and truly enjoy this blessed event of Christ's birth.

December 4

"Emmanuel"

Scripture: The LORD looked and was displeased there was no justice. He saw that there was no one, he was appalled that there was no one to intervene; so his own arm worked salvation for him, and his own righteousness sustained him. (Isaiah 59:15b-16)

In the midst of this Christmas season it is easy to overlook what has taken place. Jesus, His birth, death, and resurrection all happened so long, long, ago that they are hard to fathom. Our lives are filled with ourselves, work, family, and we go about never grasping the full impact of what God did. He loves us, cares for us, and does not want even one of us to perish.

This season take time to understand what God has done and how He loves us. He came to earth in the form of man to experience what we experience. He experienced the same temptations, the same perils, and the same rejections we face. Then, knowing that we could never remain sinless, He made provision for us. Jesus took our sins and bore them so that we would know He loves us even unto death and that He wants to spend eternity with us.

Thank you, God for loving us. I thank you Lord for coming to this earth, for understanding our shortcomings, and for overcoming the power of sin. In Jesus' name, Amen.

December 5

"Cheerful Giving"

Scripture: So when you give to the needy, do not announce it with trumpets, as the hypocrites do in the synagogues and on the streets, to be honored by men. I tell you the truth, they have received their reward in full. But when you give to the needy, do not let your left hand know what your right hand is doing, so that your giving may be in secret. Then your Father, who sees what is done in secret, will reward you. (Matthew 6:2–4)

Have you ever noticed the large number of requests made by charities during the Christmas season? Calls, pleadings, and advertisements fill the air to entice people to give. I guess people's hearts ache to do something during this season and all of the charities capitalize on that. I am not saying that their beckoning is not needed and that they shouldn't ask while the hearts of people are prone to giving, but I do wonder why people miss the opportunity to give at other times of the year. Evidently, they feel good about giving at the holidays. They feel cheerful, the act is pleasant, and they feel the blessing they get is far more than the gift given.

Give as your heart directs but sometimes, when no one's around, give $5.00 to the poor guy on the corner. Let the experience of giving be a blessing to you and to your fellow man. Don't judge the person receiving on what he may or may not do with the money, just give it with a cheerful heart and let God do the rest.

December 6

"On Fire for Jesus"

Scripture: After John was put in prison, Jesus went into Galilee, proclaiming the good news of God. "The time has come," he said. "The kingdom of God is near. Repent and believe the good news!" (Mark 1:14–15)

We got word this morning that our church had caught on fire. In disbelief, I questioned the caller about the time, the cause, and the extent of the damage. The good news was that the damage was localized and minimal. Even knowing things were alright, the fire still made me realize how vulnerable we are and how catastrophe can strike us at any time. It is a comfort to know that God is there to keep us going and to support us.

What do people do who do not have Jesus in their lives? How do they face the challenges of life without a loving God?

Make today your day to share the Good News of Jesus. Let people know that God has seen you through many trials and that He is there to help them as well. Don't let another person suffer the anguish of this world, when you have the answer. Be on fire for Jesus and share His love with all you meet.

December 7

"Holiday Family"

Scripture: You are all sons of God through faith in Christ Jesus, for all of you who were baptized into Christ have clothed yourselves with Christ. There is neither Jew nor Greek, slave nor free, male nor female, for you are all one in Christ Jesus. If you belong to Christ, then you are Abraham's seed, and heirs according to the promise. (Galatians 3:26–29)

Last night we put up our Christmas tree. The whole family worked together; we trimmed the tree, played Christmas music, sang songs, and simply enjoyed the evening.

Family is important. It gives us a sense of belonging and togetherness, even when we are apart. God offers each and every one of us an opportunity to be part of His family. God has bestowed upon us the right of heir with Jesus and the ability to receive the inheritance of eternal life. There is no greater feeling than to be part of God's family. He loves us no matter what our faults and in spite of ourselves.

If you want a family for the holidays, even if you don't have one, God is waiting, wanting, and willing to make you part of His.

____

____

____

December 8

"The Ultimate Price"

Scripture: God presented him as a sacrifice of atonement, through faith in his blood. He did this to demonstrate his justice, because in his forbearance he had left the sins committed beforehand unpunished—he did it to demonstrate his justice at the present time, so as to be just and the one who justifies those who have faith in Jesus. (Romans 3:25–26)

My wife and I enjoy going to antique and collectible shops. We find it interesting to look at how our lives have progressed over the years and how these old trinkets have increased in value. We do collect some pieces and others have been given to us as gifts, which we have found to have great value, both financially and sentimentally. The value of such things is seldom based on their appraisal, but rather on what someone is willing to pay for them. The greatest valued piece demands the highest price.

So too it is with our salvation. If it was given without payment it would be worth nothing, but Jesus paid the highest price ever—His life. God paid for our salvation with His only Son that we might be saved. A life is the ultimate price given on behalf of someone and what it purchased was of great value—our eternal salvation.

I thank you Lord for paying for my sin and for granting me life eternal.

December 9

"Our Navigator"

Scripture: After the men had gone a long time without food, Paul stood up before them and said: "Men, you should have taken my advice not to sail from Crete; then you would have spared yourselves this damage and loss. But now I urge you to keep up your courage, because not one of you will be lost; only the ship will be destroyed. Last night an angel of the God whose I am and whom I serve stood beside me and said, 'Do not be afraid, Paul.'" (Acts 27:21–24)

It is extremely difficult to navigate through a troubled world. We all face certain perils, uncertainties, and unexpected circumstances in life and we often find that most of what we face is unknown and not seen ahead of time. When we face things of this nature, the only thing we can do is try to survive.

Surviving takes courage though and where do we get this courage? Do we rely on our own experience or the experience of others to help?

Having gone through many storms and disasters in my life, I can tell you there is only one who you can fully trust and rely on and that is Jesus. Jesus will guide you through the storm, He will help you navigate the rocky shores, He will overcome the wild sea and will give you a safe haven. He is the only one who knows the final outcome, so have courage and face the storms of life with the most knowledgeable navigator ever—Jesus.

December 10

"God's Plan"

Scripture: Many are the plans in a man's heart, but it is the LORD's purpose that prevails. (Proverbs 19:21)

Life can be very frustrating at times. We make plans and much to our dismay our plans get upset. I don't know about you, but when my plans fall apart it affects my whole attitude. As a matter of fact, when I was younger failed plans had a horrible effect on me and I let everyone around me know it.

Now that God is an integral part of my life, I strive to seek His plan. His leading lessens the chance of plans being derailed, but does not eliminate the chance due to this chaotic world outside our control. However, knowing that God is in control the effect of ruined plans on my attitude is much different. I take a different approach by being more flexible and by watching God handle the plans. It is amazing to see how God molds, changes, and unfolds His plan to achieve a desired outcome. At the end of the day I can look back and see God's marvelous plan at work, because He took charge and made the plans work to my benefit and according to His will. Praise be to God.

December 11

"Choices"

Scripture: But we ought always to thank God for you, brothers loved by the Lord, because from the beginning God chose you to be saved through the sanctifying work of the Spirit and through belief in the truth. (2 Thessalonians 2:13)

Life has many choices: we can choose where to live, where to work, who our friends will be, and what we believe. With so many choices in life, how can we be sure to make the right ones?

God has granted each and every one of us free will. He wants us to have the ability to choose our course and to follow what we believe. Even with our right to choose our destiny, God is never too far away. He is there and will be there every time we choose right or wrong. He will rejoice in our good choices and will help us in our wrong ones. He will be there to mend a broken heart, help with a career, and guide us in every aspect of our lives—that is if we have chosen Him to be part of our lives.

Choose wisely!

December 12

"Abundant Life"

Scripture: To those who have been called, who are loved by God the Father and kept by Jesus Christ: Mercy, peace and love be yours in abundance. (Jude 1:1b-2)

Last night I watched a very interesting program on TV. The program was about the last century from 1900 to 2000. The program interviewed people who were born in 1900 or just before. What amazed me was their discussion about what they had seen in their lives and in America over the last 100 years. Each one was humbled by the world and grateful to have grown up during this period. They all remarked about the changes, the abundant life they lead, and as one lady put it, "I have seen the country go from a straw broom to the moon." The mental and physical capacity of the folks at their age was remarkable. Needless to say, it made a profound impression on me as I watched and listened.

God wants each and every one of us to live a full and abundant life. He wants us to live life with joy, peace, and clear understanding. We may face perils and setbacks, but if we rely on God He will give us the abundant lives we seek. I know I want to live a long, abundant life like the folks on the program and be able to relay the changes that have occurred in my one hundred years, but not without God being a part of it.

December 13

"ETERNAL FAMILY"

Scripture: How good and pleasant it is when brothers live together in unity! It is like precious oil poured on the head, running down on the beard, running down on Aaron's beard, down upon the collar of his robes. It is as if the dew of Hermon were falling on Mount Zion. For there the LORD bestows his blessing, even life forevermore. (Psalm 133:1–3)

What a wonderful Christmas. We had several occasions to get together with family, to laugh, to reminisce, and to just enjoy each other's company. It is a glorious time to draw close together in love.

God wants us all to have a family. He wants us to be part of a family of love, joy, peace, and contentment. Our earthly families, at Christmas, are a glimpse of what our heavenly family will be like throughout eternity. God wants the love granted to us through the birth, life, death, and resurrection of His Son to draw us into His family. He wants us knit together in unity and in one accord knowing that He is God and is creator of all.

Come today and be united with God's family through Jesus Christ.

____

____

____

December 14

"ALWAYS THERE"

Scripture: Then Jesus told them, "This very night you will all fall away on account of me, for it is written: 'I will strike the shepherd, the sheep of the flock will be scattered.' 32But after I have risen, I will go ahead of you into Galilee." Peter replied, "Even if all fall away on account of you, I never will." "I tell you the truth," Jesus answered, "this very night, before the rooster crows, you will disown me three times." (Matthew 26:31–34)

We recently got a new puppy as a pet and now that I have fully accepted him into the household, it has caused me to recall other dogs I have had. I remember how loyal they were. They would be at the door waiting to greet me. They were always happy to see me no matter what. They seemed to pick up my day even when I was at my worst.

That type of loyalty is hard to find in people. It seems that people switch jobs often, people file for divorce for virtually no reason, and friends seem to abandon you if you are having problems for fear that you might need or want something from them. If loyalty is virtually non-existent, who can you count on?

Jesus knew human nature was to put one's self before anything or anyone. He told Peter he would deny him. Jesus knew, even though we would forsake Him, that He would never leave or forsake us. He is loyal to the end and will never ever leave us no matter what our circumstance.

____

____

____

December 15

"Old Testament Lessons"

Scripture: "'If a member of the community sins unintentionally and does what is forbidden in any of the LORD's commands, he is guilty. When he is made aware of the sin he committed, he must bring as his offering for the sin he committed a female goat without defect. He is to lay his hand on the head of the sin offering and slaughter it at the place of the burnt offering. Then the priest is to take some of the blood with his finger and put it on the horns of the altar of burnt offering and pour out the rest of the blood at the base of the altar. He shall remove all the fat, just as the fat is removed from the fellowship offering, and the priest shall burn it on the altar as an aroma pleasing to the LORD. In this way the priest will make atonement for him, and he will be forgiven. (Leviticus 4:27–31)

Old Testament books and stories can be very disturbing. We read about wars and battles. God's word showed the Promised Land to be taken by force and all of the rules and regulations even beyond the Ten Commandments creates cause for alarm. All of these books of the Bible seem strange to us today, so we search for the purpose and how to use them in our lives.

God uses His word to teach. During the early years of establishing His Holy Nation (Israel) He gave them rules to mold them into one nation, to establish His kingdom on earth, and to reconcile them to Him.

The most important part was the teaching of reconciliation. The chosen people did not have the benefit of Christ, but God, even then, did not want to lose even one, so He gave them a way to be forgiven.

I thank God for making provision once and for all for my sin. The sacrifice and atonement was made for my total and undeniable reconciliation forevermore. I thank you God for providing the sacrificial lamb on my behalf.

December 16

"Revenge"

Scripture: "You have heard that it was said, 'Eye for eye, and tooth for tooth.' But I tell you, Do not resist an evil person. If someone strikes you on the right cheek, turn to him the other also. And if someone wants to sue you and take your tunic, let him have your cloak as well. If someone forces you to go one mile, go with him two miles. Give to the one who asks you, and do not turn away from the one who wants to borrow from you. (Matthew 5:38–42)

Today the world seems to be totally geared toward revenge. Visualize the gang wars, school violence, and car bombs—all because people feel the need for revenge. They want to right a so-called wrong and try to instill some kind of order in their lives.

There is only one who can turn chaos into order, only one who can right the wrongs of the world and put peace in place: Jesus. Jesus is the peace and the avenger of us all. He teaches us to offer those who feel that they need to receive more -more than they expect, to give them love in the time of lovelessness and to pray for those who want to do us harm. Jesus does not want us to take revenge on anyone, but rather wants us to give them to God and let God alone deal with them. Jesus always wants us to look for the good in all people, to love them in spite of themselves, and to leave the revenge to God.

December 17

"Directions"

Scripture: At the LORD's command the Israelites set out, and at his command they encamped. As long as the cloud stayed over the tabernacle, they remained in camp. When the cloud remained over the tabernacle a long time, the Israelites obeyed the LORD's order and did not set out. Sometimes the cloud was over the tabernacle only a few days; at the LORD's command they would encamp, and then at his command they would set out. Sometimes the cloud stayed only from evening till morning, and when it lifted in the morning, they set out. (Numbers 9:18–21)

In traveling extensively for my employer I often find myself in unfamiliar towns and cities. I have found that getting directions from my customers saves time and prevents headaches. They can tell me landmarks to look for, how to avoid traffic problems, and which areas are undergoing road work. Each of these tips helps ensure that I get to their location safely and without delay. Using their directions and following them step by step guides me to where I want to go in a way that is both timely and hassle free.

God tries to guide us as well. He gives us direction through His Word and through His spirit. He provides these directions to eliminate wrong turns, problems, and delays to what He wills. God, providing we follow His directions step by step, will guide us directly to where He wants us to go.

The next time you take a trip get directions and the next time God leads you follow Him completely. In doing so, you will arrive at the end safely.

December 18

"Fragile Jars of Clay"

Scripture: But we have this treasure in jars of clay to show that this all-surpassing power is from God and not from us. We are hard pressed on every side, but not crushed; perplexed, but not in despair; persecuted, but not abandoned; struck down, but not destroyed. We always carry around in our body the death of Jesus, so that the life of Jesus may also be revealed in our body. (2 Corinthians 4:7–10)

We humans think we are so strong. I remember as a young man, thinking how strong I was. There was nothing that I could not handle and nothing I could not do by my own strength. I could do it all. Give me a task, get out of the way, and I would make it happen. All of this was fine for awhile until I got older. The situations I faced became more complex and more complicated. Eventually, I could not overcome the obstacles, issues, and problems, because they where stronger than I. No matter what I tried nothing worked.

A friend led me to a Christian counselor who shared a prophecy for my life. As he shared what was to come, I knew in that instant that I was incapable of handling the situations in my life alone. I realized that I no longer had (nor ever truly had) the strength to carry out my plans. The good news is I found Jesus and with Him all things are possible. I learned that there is nothing I can do on my own, with my own strength and with my own knowledge, but that instead I must fully rely on my relationship with God.

Our own strength is fragile and we are housed in jars of clay. We have a treasure on the inside of us that enables us to do as God wants, but He and only He can keep us from being crushed by circumstances and the pressures of this world. He did it for me and He can do it for you, just trust in Him and He will not forsake you.

December 19

"Innocent by Faith"

Scripture: You, then, why do you judge your brother? Or why do you look down on your brother? For we will all stand before God's judgment seat. It is written: "'As surely as I live,' says the Lord, 'every knee will bow before me; every tongue will confess to God.'" So then, each of us will give an account of himself to God. (Romans 14:10–12)

Have you ever watched court TV? It seems every channel has its version of the virtual courts. We have People's Court, Judge Judy, Judge Brown, Divorce Court, and Court TV on cable. Each of these programs allows individuals to come before the TV judge for a hearing and ruling on their case. The evidence is presented and the judge issues the verdict typically along with a stern talking to. The verdict given leaves one party unhappy, but the judgment is final.

Someday we will all have to appear in court. We will have to appear before the judgment seat of God and give an account of ourselves. I know that when I appear before God He will ask, "How do you plea?" I know if I stand there on my own record the plea must be guilty, but because of my salvation, I can say, "I plea the blood of Christ. Jesus paid the price for my sin-filled record by His blood, therefore, I plea innocent."

Jesus paid the price, so when God calls me before His court He will recognize my advocate and will have to rule me innocent by reason of faith.

December 20

"Center Of Life"

Scripture: I press on toward the goal to win the prize for which God has called me heavenward in Christ Jesus. (Philippians 3:14)

Now that we are approaching a new year everyone is working to set new goals and make new resolutions. We all sit down and look back at what we have accomplished over the previous year and then over our lifetimes. At this time, we seek to determine how many life goals we have truly reached. Either disappointed or joyous over our findings, we realize that tomorrow is another day and what we did yesterday really doesn't matter.

As we take stock of our New Year's objectives, let us not forget to put God at the center of everything we do. God has offered us the only option that is everlasting, so make it a point to spend time daily in His word and in prayer. These steps, along with setting your own goals, will make all of your objectives attainable and possible through His glory. God and God alone is at the center of abundant life.

December 21

"God's Cure"

Scripture: But the fruit of the Spirit is love, joy, peace, patience, kindness, goodness, faithfulness, gentleness and self-control. Against such things there is no law. (Galatians 5:22–23)

Over the summer of 1999 I built a new home and did a lot of the work on it myself. Since the task was so monumental, I got used to eating only when I was hungry. Sometimes I would work all day on one meal, while on other days I ate several times. It was as if my body told me what it needed and when it needed it.

Our spirits are exactly the same way. They need to be fed daily either by God's Word, prayer to the Heavenly Father, or worship. Our spirits, like our bodies, sometimes need to be fed more than once per day and other times they need an all-day feast.

The next time you don't feel quite right and you can't put your finger on what is wrong, try feeding your spirit and let God be the cure

December 22

"Faithfully Loyal"

Scripture: Your kingdom is an everlasting kingdom, and your dominion endures through all generations. The LORD is faithful to all his promises and loving toward all he has made. The LORD upholds all those who fall and lifts up all who are bowed down. (Psalm 145:13–14)

We have a new puppy in our family and our youngest son Nathan is responsible for taking care of him. He feeds him, walks him, and plays with him. The puppy, because of my son's faithfulness, has become extremely loyal to my son. My son exclaims everyday how loyal his puppy is.

Our God wants loyalty from us. He wants us to put him first and to have no other God's or idols before Him. For our loyalty, He will be faithful. God will provide all of our needs in abundance. He has already provided for our forgiveness of sin through His Son, Jesus. He has prepared a place for our eternity and has taken care of every detail of our lives for now and forevermore.

Loyalty and faithfulness go hand in hand. If you want to experience that type of true loyalty in a world of broken promises, come to God and receive His faithful gift—life everlasting.

December 23

"Let God be God"

Scripture: "Lord, if it's you," Peter replied, "tell me to come to you on the water." "Come," he said. Peter got down out of the boat, walked on the water and came toward Jesus. But when he saw the wind, he was afraid and, beginning to sink, cried out, "Lord, save me!" Immediately Jesus reached out his hand and caught him. "You of little faith," he said, "why did you doubt?" (Matthew 14:28–31)

Many of us face obstacles that seem impossible to overcome. We face them with fear and trepidation. We doubt whether we can handle them, let alone overcome them. But if we stop and evaluate, doubt and fear are the obstacle, not the obstacle itself.

Jesus helps us whenever we ask. He will take away our doubt and fear. He will sustain us in the face of adversity and will help us overcome. He will give us the courage to face our greatest problems, issues, and obstacles without concern for the outcome. It will not matter what happens, because Jesus will be there. Jesus will encourage us each and every step of the way no matter how difficult those steps may be.

I do not know what you face in your life, but with Jesus you can face whatever it is with confidence and boldness. You can rest assured that if the worst happens, He will rescue you. All you need to do is accept His offer, proceed in faith, and let God be God.

December 24

"Christmas Eve"

Scripture: But the angel said to her, "Do not be afraid, Mary, you have found favor with God. You will be with child and give birth to a son, and you are to give him the name Jesus. He will be great and will be called the Son of the Most High. The Lord God will give him the throne of his father David, and he will reign over the house of Jacob forever; his kingdom will never end." (Luke 1:30–33)

Christmas Eve is a wonderful time as the hustle and bustle of shopping, parties, and school events are behind us and the day is yielded to the celebration of Jesus birth. My thoughts and spirit are drawn back to that night in Bethlehem, back to the stable, and to the lowly manger where Jesus would be laid. I think of the King of Kings born into this world and ponder why He was born into such humble surroundings.

I always become excited when I think of what his birth means and how through this babe the world can be reconciled to God. God in His infinite wisdom knew that He had to provide for our salvation, so He sent His one and only Son. God loved us so much that He sent Jesus to be born, to change the world, and to lay His life down for our sins.

Christmas Eve was just the beginning and not the end. Praise be to God.

December 25

"The Special Gift"

Scripture: Children's children are a crown to the aged; parents are the pride of their children. (Proverbs 17:6)

Christmas Day is a joyous time of presents given and presents received. It seems that every year I receive one gift from my family that is special. This year my son Jordan gave me a pen. The pen was very nice, all gold with a cross on the clip. The pen was a wonderful gift, but what made it special was a little card that he attached that read:

"I want to thank you, Dad, for all you've done throughout the years.

How you girded me through childhood and helped me face my fears.

No matter how life changes and no matter what I do,

I will always thank the Lord for the Dad I've found in you."

By Robert Fogle

If you are a parent, you know exactly what a gift like this means. I thank God for the knowledge, wisdom, and courage to be a Dad; and for giving me this special gift of children.

December 26

"Christmas Love"

Scripture: For the wages of sin is death, but the gift of God is eternal life in Christ Jesus our Lord. (Romans 6:23)

After Christmas morning I look over the mountain of presents, wrappings, bows, and boxes, and I realize how truly blessed we are materially. The children have the latest and greatest gadgets, my wife and I exchange those special gifts we had been hinting about for months, and everyone receives more presents than they had ever anticipated. Giving these gifts at Christmas is a special event at our house because the gifts are not just gifts, they are an expression of our love for one another.

God's gift of Jesus is an expression of His love for each and every one of us. He knew that we could never enter the Kingdom through our works, by the law and commandments, so with love He sent His Son to abolish the law and give us our salvation from sin. There has never been or ever will be a greater gift of Christmas love than this.

December 27

"What is Right in God's Sight?"

Scripture: As Jesus and his disciples were on their way, he came to a village where a woman named Martha opened her home to him. She had a sister called Mary, who sat at the Lord's feet listening to what he said. But Martha was distracted by all the preparations that had to be made. She came to him and asked, "Lord, don't you care that my sister has left me to do the work by myself? Tell her to help me!" "Martha, Martha," the Lord answered, "you are worried and upset about many things, but only one thing is needed. Mary has chosen what is better, and it will not be taken away from her." (Luke 10:38–41)

I do not know about your house, but in ours, with four children, it seems there is always one child in dispute with another. It almost seems that they argue as a way to compete for attention from my wife or me. They sometimes get attention in a proper manner and sometimes they do not. They sometimes get confused about what is the right way and what is the wrong way to obtain our affection.

We as Christians are sometimes conflicted by worrying about what needs to be done rather than doing God's will. God wants us to seek His will and then allow Him to lead the way. So the next time you feel frustrated by a person, a circumstance, or what has to be done, seek God and do what is right in His sight. It may be that God wants you to focus differently than what you expected and in doing so you will receive His blessing. You can never go wrong by seeking God's will and doing what's right in God's sight.

December 28

"Leave Your Mark"

Scripture: The body is a unit, though it is made up of many parts; and though all its parts are many, they form one body. So it is with Christ. For we were all baptized by one Spirit into one body—whether Jews or Greeks, slave or free—and we were all given the one Spirit to drink. (1 Corinthians 12:12–13)

Significance—we all seek to have it. We all want to leave our mark on the world, but the truth is few of us will. In today's world, only a handful will have any significant, recognizable accomplishments. When we examine the world more closely however, we find that many things cannot function without all of their parts. It's true that the one at the top is who gets recognized, but it's the inner workings that make the success of the one at the top possible. For example, a machine with gears and wheels would be a useless piece of junk with a gear missing. Even a molecule without positive and negative particles cannot exist, so each of us are significant to the world's progress and to the progress of Christianity.

The Kingdom of God doesn't grow or develop without a believer spreading the Gospel. A group of twelve, commissioned by Jesus, spread the Gospel impacting the world for more than 2000 years. You too can make a lasting mark on the world by telling one person, who tells another, who tells another about the love of Jesus. The mark on the world made by the twelve was good enough for eternity and it will be good enough for me.

____

____

____

December 29

"Unwavering Love"

Scripture: 1We know that the law is spiritual; but I am unspiritual, sold as a slave to sin. I do not understand what I do. For what I want to do I do not do, but what I hate I do. And if I do what I do not want to do, I agree that the law is good. As it is, it is no longer I myself who do it, but it is sin living in me. I know that nothing good lives in me, that is, in my sinful nature. For I have the desire to do what is good, but I cannot carry it out. For what I do is not the good I want to do; no, the evil I do not want to do—this I keep on doing. Now if I do what I do not want to do, it is no longer I who do it, but it is sin living in me that does it. So I find this law at work: When I want to do good, evil is right there with me. For in my inner being I delight in God's law; but I see another law at work in the members of my body, waging war against the law of my mind and making me a prisoner of the law of sin at work within my members. What a wretched man I am! Who will rescue me from this body of death? Thanks be to God—through Jesus Christ our Lord! (Romans 7:14–25)

We have recently added pets to our family and it has been great. The presence of the animals has had a profound effect on each and every one of us. We enjoy their company and they bring a new joy to our household. The joy they bring, however, quickly fades when the pets do mischievous things over and over again, especially when we have worked so hard to teach them differently. We all are disappointed when a pet hasn't learned the lesson we have tried to teach it. Even though disappointment comes, the pets are still a part of our family; we still love them and continue to help them do better. Once they have learned to behave as instructed, we all rejoice and praise them for their accomplishment.

In much the same way, God loves us in spite of the sins we commit time and time again. He is greatly disappointed when we do these things, but nonetheless He never leaves us or forsakes us. God just waits patiently while we learn for ourselves that the wages of sin is death. Once we realize this, learn our lesson, and are victorious over our sin through Jesus, God rejoices, praises us, and welcomes us with a warm embrace.

December 30

"Forgiveness Simplified"

Scripture: "He shall then slaughter the goat for the sin offering for the people and take its blood behind the curtain and do with it as he did with the bull's blood: He shall sprinkle it on the atonement cover and in front of it. In this way he will make atonement for the Most Holy Place because of the uncleanness and rebellion of the Israelites, whatever their sins have been. (Leviticus 16:15–16)

With it being just a few days past Christmas, I wonder how many of you have had to put together a toy or game for your child, grandchild, nephew, or niece. I am sure each of you followed the instructions to insure that the toy was assembled correctly. Most of you have probably learned from experience that without instructions steps are often skipped and the project risks turning out wrong.

The early Israelites were given certain instructions in order to receive forgiveness for their sin. They had to follow step by step a complete instruction (the law) or God would not make atonement for their sin nor save them from eternal separation from Him. Thankfully God, in His infinite wisdom, realized that they could never follow those instructions without mistake or error, and He abolished the law of instruction through Jesus. He took all of the law and the commandments and simplified them into one—LOVE.

The instructions for forgiveness include only three steps: 1) accept Jesus as your Lord and Savior, 2) believe Jesus loved you so much that He died on the cross for your sins and 3) believe He was raised from death on the third day and that He reigns with God in Heaven today. One, two, three: forgiveness simplified.

December 31

"The Past 3000 Years"

Scripture: For God did not send his Son into the world to condemn the world, but to save the world through him. Whoever believes in him is not condemned, but whoever does not believe stands condemned already because he has not believed in the name of God's one and only Son. (John 3:17–18)

The last day of the century and the last day of the millennium have spurred some interesting thoughts in my mind. I have thought about the changes I have seen in my lifetime, but the one thing that continues to astonish me is how after 2000 years Jesus is still Lord. He came to earth on a mission of mercy and through His life of 33 years, His death, and His resurrection He has had an impact on the world that has withstood the test of time. It is not a myth or a story, but God's way of showing us His love.

As we head into the next 1000 years, let's continue the legacy by telling everyone about Jesus. Let's tell them that He has come to save the world to keep both it and us from eternal condemnation. He gave His life so that we can face judgment with the confidence knowing that He paid the price for our sins and forgives us no matter what we have done.

I look forward to the part of the next 1000 years that I will live and I can live it with the assurance of Jesus as Lord and Master of my life.

Common Man Ministries was established by Rick Bowman as a way to share his faith with others. He has plans for several other books and does speaking engagements where requested. Please feel free to check out the website at www.commonmanministries.org.

Common Man Ministries
824 Valley Vista Court
Avon, IN 46123
317–718–0290
Email: rick@commonmanministries.org

To order more copies of this book contact:

TATE PUBLISHING, LLC

127 East Trade Center Terrace
Mustang, Oklahoma 73064

(888) 361 - 9473

Tate Publishing, LLC

www.tatepublishing.com